A History Of
The Matlocks

Peter J Naylor

For Keith
with best wishes
[signature] Peter Naylor GSC
2007

Above: *Matlock Bath from the war memorial at Starkholmes*

Opposite page: *South Parade, Matlock Bath. C. 1900. This view looks north up the A6. All the buildings on the left of the road side survive. Note the hanging sign for Hodgkinsons Hotel. The buildings on the right of the road have all gone but have been replaced with modern ones, note the Petrifying Well - and Aquarium! (Yeomans)*

LANDMARK COLLECTOR'S LIBRARY

A History Of The Matlocks

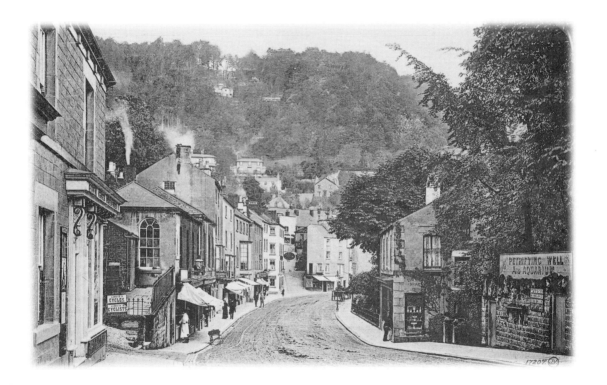

Peter J Naylor

Landmark Publishing

Published by

Ashbourne Hall, Cokayne Ave
Ashbourne, Derbyshire DE6 1EJ England
Tel: (01335) 347349 Fax: (01335) 347303
e-mail: landmark@clara.net
web site: www.landmarkpublishing.co.uk

1st edition

ISBN 1 84306 081 7

Printed by Bath Press Ltd, Bath

Design & reproduction by Simon Hartshorne

Cover captions:

Front cover: South Parade, Matlock. C. 1900
Back cover Top: St John's Chapel of Ease built 1897 this picture C. 1920
Back cover bottom: Matlock Bath from the Old Bath Terrace

Opposite inset: Rockside Hydro, built 1903-6 and taken shortly afterwards note the newly planted trees. This gives an impression of the grandeur of this building

CONTENTS

Introduction	6
1 – Lost in the mists of time	8
2 – Church and Chapel	16
3 – Lead Mining and Quarrying	27
4 – Matlock Bath – the Spa village	36
5 – Matlock Bank – the Hydropathic town	46
6 – Transport	59
7 – Services	71
8 – Leisure activities	82
9 – Famous persons	107
10 – The Buildings and Parks	117
11 – Employment	138
12 – Education	151
13 – The Two World Wars	157
14 – Local Government	162
15 – Epilogue	163
Appendices	169
I – Incumbents of the Church of England	169
II – War memorials	172
III – Population	177
IV – Mayors & Chairpersons	179
References	181
Acknowledgements	183

INTRODUCTION

The "Matlocks" is a portmanteau name for a group of villages and settlements that lie in the centre of Derbyshire, in an area known as the White Peak and firmly located in the southern Pennines. They lie in or near to a beautiful, natural and narrow gorge having the River Derwent at its core with a tributary, the Bentley Brook. These waterways have been and still are exploited.

Geologically the lower levels are of limestone, which contains numerous mineral veins, the upper levels are of Millstone Grit or Gritstone. The limestone is heavily mineralised mostly with lead ore (galena), barytes (caulk), zinc (wad) and fluorspar, all of which have been exploited over the centuries. The limestone has also been exploited for the stone is of value in road making and for chemical use, the gritstone was used for the manufacture of grinding stones and building stone. All these industries are now consigned to history.

Within memory the local spring waters have been used to create a hydropathic industry of some size now gone. The legacy of this is a number of fine buildings now used for other purposes, the Derbyshire County offices, a home for the elderly, a convent and other uses.

The area now comprises the following:

Old Matlock	the original Matlock with the church of St Giles as its focal point
Matlock Bridge	the site of an ancient crossing of the River Derwent
Matlock Bank	an elevated part of the area which grew out of the hydropathic industry
Matlock Green	the original Matlock market area
Matlock Bath	an area in the gorge where the "thermal" springs occur
Matlock Moor	the uplands above Matlock Bank
Lumbs Dale	the upper valley of the Bentley Brook
Riber	the highest area dominated by Riber "Castle"
Hearthstone	a farming community near to Riber
Upperwood	a hidden hamlet overlooking Matlock Bath
Willersley	a lost village destroyed by Sir Richard Arkwright
Scarthin	adjoining Cromford
Masson	a hill overlooking Matlock Bath and Matlock Bridge.
Dimple	

Masson is the name of a large hill euphemistically called a mountain by Victorian writers. The same name was also applied originally to the Derwent valley below the hill, which was known as Masson Dale until the time of Arkwright and first mentioned as "le Masseden" translated to "Maessa's valley". One cannot ignore the similarity with Mestesford. (PND p389). The area comes under the stewardship of the Soke, Wapentake and Hundred of Wirksworth and the See of Derby, previously Southwell, Nottinghamshire and, before this, Lichfield, Staffordshire.

The area attracts many day visitors and holiday makers who treat the Matlocks as an inland resort, others enjoy the hill walking and the speliologists explore the mines and caves. Matlock Bath is a Mecca for motor cyclists at weekends, and the area is used as a dormitory for those who work in Sheffield, Derby, Nottingham and further afield.

Some condemn Matlock Bath for its Blackpool-like atmosphere. Admittedly it seems to have too many fish fryers but overall it is a pleasing spot and in stark contrast to the cities the visitors hail from.

The writer well remembers his childhood visits during World War II and the later delight of living on the slopes of Masson Hill, which is a world apart from the riverside.

Today, the quarries are reverting back to nature, hotels and bed and breakfasts prosper as do the ice cream parlours, fish fryers and souvenir shops. The crowds congregate to enjoy a stroll along the promenade at Matlock Bath or to let their children play in Hall Leys Park, Matlock Bridge.

Also of recent date, the Derwent valley has been designated a World Heritage Site, which runs from the Silk Mill in Derby up to and including Masson Mill at Matlock Bath. Also at the time of writing it is intended to spend a small fortune on Hall Leys Park, High Tor, the Lovers' Walks and Derwent Park. Whilst hydropathy is a thing of the past, the Derbyshire Dales are still members of the British Spa Federation along with Bath, Buxton, Cheltenham, Droitwich Spa, Harrogate, Malvern, Royal Leamington Spa, Royal Tunbridge Wells and Woodhall Spa and, at the time of writing, it looks as if the spas will be exploited again, centred on the Matlocks. This gives a total of ten spa towns; originally there were 220. (MM 07.03.2002)

There is a little farming in the area, mostly cattle and sheep with cereals, mainly barley. The land varies from 94m ASL in the valley bottom on the road outside Tor House and 338m ASL at the summit of Masson Hill. This along with its long distance from industry, makes the area a healthy place to live due to the clean air and clean water, attributes recognised by the old hydropathic industry.

We must not forget the other Matlocks in the United States of America. One originally called Maurice, which they renamed after our Matlocks when they found that this name already existed in the same state, Iowa. In 1999 it had a population of 92 being founded in 1883. The two top employers are Maggert Machine and Matlock Electric. The locals have dubbed it "Firetown" after a conflagration in 1909 that destroyed half of the main street. It lies in Sioux County about 200 miles northwest of the State Capital, Des Moines. The other Matlock is in Mason County, Olympic Peninsular in the State of Washington an area of some 26,000 hectares, its only industry being logging under the control of the Simpson Timber Company, the largest company of its kind in the United States of America. This Matlock is more of an area than a "town" and comprises a church, garage, meeting hall and a small convenience store having a post office. It boasts 450 registered voters and 220 students attend the Mary Knight School. (Hall, In Lit)

Matlock also gives its name to two scarce minerals found in the area; Phosgenite ($Pb_2(CO_3)Cl_2$) and Matlockite ($PbFCl$) found in Bage Mine, Little Bolehill. Of interest there is also a Cromfordite. These very rare minerals can be seen in the British Museum of Natural History who have the best specimens: others are in private collections.

(Burr P S p.377-86)

Finally, this history is to be published a century since the only previous one, *Matlock Manor and Parish* by Benjamin Bryan, London, 1903, an excellent book to which the writer owes a considerable debt.

Peter J Naylor GSC IEng BA BSc
Cromford
February, 2003

Most of the sources consulted give measurements and money in the now defunct Imperial Units. These have been retained in order to keep the flavour of the times but a conversion to SI units is given in most cases in brackets thus – 10 acres (4 hectares). The larger measurements are converted to two or less decimal places.

Today's trend to use BCE (Before Common Era) and CE (Common Era) has been used.

① LOST IN THE MISTS OF TIME

Stone age man has left evidence of his presence in the area, for there was a stone structure (similar to Kit's Koty House, near Eccles – itself a Celtic place name – in Kent) near to Riber Castle which Smedley caused to be removed, as it disturbed his Christian susceptibilities in harking back to pagan times. A cromlech with a water stoop stood at the summit of Bilberry Knoll, the ruinous remains of which are scattered about, and said to be similar to the Logan Stone, St. Agnes Island, Scilly, yet another casualty of Mr Smedley? A couple of cottagers (man and wife, when aged 80 and 84 respectively) in 1866 recalled to the eponymous Dr Cox that this and a stone chair (similar to the one on Carsington Pastures?), was also on this site and remained long after the ruination. A further circle once stood at the summit of Cromford Hill on Barrel Edge where the abandoned quarry now is but this was quarried away during Arkwright's time. The summit of Masson Hill has a small barrow. The Celts however, made use of these Megalithic remains with which Derbyshire is well provided.(DAJ XXXVII p.59 and IX, January 1887).

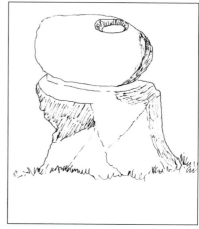

It is recorded that another stone age edifice existed on Matlock Moor called The Seven Brideron, cleared in the 19th century, possibly by quarrymen for the stone. It was recorded in October 1764 as being a seven-stone circle, but another observer recorded it as a nine-stone circle with some of the stones standing higher than a tall man on a diameter of 7.5 m. There is no trace of this circle today; it stood a few hundred meters due north of Palethorpe Farm.(Morgan and Morgan p.88)

Animal remains of ancient origin have been found in the Matlocks. When the tufa bank at Matlock Bath was being quarried – it was a great favourite with Victorians for their grottos – an arrow head was found thought to be of Roman or Saxon origin.(Mello p.9) Also, when the same tufa bed was being levelled for the construction of Temple Walk, the skull and antlers of a moose were found and subsequently sent to the British Museum in London.(Adam 4 ed. p.56) When the coffer dam was being built for the erection of the bridge to the train station at Matlock Bath in 1848 the horns of a red deer were found at a depth of 8 ft (2.45m) below the river bed.(Bryan p.123) The rest of its skeleton was later found in a nearby tufa bed.

Dateable archaeological finds have been rare in the area. In 1795, whilst cutting into the limestone on Scarthin Nick, a workman found a human skeleton complete with sixty copper coins of Roman origin mostly from the time of the two Constantines and Lucius.(Naylor CaH14) These passed into the hands of Charles Hurt of Wirksworth and were subsequently sold by Sotheby's.(Bryan p.124) In 1893 a burial was found in Cawdor Quarry during the removal of over burden near to Megdale Farm. Human remains were found under a large stone cap comprising four skulls and some long bones.(DAJ 1901 p.40).

The Celts were certainly active in the area. Crich and Pentrich are both Celtic place names and Derwent is a Celtic word meaning dark water, no doubt due to the peaty nature of the river, much as it is today. By the Celts we also mean the later Iron Age, for they were skilled craftsmen in this metal.

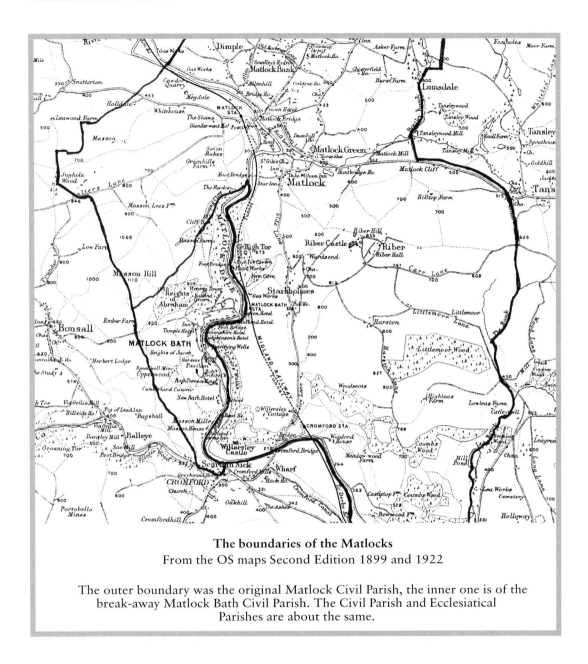

The boundaries of the Matlocks
From the OS maps Second Edition 1899 and 1922

The outer boundary was the original Matlock Civil Parish, the inner one is of the
break-away Matlock Bath Civil Parish. The Civil Parish and Ecclesiatical
Parishes are about the same.

Opposite page: A sketch by the author based on the Logan Stone, St Agnes Island, Scillies
from a sketch in Borlases's "Antiquities of Cornwall". Note the water stoop into which the locals
placed flowers. It is 3.2m high and 14.3m circumference round the middle

The nearest source for the ore would have been in the Belper area and the forge sites that exist at Belper and Alderwasley may be the descendants of ancient workings. Their hill forts can be seen at the summit of Mam Tor near Castleton and one has just been discovered near Belper.

The Celts were tribal and it is believed that either the Coritani or the Brigantes ruled the area. The truth might be that they ruled it in turn, for tribal boundaries would have been constantly changing. They were a warlike people who enjoyed fighting with each other.

It is recorded that there used to be a headless cross at Matlock, possibly in or close to the church-yard. This could have been similar to the one at Eyam, originally being a Celtic lyth carved with knot work.(WMSS 6667, f.329)

Alas, evidence of these people is scarce locally. We are still waiting for the big discovery, which will refine our knowledge of these skilled if bloodthirsty people.

These are the people who confronted Julius Caesar on his foray to our south coast in BCE 55, followed a year later by an invasion force. He has left us with a very revealing insight into these peoples in his *Gallic Wars*. The Romans had arrived and they came to stay for over 400 years. They reached our area in circa 71 CE and exploited the local lead deposits to satisfy their need for bathing and sewage disposal. Indeed, lead from Derbyshire found its way to Rome and beyond, and there was a time when our local lead was rationed as it fetched a lower price in Rome than their locally pro-duced and Spanish metal. Romans did not do the mining, this would have been contracted out to a local petty chieftain in return for protection and the advantages offered by the Romans in a Roman colony. Most of the army were Spanish mercenaries; one's heart goes out to them when patrolling the local hills on a cold January day.

They would have exploited the fresh water pearls for which Britain was famous and which at-tracted them greatly. These were collected until recent memory by a Yorkshire pearl fisher. Alas, the Swan Mussel the source of these excellent pearls has suffered serious decline. These prized gems were popular at that time and much coveted, indeed pearls along with gold and slaves are why they came.

The road from Rocester to Chesterfield was Roman and is now known as Hereward Street. It came down Cromford Hill and forded the River Derwent just downstream of where Cromford Bridge now stands, then climbed the hill to Starkholmes. The lead produced in the Matlocks would have been easily moved along this road and on to Brough on the Humber Estuary.

Claims have been made that certain lead mines in the Matlocks are of Roman origin. This may be so, but there is little evidence to support it. Any ancient workings would by now have vanished due to the work of later miners. As the lead veins are vertical or nearly so and as the ore lies just below the sub-soil the Romans may well have exploited it from the surface thus avoiding the digging of mines. The best contender for this may well be the "Roman" mine on High Tor.

The best evidence we have of Roman lead production is the several pigs of metal found in the Matlocks. Of the pigs traceable to this area most have been found elsewhere and these can be identi-fied by the inscription LVT for Lutudaren(m) a location which puzzled historians for many years. Some placed it as Wirksworth, some as Chesterfield, Templeborough near Rotherham and unbelievably at Church Wilne. Prior to the filling of Carsingtom Water it was established that this heretofore mythical site was where the water is now. This was the author's own belief for many years for it is located where the Street (Buxton to Little Chester) crosses Hereward Street.

Most of our lead, as ingots or pigs, was transported to Brough on Humberside – a large number have been found

Right: A sketch by the author based on Kit Koty's House, Kent. It is approximately 4.0m high overall

at South Cave nearby. These may well have come from the Matlocks. They would have used pack animals or floated the lead on rafts down the River Derwent and thence to the Humber via the River Trent.

During Anglo-Saxon times the area lay on the borders of Mercia and Northumbria, with the emphasis on Mercia and its then capital Repton. After the Norman conquest the new king took the manor from the old one. The Domesday survey of 1086 gives us our first insight into the Matlocks, for it records:

In Matlock (Mestesford) King Edward had 2 carucates of land without tax. Waste. Meadow, 8 acres; 1 lead mine; woodland pasture in places, 3 leagues long and 2 wide. (This was approximately 3,237 hectares).

To this manor are attached these outliers, Matlock (Meslach), Snitterton, Wensley, Bonsall, Ible, Tansley. In them 7 carucates of land taxable. Land for 7 ploughs.

11 villagers and 12 smallholders have 6 ploughs.

Meadow, 22 acres (8.9 hectares); *woodland pasture 2 leagues long and 1 league wide* (777 hectares); *underwood as much.*

A further entry for the Wirksworth Wapentake refers to the manors of "Darley, Matlock (Mestesforde), Wirksworth, Ashbourne and Parwich, with their outliers, paid £32 and 6 sesters of honey before 1066, now £40 of silver."(Morgan pp 272b,c & 272 c.)

This suggests that Mestesforde and Meslach were separate communities and the Morgan edition of the Domesday Survey calls the former Matlock Bridge. This is unlikely as the ford in question is at Nestes or Nestus – a corruption of new stowse or windlass – the mine on the Heights of Abraham (Nesterside), which would place this river crossing where the bridge to Matlock Bath station is today, the banks being built up at the coming of the railway. Meslach therefore must be Matlock Bridge, a location which would not have been fordable and which name over the centuries became corrupted to Matlock. The reference to a lead mine is dealt with in Chapter 3. The silver, which had to be found as an annual tax valued at £40, is a considerable amount of metal, which had to be separated from the lead when being smelted. It also suggests that, at approximately 20 ounces to the ton of lead, a large amount of lead was being extracted. This lead would have been sent to the new churches that were being built and the new monastic houses that were being founded under the aegis of the Conqueror; not forgetting the coffin linings for the better off. The area seems to have been well wooded, possibly as the northern limit of the Duffield Frith, a hunting forest dominated by a castle at Duffield, having the third largest keep in the country after the Tower of London and Colchester. The reference to waste may be due to the harrying of the north which touched this area and probably not to moorland which is a more recent phenomenon following deforestation.

At the time of Edward the Confessor (reigned 1042-66) the manor of Matlock was worth £11 2s 6d (£11.12).

A Jordanus de Sutton died 16 Edward I (1280) possessed of lands which he left to his son John who died 33 Edward I (1288) who then left it to his son John. During the reign of Edward I a quarter of the manor was held as a knight's fee under Ralph Bakepaire. The Leches and Poles held lands at Matlock under Henry VIII (reigned 1509-47).

The most important family for centuries was the Woolleys of Riber who bought vast tracts of land during the reign of Henry VII. This wealth originated with an heiress of the Ribers or Riberghs, who married a John Robotham and whose daughter Margaret married William Wolley. The Wolleys (et. Var. De Woley, Wolegh, Woleghe, Woleigh) were in 1313 of Wolegh in Hollingworth and Broadbottom in the Parish of Motterham in Longdendale, near Glossop. They held the Riber estate for some seven generations and were memorable for their lengthy marriages, numbering many silver, golden and diamond wedding anniversaries. An Anthony who died in 1578 was the father of a William of Overton Hall, Ashover, also John of Allen's Hill, Dimple, and Thomas of Bonsall. The Marston-on-Dove branch is descended from John, which family produced William the antiquary and Adam the genealogist and topographer. The last of the Riber Wolleys was Anthony who died without issue in 1668 and whose sister sold the estate to Thomas Statham, to be bought in 1681 by a John Chappell. In 1724, the estate was divided into two moieties to two heiresses of the Revd John Chappell when one moiety was sold to the Wall family and the other to a Joseph Greatrex which then passed to the Allens, causing Riber Hall to be divided as it still is.

This longevity amongst the Wolleys is best described by the lives of Adam and Grace Wolley of Allen's Hill. Adam was married to Grace for 76 years – Grace being only sixteen years of age when she married Adam. She survived him by 12 years, dying in 1669 aged 104 years old. Family tradition had it that she was 110 years old when she died and Adam was 100 years old when he died. They share a table tomb of Derbyshire alabaster located in St Giles' Church, Matlock Town. A William Woolley recorded that in his lifetime – he died in 1732 – there were only three or four good stone houses, which suggests a population of about 20. This cannot be true, he appears to be ignoring the majority of the people who would have lived in hovels.

The manor of Willersley has had a mixed ownership. Several baronial families have had possession: the de Ferrers, Talbots, Pierpoints and Lascelles, of which curiously all the lines died out! Henry Talbot, Bess of Hardwick's stepson was in possession in the late 16th century and he died without a son. His heiress and daughter Gertrude married Robert Pierpoint, created Viscount Newark and Earl of Kingston by Charles I. Robert gathered 4,000 soldiers to follow the King's standard and was made a Cavalier lieutenant-general, being much hunted by the Roundheads. He was accidentally shot by one of his own side when attempting to escape the opposition in a boat. His mother was Frances, sister of the first Earl of Devonshire. The manor devolved to a younger branch of the Pierpoints who gave it to Sir D'Arcy Dawes of an old Putney family. Sir William D'Arcy DD MA, the father Sir D'Arcy, was an Archbishop of York and a Fellow of St John's College, Oxford later Master of St. Catherine's Hall, Cambridge. After succeeding his brother as the third baronet, he married Frances heiress of Sir Thomas D'Arcy, becoming Chaplain to William III to become the prebend of Worcester Cathedral, later becoming the Bishop of Chester and thence Archbishop of York in 1713. He was one of the regents of the kingdom on the death of Queen Anne. The son of Sir D'Arcy became the fifth baronet and died without issue. The manor then fell to Edwin Lascelles who was made a peer in 1790, dying five years later without issue. His cousin was Baron Harewood, Viscount Lascelles and Earl of Harewood. In 1778, Harewood sold the manor to Edmund Hodgkinson, who sold it on to Thomas Hallett Hodge who – in turn – sold it to Richard (later Sir Richard) Arkwright in 1782. In 1924, the Arkwrights auctioned the Willersley and Cromford estates in parcels.(Tilley p.255-7)

The Manor of Matlock has been owned as follows:

1066	King Edward the Confessor
1086	King William the Conqueror
1138	King Stephen passed it to Robert de Ferrers when he was made Earl of Derby
1199	William, Earl of Derby with his heirs was granted the fee farm of the Manors of Wirkesworth (sic) and Esseburne (Ashbourne) together with the whole Wapentake (of Wirksworth) paying £70 sterling to the exchequer per annum in equal amounts at Midsummer and Easter.
1204	King John gave a grant of inheritance of the same manors as for 1199 for which he paid 500 marks.
36 Henry III (1252)	William son of William obtained free warren at Matlock. (This allowed William to impound an area for the raising and keeping of deer and rabbits. Both were delicacies at that time).
7 Edward I (1275)	Reverted to the crown after Robert son of William de Ferrers sided with Simon de Montford, Earl of Leicester, the King granting the manor to Edmund, Earl of Lancaster.
	John of Gaunt inherited it as part of the Duchy of Lancaster with which it remained until:-

1628	Charles I granted the manor by letters patent to Edward Ditchfield, Humphrey Clark, ffrancis Mosse and John Highlow, all citizens of London in trust for the Corporation of London.
1629	Early January, an indenture was made between the above named trustees reselling the manor to John Middleton Esq. of Wannesley (Annesley) Nottinghamshire, Arthur Moore of Milthorpe, Derbyshire, Gent., Richard Senior of Cowley, Derbyshire and George Heathcote of Cutthorpe, Derbyshire in trust as copyholders.
1630	January 14th – articles of agreement entered into between the above and William Walker, Adam Wolley with others as copyholders and with Elizabeth Wolley (widow of Adam Wolley of Riber on behalf of William Wolley her infant son) declaring that the said William Middleton and others stood seized in trust for the benefit of William Walker *et al*, the copyholders according to their several shares. The rent paid to the Duchy of Lancaster was £16.10s 3d (£16.51) payable at the feasts of the Annunciation and St Michael the Archangel, the profits being divided equally amongst the copyholders. Of this payment, £14 13s 5d (£14.67) was the total of the rents payable to the copyholders, the balance being payable to the Crown. It is of interest to give the individual rents received by the copyholders:

William Wolley Gent.	£2 8s 8d (£2.43)
Anthony Woodward	£1 14s 1d (£1.70)
John Mellish	£1 7s 0d (£1.35)
William Walker	£1 5s 0d (£1.25)
Remainder	£1 or less the least being
Thomas Walker of Wirksworth	21/2d (£0.01)

Even by the standards of those days these rents are small, thus vacancies of copyholders were not filled and this came to a head after they had all died in:

1699 Thomas Statham the largest holder of the royalty had new trustees appointed.

1700 October 17th – an indenture was made between Thomas Statham and John Thornhill with Ann his wife (grandchild and heir-in-law of William Booth Gent.) the manor was conveyed to William Turner, Michael Burton, Arthur Dakeyne and Expurius Turner, Gent. (we do not get names as exotic as this one today!) in trust for the copyholders.

1701	Same year, proceedings were instituted in the Court of Chancery against the proprietors of the manor by Sir John Statham Kt. which proceedings were sustained until;
1716	June 25th when an award was made by John Port and John Beresford, Esq. who had been appointed arbitrators for settling disputes in the High Court of Chancery between these parties. They found for the copyholders and that the profits of Lomas's (Lumb's) Mill to be paid to the proprietors of the manor.

The trustees for the manor from this date forward were:

1716	John Beresford, John Port, John Chappell, Charles Greaves
1738	Bache Thornhill with others
1760	Francis Radford with others
1769	Bache Thornhill, Brooke Boothby, Francis Hurt, William Milnes, Alexander Barker

1785	Brooke Boothby, Bache Thornhill, William Milnes
1798	Bache Thornhill, Francis Hurt, Philip Gell, John Toplis, John Holland
1817	Bache Thornhill, Philip Gell, John Toplis
1830	Bache Thornhill the sole survivor – there were 190 copyholders in this year.
1971	William Bache Thornhill
1880	The courts had lapsed but were revived in this year by James Potter (solicitor)
1899	Revd. Fielding, Arthur Wolfe, Hamilton Gell, John Gilbert Crompton, Esq.

In 1903, James Potter, solicitor of Matlock Bridge was the court steward and the court-leet and view of Frankpledge (members of a tithing being responsible for each other) with the Great Court Baron were held every six months at Matlock and Matlock Bath in turn.

The lands which the Matlocks comprise have been owned by local families of note and as follows:

1527	Roger Foljambe – meadows, pasture, four messuages in Bonsall and Matlock
1528	Roger Leche of Chatsworth – three messuages
1541	Radulphus Leche had a messuage and ten acres (40.5 hectares) of land
1549	Thomas Agard Esq had three messuages and 20 acres (81 hectares)
1551	Godfrey Foljambe – messuages and lands in two places
1558	Sir William Cavendish Kt had a messuage and tenements
1663	Freeholders were: Anthony Bourne, Anthony Cotterell, Thomas Flynte, William Ludlam, Anthony Woodward, Adam Wolley and William Wolley as freeholders.

A return of 1873 resident owners of more than ten acres were 32 in number, those having 100 acres or more are as follows, with areas and annual values:

Frederic Arkwright	1,782 acres (722 hectares) plus
	656 acres (266 hectares) as executor of Peter Arkwright
	£4,794 14s (£4,794.70)
Mrs Charles Clark	212 acres (66 hectares) co-heiress of Adam Wolley
	£393
Mrs John Greaves	105 acres (42.5 hectares) £215
Revd W R Melville	210 acres (85 hectares) £665
W E Nightingale	2,238 acres (906 hectares) Lea Hurst £3,966
W H Nightingale	176 acres (71 hectares) £70
John Nuttall	192 acres (78 hectares) £398
C Childers Radford	1,117 acres (452 hectares) £1,218

Only one person had less than 10 acres (4 hectares) and that was William Nightingale who held 1 acre, 1 rood, 6 poles (0.62 hectares) worth £1 7s (£1.35).

As can be seen the Arkwrights and Nightingales held the largest portions by far and in total 4,853 acres (1,963 hectares), the latter family having been landed proprietors since 1777 when Peter Nightingale bought land, called Coumbs and Bow (Bough) Woods, on the south-east slope of Riber Hill from an Edmund Morphy. Part of this estate was sold in 1901 to Mr S E Marsden-Smedley.

Lea Mills were built by Peter Nightingale, Yeoman, who owned the lead smelter which used water wheels on the same stream to drive the bellows at the latter and the machinery at the former. As the boundary runs down the centre of this stream the mills lay half in the parish of Matlock and half in the parish of Ashover at that time. The mill originally spun cotton but was adapted after purchase by John Smedley in 1807 to make hosiery. Florence Nightingale of nursing fame was from the same family, being a great niece of Peter Nightingale.(Bryan ps 7-20)

Whilst the Matlocks had a reputation for their health-giving waters and atmosphere, there was a down side for the local inhabitants. A condition commonly known as "Derbyshire Neck" or Goitre or Bronchocele was not uncommon at Matlock Bath caused by drinking the warm spring water. It is a swelling of the thyroid and can become very large and unsightly. The condition cleared up after the laying of mains to the village using water from a different source to that used at Matlock Bath. However, the area must have had many benefits the least of which was longevity. It was recorded in a guide book of 1902, that the Matlocks had the lowest death rate of any resort in the United Kingdom at 10.5 deaths per 1,000 of the population compared with the rest of the country with an average of 20 deaths per 1,000 persons.

The origins of the place names are of interest, Matlock being dealt with elsewhere. Riber originated as Ryberg(h) meaning "Rye Hill", Willersley was "Willheard's clearing" and Scarthin is unclear. Masson was known as "le Masseden" translating as "Maessa's valley".

WEBSITES

There are numerous websites which cover the Matlocks. At 0900hrs on 30 December 2002 there were 85,645 pages available! The overwhelming number of trade pages are not included here but those that deal with the Matlocks historically or topographically are listed below.

www.andrewspages.dial.pipex.com/matlock/
www.cressbrook.co.uk/matlock (based on "P.D. Multimedia Guide")
www.derbyshireguide.co.uk/travel/matlock-bath
www.genuki.org.uk
www.knowhere.co.uk/3879 (based on "Knowhere Guide to Matlock")
www.matlockmercury.co.uk
USA
www.matlock.washington.city.guides.com

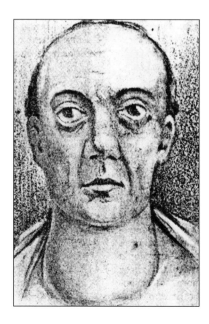

Left: A Sketch of a Goitre. This condition also known as "Derbyshire Neck" and its full name "Exophthalmic Goitre" was once common in Matlock Bath. It could be much more disfiguring than this sketch suggests. (The Universal Home Doctor, Odhams, London n.d.)

Church of England

The ecclesiastical parishes are as follows:

> Matlock (St Giles) – the Matlocks excluding Matlock Bath and Bank
> Matlock Bath – Matlock Bath (Holy Trinity), Matlock Dale (St John – a chapel of ease),
>   Scarthin (Mission Room)
> Matlock Bank (All Saints).

St Giles' Church, Old Matlock

There is no mention of a church in the Domesday Survey. The original Matlock church dedicated to St Giles is the oldest, dating from the 12th century, for it is recorded that the patronage of the Rectory was granted to the Dean of Lincoln in 1130.

By the end of the 15th century the original church had been substantially rebuilt of which the tower and some rubble are all that now remain. In the 18th century the church was extensively rebuilt: the north aisle in 1760 by Peter Nightingale, a lead merchant of Lea and uncle of the famous Florence Nightingale, and the south aisle by Richard later Sir Richard Arkwright, in 1783. This latter made the church appear as if it were "something like a mill or factory with battlements" (MPCG)

The chancel and nave were rebuilt in 1871, the architect being Benjamin Wilson of Derby. The south aisle and south chapel were added in 1898, the architect being P H Curry of Derby.(Pevsner p 272) A remnant of the 17th-century church can be seen in the churchyard as the façade of an earlier porch with the date 1636 cut into it. The font is large and Norman in origin and was buried in the rectory garden until 1924 when it was happily restored to the church. Immediately above the font is a roof boss of a king's head, the only survival from the medieval church. There is some good plate given in 1791 comprising a Chalice, Paten and a Flagon.

The Lady Chapel at the east end of the south aisle has a modern aumbry (a recess for church vessels) to contain the blessed Sacrament, set in a pillar to the left of the altar. Another chapel in the north aisle is a revival of a medieval guild chapel dedicated in 1955 and paid for by gifts from local industry. It is carved from Hopton Stone and designed by Colin Shewring. The stained glass by Lawrence Lee ARCA in the east window was installed in 1969 and the two light chancel window is by Heaton, Butler and Bayne of 1920.(Pevsner p 272) The glass by Lee is probably one of the finest pieces of modern glass in the county and was presented in memory of the Bailey family of the Butts, Matlock, 1838-1938.

Of the monuments, the one to Anthony Woolley dated 1576 is of note and made by the Royleys.

He is featured in a fur-lined gown, fashionable at that time with the better off. A tomb to Adam and Grace Woolley is located under the west window of the south aisle. This was placed here by their descendent, Adam Woolley of Riber in 1824, their four times great-grandson. Adam died in 1657 at the age of 100 years and his wife Grace died in 1669 aged 110 and they were married for 76 years. Another Woolley memorial is in the form of an altar tomb placed under the west window of the south aisle and dedicated to Anthony Woolley who died in 1578, together with his wife Agnes. The alabaster top slab – probably from Chellaston in the south of the county – shows Anthony and his wife with their six children – four boys and two girls. The edge of this tomb slab has been inscribed with the words, "Here lyeth the bodies of Anthonie Wolley and Agnes his wyffe wch Authors dyeth IV day of September in the yere of our LORD MDLXXVIII aged LXII and whose souls GOD hath taken mercy on". The Woolley hatchment can be seen in the Lady Chapel.

A permanent lamp in a ruby glass is located in the chancel as a lasting memorial to those who died in World War II. The kneelers at the altar rail were designed by the Rev. L N Childs and were embroidered by seven people.

This church still has its Maidens Crantses (Maidens Garlands) – there are others at Trusley and Ashford in the Water. They comprise a crown made of wood wrapped with paper together with paper cut-outs of a glove, collar and kerchief. Shakespeare refers to them as "Virgin Crants" which the priest objected to at the funeral of Ophelia. The crantse was carried before the coffin of the maiden who had been betrothed but robbed of her marriage by her untimely death. The carrier was a maiden of the same age and of similar presentation. After interment the crantse was hung above the pew of the bereaved parents. The crantses at Matlock and Trusley are contained in glazed frames, those at Ashford still hang in the church.(Naylor CD pps 29/30)

The organ has three manuals with pedals and 29 speaking stops and was built by J H Adkins of Derby in 1908. This replaced an earlier one, dated 1873, by Brindley and Foster of Sheffield who installed a two manual instrument, replacing one by Flight and Robson circa 1820, which was probably a barrel organ. The first organ proper was probably the one installed in 1844, it being reported that in 1870 it was played in accompaniment with fiddles, clarinet and a trumpet, no doubt played with cacophonous enthusiasm. The most recent organ was adorned with a Great Glory case by the Derbyshire "Grinling Gibbons", Advent Hunstone.(Tomkins ps. 84-6) This recalls the church "band" of the 19th century. The eponymous Phoebe Bown of whom more later, "played the viol (cello) for many years."

The bells are nine in number and hang in the tower, for details see Appendix VI. A custom was established in 1949 to ring the Angelus on the Feast of Annunciation. Another tradition was started in

Opposite page: St Giles Church. This sketch of the Parish Church predates the many alterations that took place in the 19th century. Of particular note is the external stair way to the gallery. Circa. 1850 (Adam W p.86)
Right: St Giles Church

St Gile's Parish Church. Seen from Bentley Brook, all the buildings in the foreground have been consigned to history. This view is Circa 1850 (Author's Collection)

St John's Chapel of Ease built 1897 this picture c. 1920
(Derbyshire County Council, Libraries and Heritage)

the mid-16th century by a Mr Davis of Davis's Lot, Matlock Bank when he asked that the bells be sounded on his burial day (26 September 1860) and on the death of any of his descendents. This has now either fallen out of use or his descendents have lost interest as there is no-one who can recall this custom.(Bryan p.48)

The church is dedicated to St. Giles, the patron saint of cripples, beggars and blacksmiths. This St. Giles – there are many others – was popular in the middle ages and his shrine was much visited by pilgrims, there being at least 160 in England alone. A small statue of this saint can be seen on one of the clergy stalls in the chancel, which shows St. Giles with his pet hind. His only companion was a hind; he had rescued it from huntsmen led by Flavius Wamba, king of the Visigoths. The king so admired St. Giles's humanity that he built a monastery for him on the river Rhone in France now the site of Saint-Gilles. We have to be cautious with this story for there are many events ascribed to this saint. This one sounds the most plausible. He died in 712 and his feast day is September 1.(Book of Saints pps 267/8)

By 1896 the churchyard was full and the churchwardens bought a 1.25 acre (0.51 hectares) plot of land to extend it. This was sold by F C Arkwright for £50, another £90 was spent in planting and laying it out. The Right Rev. Dr Ridding, Bishop of Southwell consecrated this extension in April of the following year.(Bryan p.40-1) In 1880, an Act was passed whereby non-conformists were allowed to be buried in Anglican churchyards. The first such burial in the Matlocks was on Christmas Day 1880 when Drill Sergeant O'Brien (a Roman Catholic) was interred, the officiating priest being the Rev. Canon McKenna of Derby. The incumbent of the church caused a bell to be rung.(Bryan 48-9)

All Saints' Church, Matlock Bank

With the growth of Matlock Bank, based on the arrival and expansion of the hydropathic industry, a need arose for a separate parish with its own church. It was decided that this new church should be funded by the parishioners without a charge on the rates. They started with a school and mission room.

Mr James Arkwright laid the foundation stone on 6 November 1874 for the school room and mission room on Dimple Road/Woolley Road junction, Matlock on land provided by the Rev. John Wolley, for which he was paid the lowly sum of £100. This was opened on 10 August 1875 by Captain Arkwright MP in the presence of the Archdean of Derby, the Rural Dean and Rector of Matlock, who presided over a lunch for 70 people. The total cost was £1,200, which carried a debt of £270. A Mr and Mrs Wright of Bradford donated the school desks, a reading desk for the school and a pulpit for the Mission Room. The Arkwright family provided £100 per annum for three years for the benefit of the curate. The school opened for pupils in time for the Autumn term on 30 August 1875.

In January 1880 the Rev. John Higgs (a native of the parish) gave a plot of land for the church on Smedley Street West, the architects T H & F Healey of Bradford were appointed and their plans were approved on 7 June 1882. The foundation stone was laid, complete with the customary time capsule – which contains a Bible and a prayer book. The Bishop of Lichfield was present along with local non-conformist ministers and the Salvation Army. Only a part was built initially due to a lack of funds.

This new church was opened on Easter Day, 15 April 1884 and was consecrated on 17 September of the same year. It housed 360 worshippers and cost over £3,000 (about £300,000 in today's money!).

The previously mentioned Rev. John Higgs gave land for the vicarage in 1889, and the local Co-operative Society Shop was bought for £630 for use as the church house and meeting room with accommodation for a caretaker.(Mitchell)

The organ built in 1886 by Foster & Andrew of Kingston-upon-Hill was a gift from a Mr Cole of Southport. The organ costing £500 was only one of many gifts donated to this church. In 1961 it was modified by J W Walter of London and in 1982 it was overhauled by Midland Organ Builders of Derby.(Tomkins)

Of particular note in this beautiful church are the stained glass east windows, designed by Sir Edward Coley Burne-Jones and built and installed by the William Morris Company in 1905. This comprises three lancets with a rose above of the saints and prophets.(Pevsner p274)

Chapel of St John the Baptist

This exquisite little chapel – it has only 80 sittings – on St John's Road was built as a chapel of ease for St Giles' Church by the architect Sir E Guy Dawber, one of only two churches by him. Sir Guy lived in the parish at that time. This was built in 1897 at the expense of a Mrs Louisa Sophia Harris who lived at "The Rocks" just below the church, daughter of Brooke Leacroft who resided at Cliff House.(Bryan p.176) The exterior is of local stone with mullioned windows and a pyramidal turret; internally it has fittings and plasterwork having touches of the arts and crafts movement.(Pevsner p 274)

This chapel sits into the hillside with a stone trough at the roadside fed by a spring. This trough always seems to support a small colony of frogs. This charming gem of a chapel, now over a hundred years old should be preserved for it seems to be a little neglected, it would be a tragedy if it became vandalised.(Derbyshire Countryside September, 1978)

Church of the Holy Trinity, Matlock Bath

This church was built to provide both the inhabitants and the many visitors with their own place of worship. It was built in 1842 by Weightman & Hadfield, the south aisle and the chancel being enlarged in 1873-74 by T E Streatfield.(Pevsner p 273) This church has a very fine crocketed spire. The first stone was laid by the Venerable Walter Shirley, Archdeacon of Derby on 9 June 1841 and it was opened for worship on 5 October 1842, being consecrated by the Bishop of Hereford acting for the Bishop of Lichfield. Bevington & Sons of London built the first organ at this church, modified in 1876 by W. Hill & Son, a tremulant being added in 1906 and a bass flute in 1930. An electronic organ was bought in 1975, since removed.(Tomkins)

Scarthin Mission Room

This was built as a satellite of Holy Trinity Church, being in the same parish. The intention was to tempt parishioners away from the rash of non-conformity in Scarthin and adjoining Cromford. The foundation stone was laid by Mr Charles Clarke on 5 August 1868 and it opened for worship on 8 April 1869, having been built by the vicar and churchwardens of the mother church. The architect was John A Whyatt of Manchester. This chapel was known as the Scarthin Mission Room. It closed for worship in 1955 when it was sold for the sum of £400 to a Mr and Mrs Gerald Needham, road hauliers whose planning application for a roadside canopy and petrol pumps was happily refused. It is presently used for a motor car repair garage and has been spoiled, but not by the present user.(Naylor CaH p 74)

Non-Conformist

Lady Glenorchy Chapel – Congregational

Now lost. Willielma, Viscountess Glenorchy, wife of John, Viscount Breadalbane, when travelling south in the Matlocks had to rest for a day and night due to her carriage breaking down. Whilst here she enquired after the spiritual welfare of the locals and did not like what she was told. In August 1784, a day after the above mentioned event, she organised the purchase of a chapel to seat 300 persons, which had been built near to the present Masson Mill at Matlock Bath. This was swept away by a road widening scheme in 1961. She resided in the area until the purchases were finalised and intended to continue living locally but ill health dogged her and she died a year later.

She made over the house, chapel and furniture to the Rev. Jonathan Scott, one of her protégés, as a deed of gift being without limitation and restriction to himself and his wife. She also bequeathed to him a fortune of £5,000 to be spent on the training of young men for the ministry. In addition she presented the chapel, dated 1777, with its communion plate which bore her arms. Lady Glenorchy was sincere in her approach for she endowed many chapels throughout Britain, the principal of which in Edinburgh contains her tomb.

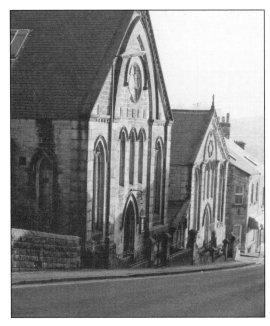

The original intention was that this chapel would have Anglican principles but it was invested with Independent ideas and by 1900 it was known as a Congregational chapel. The adjoining house was the residence of one of Sir Richard Arkwright's partners, Samuel Need (an Independent) and, at his death in 1781, the house was bought and used as the incumbent's residence – the first, from 1790, being the Rev. Joseph Whitehead, who spread his work over nearby parishes. He retired in 1794 to be succeeded by the Rev. Jonathan Scott, who having been in the army was dubbed Captain Scott. He suffered an injury in an accident and retired to Nantwich, Cheshire where he died in 1807, bequeathing his library of 700 books to the Glenorchy Chapel. He was succeeded by the Rev. John Wilson of Huddersfield in 1797; retiring to Nottingham in 1931 he was followed by the Reverends R Littler, T M Newnes, W Tiler and F R Bellamy which latter took office in 1867. Newnes was the father of the publisher, see Chapter 9.(Bryan p.177-180) The Rev. Newnes's son was George Newnes who created a magazine and newspaper empire, including the periodical *Titbits* and a progenitor of the Matlock Tramway.

Lady Glenorchy is remembered by a conference centre in her name on Chapel Lane, Wirksworth which is managed by the United Reform Church that absorbed the function of her chapel at Matlock Bath on its closure.

Methodism and its variants

Methodism was and still is popular in the Matlocks but, due to the loss of congregations, many of the original Methodist (Wesleyan *et al*) churches and chapels have been abandoned over the years and have all joined into a single congregation at the United Methodist Church on Bank Road.

Most of the information herein has been gleaned from the histories which can be seen on the back wall of the above mentioned church which was renovated, updated and re-opened in February 1987 after four years of deliberation and building works.

Methodism

In 1746, England was divided into seven Methodist circuits with Derbyshire forming part of the Yorkshire one. Due to the rapid expansion of the movement in the country it was divided again two years later into nine circuits of which Derbyshire was transferred to the Cheshire one. In 1765 Derbyshire joined with Nottingham and Leicester to form its own circuit and, by 1782, Derby had its own circuit including Ashby-de-la-Zouch in the south and Winster in the north. 1803 found Belper in

Above: The original non conformist chapel with its school room

a separate circuit that included, apart from Belper town, local societies at Cromford, Winster, Milltown and Wirksworth.

Cromford was the location of the home mission station by 1807, which exists on Chapel Hill and is now a private house. Four years later Cromford had its own circuit. This village also had its chapel located in Scarthin, dated 1853 and accommodated 300 worshippers This is now an engineering works.

In the early years the Methodists were meeting in peoples' homes and any other convenient buildings. The year 1840 was possibly the most significant date for local Methodists as they built their first Wesleyan Church on Snitterton Road. On 13 February 1867, Matlock Bath became head of the Matlock Circuit with a new chapel at a cost of £1,800 (a furniture store today). By 1882 Matlock had its own circuit and a new church was built on Bank Road, which is in use today. The congregation moved to this church from Snitterton Road.

A Deed of Union was signed in 1832 bringing together the Wesleyan, primitive Methodist and United Methodist and in 1866 the Matlock Methodist Church was formed. This church on Bank Road has undergone changes during its successful life; 1904 saw the addition of a tower and porch designed by the architect, Horace G Bradley of Birmingham and major works carried out later.

Primitive Methodism

The first "camp meeting" was held in 1807 at Mow Cop, Stoke on Trent, Staffordshire and was promptly condemned by the Wesleyan Conference as "highly improper and likely to be productive of considerable mischief". In spite of this, Hugh Bourne and William Clowes continued evangelising and were expelled from Methodist societies in 1808 and 1810 respectively. Three years later Clowes set up his own society and by the following year the "first class tickets" were issued having the text "but we desire to hear what thou thinkest, for as concerning this sect, we know that everywhere it is spoken against" (Acts 28 v 22).

The first plan of preachers was established in 1820 when missionaries were sent from Belper to the Matlocks. The first church was built on Winster East Bank in 1823 to be enlarged in 1850. The Winster circuit was set up by dividing the Belper circuit.

The Matlock Primitive Methodist Church was built in 1838 having 50 members, which was to reduce to ten by 1836; the initial enthusiasm seems to have faded. However, in 1856 it was rebuilt and a Sunday School was added in 1878. This new chapel sat 550 worshippers and the cost was, complete with the manse, £3,424 and £1,101 for the school. This is the building higher up Bank Road opposite the Derbyshire County Offices. A school room was added in 1885 and the whole has the appearance of two chapels side by side.

This church had an organ by Brindley & Foster in 1886, rebuilt twice by J H Adkins in 1904 and 1926 on which latter date it was equipped with a pneumatic action. Whilst this organ is now lost, the old school room is equipped with a full Werlitzer organ which is sometimes played in concerts.

Matlock Moor was not forgotten as this had its own chapel by September 1903 which is still used, followed by Ward End, Starkholmes two years later, alas no longer in use.

The Primitive Methodists signed the deed of union of 1932 already referred to.

Wesleyan Methodist Church, Matlock Bath

This church was opened in 1865, the premises being designed by Henry Fuller of Manchester. It is now a furniture repository. This church had an organ by Lloyd of Nottingham in the 1870s. (Tomkins p.82)

Primitive Methodist, Starkholmes

This chapel, originally known as the Fox Memorial Chapel, was built in 1823 on a plot of land bought from John Higgot of Riber for £2 10s (£2.50). It was later rebuilt in 1905 and closed in 1993. It contained 180 sittings and had an organ. This instrument in the original chapel was installed in the 1840s and rebuilt in the 1870s by J M Grunwell of Derby. A new organ by J H Adkin was installed in 1905 to be dismantled in 1994 and put into storage – for some future use?(Tomkin p.89) There is a school room in the semi-basement. The first minister was the Rev. James Burton of Matlock Bank.(Bryan p.69)

Free Methodism

John Wesley died in 1791 and schisms were quickly formed one of which was the Independent Methodist Connection in 1805, mostly in Lancashire where it is still independent and successful. In 1810, the Primitive Methodist Connection was created followed by the founding of the Bible Christian Methodists five years later. In 1836, the Wesleyan Methodist Association was founded followed by the Armenian and Faith Methodists in Derby.

In 1849 the Wesleyan Methodist Reform Church movement was started, which grew out of the expulsion of three Wesleyan ministers by the Wesleyan Conference. This caused repercussions locally and mass meetings were held to support them. This support comprised 780 persons initially but this figure fell to 496 by 1852. They never again reached the 1849 figure.

In 1857 the United Methodist Free Church was formed by seceders, the majority of whom were from the Wesleyan Reform Union which is still independent.

1864 saw the founding of the Cromford United Methodist Free Church Circuit destined to be the Matlock Circuit in 1873. Yet further changes were to come for in 1907 the United Methodist Reform Circuit joined the Bible Christian Methodist New Connection to form the United Methodist Church, as a consequence of which the Imperial Road Church was built five years later.

United Methodist Free Church, Imperial Road

Built in 1912 and closed in 1977, this church is now an extension to the Matlock Town Hall and is used for meetings, etc. having been a magistrates court for some years. This church boasted a Lloyd of Nottingham organ.(Tomkins) The school rooms of this church now form the offices of the Matlock Town Council with a room for letting, it having been a magistrates court for some years, now relocated to Alfreton.

United Reform Church

In 1785 the Glenorchy Chapel was founded by Lady Glenorchy, already mentioned and this movement made its presence felt again when, in 1842, the Stevens family moved from Cheltenham Spa to Huntsbridge House, Matlock Green where Sunday afternoon services were held in a "large room connected to their big house". This room still exists. The services were conducted by the Rev. T M Newnes from the Glenorchy Chapel. The congregation must have grown for on 15 May 1848 the foundation stone was laid for a Congregational Chapel at Matlock Green at a cost of £600. The first minister was the Rev. J Whewell of Rotherham College, 1849-50.(Bryan p.69)

In 1855 a large school room was built at Matlock Green which cost £400. By 1860, a day school attracting 190 pupils became the first British School in the area, the head teacher being Edwin Davis who was to become the first head teacher of the council schools on School Road.(1872-1907).

In 1866 a new church was built on Chesterfield Road, designed by an architect from Northampton. This cost £300, the land being gifted by Thomas, Joseph, Charles and Frederick Stevens. It took four years to clear the debt on the church. It was demolished in 1969.

This newly renovated church has some interesting plaques at the side entrance.

> *This redeveloped building was opened on 22nd February 1997*
> by Ms Jan Sutch Pickard
> Vice President of the Methodist Conference

The architects:	John Davie and Associates
The main contractor:	Sadler & Turner
Special thanks to	Joseph Rank Benevolent Trust
	Methodist Church
	United Reform Church
	And many friends and members of the church

This church enjoys a thriving congregation who can worship in what is now an impressively modernised church. This church also boasts a beautifully crafted desk of oak, dedicated as follows:

Given by the family of James Arthur and Elsie F Mills in their memory.
This desk was made by their
Grandson Peter J Bennett 1993

The organ was built by Bevington and Sons circa 1885 and renovated by J H Adkins in 1909.(Tomkins p.87) In 1968, Henry Groves of Nottingham fitted a pneumatic action.

The ministers for this new church were:

Hewson Farmer	1962
Ernest Partner	1968
George Farnell	1973
Stanley Beard	1979
Edward Ager	1986
Colin Membery	1994
Dale Sherriff	1999
Barbara Savage	2002

Congregational Church, now Pentecostal

The first chapel was located in Matlock Green in 1842 having 200 sittings, to be replaced in 1866 by a larger chapel (having 500 sittings) built in the Early English Gothic style on Chesterfield Road . They were both administered by the same minister for a time.

From 1873 for the next three years the Rev. Edwin Clarke was the minister at the Farley Congregational Chapel and was later to be the chaplain at Smedley's Hydropathic Institution. In 1886 a manse was built adjoining the church at a cost of £850, to be demolished in 1970. In 1901 the foundation stone was laid for a new Sunday School on Chesterfield Road. The original school at Matlock Green had to be demolished as it had been condemned by the Education Authority prior to 1899. This building, which cost £2,500, was a "new, noble and massive structure" designed by W Hunt of Northampton – now demolished – but the school room still stands. In 1971, the former church building was demolished and the Sunday School was renovated, being rededicated as a place of worship. In 1990 the premises at Church Road was closed and the congregation joined the Bank Road Church.

Sunday School Union

The Matlock District Sunday School Union of the non-conformist churches was created in the 19th century, actual date unknown, and fell out of use in 1886 to be resuscitated in 1900. The area covered by this union was: the Matlocks, Wirksworth, Bonsall, Starkholmes, Tansley, Crich, Fritchley, Holloway and Cromford.(Bryan p.78)

Roman Catholic Church

Our Lady and St Joseph's Roman Catholic Church

A simple centre for worship was established in 1880 when 3 Holt Lane was rented for the sum of £28 per annum and an upstairs room was converted into a chapel. The first Mass was celebrated on the feast of St Dinas, 23 April 1880 – a stained glass window in the present church is dedicated to this saint.

In the same year a site was bought on Bank Road where the present church (seating 200) was built. The architect was E Fryer of Derby, the contractor being B Askew of Matlock and the cost £700. Crucifixes and furnishings were by Whitehouse & Company, Birmingham. This was opened on 16 July 1883 by the then Bishop of Derby. A choir from St Mary's of Derby sang Mozart's Mass No 1.

In 1884 an adjoining plot of land was acquired for a presbytery, which had to wait until September 1896 to be built and occupied. A stained glass window is dedicated to the memory of The Reverend Father George Le Roy, a Belgian who, from 1895 until his death in 1920, worked hard to fund the church and presbytery. The parish hall was built in 1967 and rebuilt in 2002.

The Knights of St Columba were established in Matlock in 1939. The relics of St Hedwig were embedded in the new altar, which was consecrated on 1 October 1978.

The priests who have served at this church were as follows, all being Reverend Fathers unless stated otherwise:

1890	Robert Browne
1895	George Le Roy
1920	Crowther
1926	Cossins
1931	Hugh Atkinson (later Monsignor)
1934	Cyril Restieaux (later Bishop of Plymouth)
1948	John Goodwin
1965	Hugh O'Brien
1969	Cannon Thornhill (assisted by Michael Bell)
1983	Anthony Colebrook
1990	Jonathan Cotton
1995	Paul Newman
2000	Bernard Needham

This church boasts an organ, possibly the smallest in the county, being a "Plain Song" organ dating from c.1900.(Tomkins p.90)

Religious Society of Friends (Quakers)

There were individual Quakers living in the area in the late 17th century, their names appear in the minutes of meetings at Bakewell, Chesterfield and Monyash – both the village and One Ash Grange.

There are records of meetings in Matlock from the 1720s followed by a strong presence between 1866 and 1920 with a decline from 1924. From 1933 to 1937 there was an "Allowed Meeting" in Matlock.

The Meeting House on Jackson Road was built circa 1908; this is now a private residence. There is a record of an "old Meeting House" not yet identified.(Hope)

Burial Grounds

Originally the only burial space for the Matlocks was the churchyard of St Giles. The number of monuments seen today represents a small fraction of the total.

The Society of Friends' Meeting House (Quakers) now a private residence

Note:

Most of the information above concerning Methodist and Wesleyan Churches was gleaned from a history located on the back wall of the school room in the United Reform Church, access being made available by Mr Frank Lund. Other details were found in Bryan and from other sources.

③ LEAD MINING AND QUARRYING

Apart from agriculture, the mining and quarrying of local minerals are the oldest occupations in the Peak area. The extraction of lead dates back to at least Roman times if not earlier. The metal ores are found in veins, variously known to the Derbyshire miners as rakes and scrins – mostly vertical or nearly so – whilst flats and pipes were nearly horizontal. Rakes and scrins outcrop at the surface hidden only by the overburden of soil and sub-soil; flats and scrins were more difficult to locate. The old miners, known colloquially as "t'owd man" could read the signs made by these veins in ore turned up by moles, by the discolouration of the grass, by the presence of certain plants such as leadwort, by their presence in the river bed and by dowsing. The Romans found that the metal ore could be excavated in abundance by working the veins from the top down, avoiding having to mine underground.

Lead Mining

The lead occurs as a sulphide in the mineral (galena) and invariably in the presence of other minerals such as barytes (barium sulphate), sphalerite (zinc sulphide, or blende), hydrated zinc silicate (hemimorphite), zinc carbonate (smithsonite or calamine), fluorspar (calcium fluoride) together with calcite, selenite, chalcedony, jasper, quartz, etc. Of interest is the rare mineral Matlockite of which traces have been found in Rutland Cavern. The lead ore also contains silver, the record for Derbyshire being 22 troy ounces per ton (0.06%) of lead ore and was from lead extracted from the Ball Eye Mine in Bonsall Hollow. Galena was used as an alternative to germanium as a crystal in the original radios called Crystal Sets in the 1920s.

The miners sank shafts into the veins and drove adits into the veins horizontally. Having won the ore they smelted it in boles, crude furnaces using wood as a fuel and located on hill tops, eg, Bole Hill overlooking Wirksworth and Cromford. The smelting technology improved over the ages albeit slowly, with ore hearths after 1570-72 and cupolas after 1735. This is a sketchy and brief outline for there is insufficient space in this book for the history of mining; there is a large bibliography covering the subject available locally.

It is recorded that in 1580 the Willoughby's of Wollaton near Nottingham, coal owners, had caused to be set to work 16 horses in a field – which cannot be traced – called Ashbury Croft, Matlock. This number of horses suggests that they were operating a pumping device for 24 hours a day, using four horses in shifts of six hours. This would have represented a considerable amount of water by using either buckets or rag and chain pumps.

The various types of veins in an imaginary section.
A - Bed of Toadstone, volcanic material
a - fissures parallel to the bedding in places d-d much enlarged
b - fissures vertical to the bedding called SCRINS
c - RAKES
d - PIPES
(Stokes)

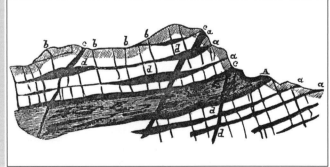

The early workings, which can be viewed, are to be seen in the Masson Cavern and Rutland Cavern show caves. These are the oldest examples of early mining to be seen in the Peak District, mostly dating before the 17th century. These could have been active in 1470-71 when a mine named the Breakholes in the Nestalls was documented of which 670 m of galleries are accessible.

The old mines have been exploited from early in the 18th century onwards as show caves for the greater enjoyment of the public. This aspect is covered in Chapter 4.

The Romans left evidence of their mining in the form of pigs of lead inscribed and found in or near to the Matlocks, see the illustration. Methods of mining were basic until the Saxons arrived and their enduring legacy is the laws and customs in Derbyshire. For the purposes of legal administration the mineral field is divided into the High Peak and Low Peak with several private liberties. The Matlocks are located in the Low Peak and more particularly in the Soke, Wapentake and Hundred of Wirksworth. The High Peak and the Low Peak are also called the King's (or Queen's) Field for lead mining purposes and this is broken down into Liberties which approximate to Parishes. Customs were integral with the industry from ancient times, and this gave the miners and the mineral owners rights to mine the lead ore upon payment of certain fines and duties. These customs were administered by a unique leat court, known as the Barmote Court, which sat and still sits in Wirksworth at a court house built for the purpose, the Moot Hall. This court is conducted by a Steward (a local lawyer), Barmaster (from Burgmiester, literally Master of the Mountain), a jury of 12 (originally 24) and it sat regularly in the heyday of mining but now sits once a year in April. This is called the Great Barmote Court, lesser courts were held in local villages when business was heavy many years ago.

The lead dues in the Matlock Liberty are the property of the Queen as her right as the Duke of Lancaster.

A lead mine (una plumbaria) is mentioned in Matlock (Mestesforde) in the Domesday Book of 1086. This is believed to be a reference to a smelter rather than a mine or possibly the Nestus Mine now a show "cave" on the Heights of Abraham, as there are only a few more listed and there must have been many more.(Morris p.272 b,c)

In 714 the Abbess Eadburger of Repton, Derbyshire (daughter of King Adulph of the East Angles), who had possession of the mines of the Low Peak, despatched lead to the Croyland Abbey, Lincolnshire for the tomb of St Guthlac whose sarcophagus was of lead. In 835, Kennewara, abbess of the same nunnery granted Aelderman Humbert her mines with the proviso that he gave assent to Archbishop Ceolnoth to have lead valued at 300 shillings (£15.00) for use at Christ Church Cathedral, Canterbury. It is almost certain that some of this lead came from the Matlocks.

A Royal Inquisition was held in 1288 at Ashbourne and the King gave leave to Reynold of Ley (Lea) and William of Memill (Meynell)

to inquire by the oaths of good and lawful men, of your county, by which the truth may be best known, of the liberty which our miners do claim to have in those parts, and which they have hitherto been used to have, and by what means, and how, and from what time, and by what warrant.

(Glover I appendix, p.35)

From this the miners were given certain rights and ratification of their customs. These customs with additions were confirmed on several occasions in the 16th to 18th centuries being codified by two Acts of Parliament in 1851 and 1852.

The earliest reference to lead mining in the Matlocks apart from Domesday is 1470 when the Nestus Mines were being worked. These mines along with others on Masson were virtually worked out by the 19th century. There were numerous mines in the Matlocks but most were at Matlock Bath. Of these, in 1809 only one had the benefit of a steam engine and this was at the Dimple Mine at Matlock Bridge.(Farey I p.252) One assumes that this was for pumping the water out of the mine. Several water wheels operated at Side Mine for unwatering this mine using the river Derwent as the driving force. This wheel pit was used when the colour works was established at the foot of High Tor,

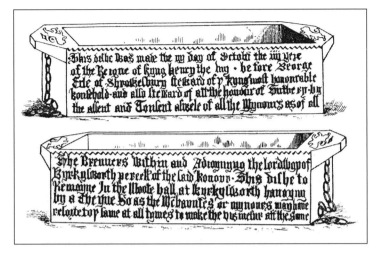

This dishe was made the viij day of October the iiij yere of the Reigne of King henry the huj . be fore George Erle of Shrouesbury stewarde of y kyng most honorable housholde and also stewarde of all the honour of Tutbe ryr by the assent and consent also ele of all the Mynors as of all

The Brenuers within and Adioynyng the Lordshyp of Byrkyswoorth perell of the said honour. This dishe to Remayne In the Moote hall at Byrkyswoorth hanaryn by a The vine so as the Mchaunte's or mynours may have relote to y same at all tymes to make the his mesur aft the same

Standard measuring dish kept at the Moot Hall, Wirksworth. Given by Henry VIII, it holds 14 Winchester pints. It is made of bronze (Stokes)

the original 80 HP (60 kW) wheel having been destroyed in a fire. This colour works was built by F C Arkwright and he restored the wheel, later to be replaced by a turbine. Originally it was used for grinding white lead (lead carbonate) using the stack process; a chimney once stood amongst the trees. The turbine was installed in 1920 being an Achilles reaction type, which drove four grind stones 1,220mm to 1,370mm diameter each, later to be used for grinding iron oxides until 1920. This site was taken over by the Via Gellia Colour Works Limited in 1897. From then on it was used for grinding bone char in water – a waste product from sugar refining. Today they grind pigments for paint manufacture.(Bryan p.303 and Wailes p.108)

Messrs Bouthman and Biscoe of Wrexham, north Wales had in the 19th century spent £10,000 on a mine under High Tor without returning a profit, and the venture was abandoned.

Fuel for smelting was a perennial problem and much timber, known as "white coal" was cut for the purpose but coal was used from about 1735-1740 at the cupolas.

Other minerals were encountered, an important one being zinc carbonate or calamine (calamy, *lapis calaminaris*) used as an ingredient of brass. A surprising encounter was also made with coal but in uneconomic quantity. Coal was also found in Lumsdale.(Bryan p.305) Zinc was manufactured in works at Bonsall and Cromford.

The miners also had other customs, more of the folk type than by statute. They used to decorate their coes (mine shelter for changing clothes and storage) annually – on May 13 the Miners' Holiday – with oak branches and garlands when a substantial dinner was laid on and, if the weather permitted, it was held outside. A rowan (mountain ash) if planted at the entrance to a mine ensured that more ore would be found, a sprig of rowan attached to the beam of a steam engine ensured that it would not break down. Some mineral owners believed that lead ore actually grew and it was therefore subject to tithe but the miners disputed this.

The naming of mines was undertaken by the miners to create a remembrance for the miner himself, or his family, or wishful thinking. In the Matlocks we have, to name but a few: Hard Rake (hard winning of the ore), Bacon Rake (Bacon is a local family name), Nestus Mine (Nestus a corruption of new stows or stoce, a stow was a mine windlass which was also a legal device confirming ownership – author's interpretation!), Coalpit Rake (coal was used here for breaking the rock by fir setting), Cardings Nestus Mine (Carding was a local family) and so on.

The mines were later worked particularly during and after World War II for their fluorspar content, a mineral that did not interest the old lead miners. It made an excellent flux when smelting steel at nearby Sheffield and contributed to the war effort. It is also used for the manufacture of hydrofluoric acid, Teflon and other industrial chemicals. Most of it was exploited by the Banks and Barton partnership and Derbyshire Stone Ltd. Later, during the North Sea oil boom, barytes became valuable as a drilling medium with the dual purpose of lubricating the drill bit and for maintaining pressure to keep the gas under control. This mineral is also used in the manufacture of paper and paint.

The story of lead mining in the county is also the story of the fight against water. As the old miners ventured deeper into the rock, the problem of water drowning the workings became a matter of great concern. Early, simple pumps such as the rag and chain variety were used – a working full size model can be turned in the Peak District Mining Museum – and there were numerous instances of the hand bailing of the water. The major breakthrough was the tunnelling of soughs (pronounced suffs locally), one of the earliest being at Cromford nearby. The Matlocks had numerous such drainage tunnels, all spilling their water gathered from the veins into the River Derwent and the Bentley Brook.

Starting at the northern end of the Parish of Matlock and proceeding south to the southern limit of the Parish of Matlock Bath there is or were a succession of soughs, some of little consequence, others providing drainage of the veins they intersected. When the veins had drained to the sough level, engines were introduced to pump the water from levels below the sough mouth, water engines or wheels and/or fire or steam engines. The term engine found in the records could easily refer to a rag and chain or similar pump so one needs to be careful with the interpretation of this word.

The Dimple mines were worked under Matlock Bank and Allen Hill boasted several soughs. On the north bank of the river Derwent was the best known of these, which can still be seen. Allenhill Sough was driven into the shale from 1734, easier than driving through rock. It can still be seen issuing

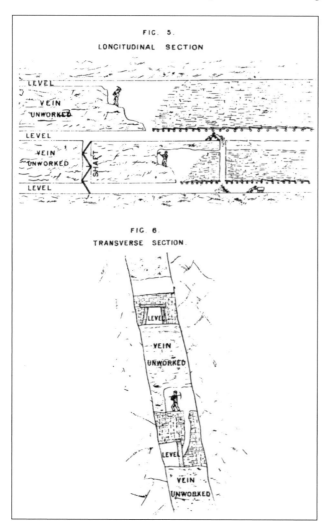

FIG. 5.

LONGITUDINAL SECTION

FIG. 6.

TRANSVERSE SECTION.

chalybeate water and is known as Allen Hill Spa, mentioned elsewhere. Sinter can be seen where the water issues to-day. Ladygate Vein was drained by a sough having an 80HP (60kw) engine on a shaft, the site occupied by Bateman's Park, now the current market area. This raised water from a depth of 450 ft (137m) below the river in the 1800s to be abandoned in 1812. These mines were abandoned circa 1830. The Dimple Level and Granby Level are other minor soughs in the area.

The Stoney Way Mines at Matlock Green were drained by two soughs: Stoney Way Level for Stoney Way Mine of pre-1800 and Jane Level, a combined wagon way and pump way for draining Hills Vein and Jane Vein, in use in 1825, but probably much older. Ladygate Level unwatered the Ladygate Vein, acting as a pump way using a water wheel in the river Derwent with pump rods to the mine.

The Seven Rakes and Cawdor Mines were drained into the west side of the river Derwent; Masson Sough, part of the Ringing Rake Sough drained Gentlewoman's Pipe and dates from early 18th century. Holt Level drained Robin Hood Vein and served as a pump

The method of working a vein (Stokes)

way for a Newcomen Engine installed in 1802 located at Seven Rakes Mine while Cawdor Level was driven from the northern end of the Seven Rakes, and "Masson Farm Level" gave a small amount of high contour drainage to the Crichman Mine.

The Hey (High) Tor and Starkholmes mines were exploited in 1541-42. The High Tor Mines drained into the River Derwent on its east bank comprising the Seven Rakes Vein here split into High Tor Rake and Slit Rake. Under High Tor the mines were worked on Hard Rake and Coalpit Rake, later this group was to be known as Side Mine. As early as 1709 the Wildersley (Willersley) Sough was being extended into this complex and again around 1748-50. In 1815, a proposal was made to run water from the Derwent along the Blackstone Level in Slit Rake to drive a water wheel in Side Mine but nothing came of it. The second decade of the 19th century saw a large 80HP (60 kW) water wheel erected at Side Mine capable of lifting 1,000 gallons per minute (750 litres/s); the flat rods connecting the wheel with the pump were 300 yards (274m) long. Side Mine Level was a pump way for the above water wheel in Side Mine, and was in use 1824-44.

The mines on the Heights of Abraham including Bacon Rake (Bacon is a local family name) were drained by soughs originally driven to drain Coal Pit Rake and other veins but extended later to seek the source of the warm water – possibly rising from the Bonsall Fault. These warm waters issue from Masson Hill in various places, both natural and artificial. The easterly flow of some of this water was along Bacon Rake, later diverted by the Wragg Sough (Wragg is yet another local family name), possibly the earliest known sough in the Matlocks, now used by the Aquarium. A similar sough aimed toward the same source exits beneath the cellar of Hodgkinson's Hotel, Matlock Bath and may date from 1686, it being abandoned when Bath Sough was completed.

The ore in this area was exploited from the Nestus (Newstowes, Nestor) Pipes as early as 1470 until they were almost worked out by 1700. The ore north and south of Bacon Rake was found in cavernous pipes now exploited as a show cave complex. During the1730s this sough was driven to the lower workings of the Nestus Pipes and before 1780 it had been extended to the Bacon Rake. The Bath Sough was driven to recover the warm water from Bacon Rake in 1785-6 being 40 feet (12m) above Wragg Sough, to serve the Fountain Baths. Gaskin Level from Long Tor is reputedly the longest level in Matlock Bath but this is doubtful if not almost impossible. Key Vein Level drained a mine of the same name under Brunswood Terrace, later to be used as a show cave. A sough was possibly exploited by Mary Whittaker for her bottling works, of which there is no trace. Owlet Hole Pipe with Woodwards Pipe, Hopping Pipe and Tear Breeches Mine were drained by Bath Sough (this does not imply warm water!), tunnelled in 1735, driven toward Owlet Hole Pipe, later to be known as the Owlet Hole Sough now in Gulliver's Kingdom. Carnhill Wife's Sough dating from the 1750s is adjacent to Cromford Court. Carnel Level unwaters Gatestoop Vein, Carnel Level, Blue John Level and together with the veins and mines on Harp Edge drained the Carnel (Carnhill) Vein and post dates Carnhill Wife's Sough, it first being recorded in 1839. The reference to Blue John is of interest as this rare mineral is only found at Castleton. Wilcock's Founder Level was intended to drain the mines adjacent to the New Bath Hotel and Upperwood. For Hollands Mine Level (Moletrap Vein, Wapping Mine) there is a vague reference to "A submerged level on the west bank of the River Derwent near Masson Mills". It is most likely to be the water used for driving a water wheel at a paper mill on an island in the river now occupied by Masson Mill.

Station Quarry veins and mines east of the river are represented by Hag Mine, used as a pump way for a water wheel in the river dating from 1761, enabling the mine to be worked 48 ft (14.6m) below river level. Moletrap or Bullestree (Bullace Tree) Mine had a shaft 420 ft (128m) deep, which would take it below sea level, the vein being an unusually generous 10 ft (3m) thick. Three pumping "engines" of the Cornish principle– therefore they were steam operated – were installed in 1843, 1858 and 1868. Hag Wood Level (Upper Hag Wood Level) mentioned in 1849 gave limited drainage to the Upper Hag Vein, used as a pump way having flat rods and a wheel in the river, pumping from c.48ft (14.6m) below river level, installed in 1761 and working 12 years later.

Bullestree (Bullace Tree) Sough was originally driven into Fillpurse Vein, an evocative name for a mine! Later it was driven to the Moletrap Vein. A pumping engine was installed using the sough as a pump way, a second engine being provided in 1848. A further extension was undertaken to link up with a Cornish pumping engine, which was sold off in 1868.

This makes a large number of water wheels on the river Derwent in the two parishes as well as wheels at Masson Mill and Willersley Smelter.

The last mining venture in the Matlocks was the opening of the Riber Mine in the 1950s behind High Tor to work a section of the Great and Coalpit Rakes. It was not at Riber as the name suggests. An inclined tunnel reached the veins only to find that the "old man" had been there before and had removed much of the ore. A legacy of this venture was made evident when a hole opened up in the back garden of a house at Starkholmes in November 1972. This proved to be mine shaft 9m wide and 18m deep. The reassuring advice to the occupant was to "leave his home if a second mine shaft moved closer".(MM 28.11.02)

There is little wonder that a visitor in the 19th century remarked that if one smote Masson Hill with a large hammer it would ring hollow. Lead mining today is just a memory kept alive by the Great Barmote Courts, the Peak District Mining Museum, show "caves" and enthusiastic members of the Peak District Mines Historical Society Ltd.

Quarrying

The excavation of the local rocks from the hillsides and moors must be as old as mining, the need arising for such material for the building of houses and churches, the laying of roads and the construction of the omnipresent dry stone fences, a major feature of the area.

It is now impossible to identify the early quarries, as later workings have obscured them just as later mining has obliterated early mining. The presence of disused quarries locally is obvious and they have been disused long enough to allow nature to re-establish itself.

Cawdor Quarry (Limestone)

This huge quarry lies between the railway and Snitterton Road comprising two benches. At the time of writing this area houses derelict and ruinous quarry buildings, fly tipping, a car park and much waste land. Its future however looks brighter, see Chapter 15.

Cawdor quarry was worked by Constable & Co later Constable Hart of London and by Derbyshire Stone Ltd until the amalgamation with Tarmac Ltd. They supplied raw stone for infill and road making, operating a tarmacadam plant for the manufacture of asphalt for road finishes, especially for London. These materials were despatched by both rail and road but by road exclusively after the railway went over to passenger traffic only. Some of the limestone was sent to Sheffield and other steelworks at Scunthorpe and Corby, for use as a flux in the smelting of iron ore. At the turn of the 20th century, Messrs Walter Drabble and Arthur Beck had sawing sheds in the station yard where they cut this stone to any shape and size and sold it as building material.

Cawdor was the parish quarry from whence limestone was extracted for road making and building in the Matlocks. A shed on this site housed a tarmacadam plant the product from which was for local use. Lime burning also took place here and was sold to farmers after slaking for use when limning (or liming), the method used for winning land from the moors by neutralising the acidity of the ericaceous peat. The name of this quarry has intrigued people for many years, for Cawdor is a village a few miles south of Nairn, Scotland made famous by the Thane of Cawdor in Shakespeare's Macbeth.

Hall Dale Quarry

This very large quarry was for limestone and is located between Salter Lane and Snitterton Lane.

Harveydale Quarry (Limestone)

This quarry is level with the A6 south of the railway bridge at the end of Dale Road. An office block, originally used by Derbyshire Stone and named John Hadfield House occupies some of this quarry. John Hadfield was the original Chairman of Derbyshire Stone Ltd, formed by the amalgamation of smaller quarry firms later taken over by Tarmac Roadstone Ltd. before they withdrew from the area. This 1960s' building is now occupied by Derbyshire County Council.

Lumsdale and Cuckoostone Quarries (Millstone)

This stone was made into millstones for the grinding of wheat, corn, etc. The stones were shaped in the quarry and despatched to the customer on horse drawn wagons, later by railway from Matlock goods siding near to Matlock Station. A quarry not in the parish but worthy of mention is the Poor Lots Quarry at Tansley – owned by a Mr George Boden of Matlock at the turn of the 20th century. Blocks of stone were brought down from here to the goods siding for shaping into mill stones for export to Scandinavia and Switzerland, where they were used for pulping wood for the manufacture of paper.

Long Tor Quarry and Station Quarry

There are other much smaller limestone quarries in Matlock Bath: Long Tor Quarry near to the County and Station Hotel and Station Quarry where the Willersley railway tunnel emerges at Matlock Bath – used by the railway contractors for fill and embankments. A small quarry adjacent to Tor House off the main road down the Matlock gorge was also worked by a Boden.

Masson Fluorspar Opencast

This large scar, which thankfully cannot be seen from the Matlocks, occupies a large site off Salter Lane. This was worked extensively on and off over the latter half of the 20th century. Many tons of fluorspar were extracted and in the process many old lead mines were uncovered.

By-products

Ironically a by-product of quarrying limestone is lead ore, which has to be declared through the Barmote Court. Several thousands of tons of galena has been smelted at H J Enthoven & Sons at Darley Bridge and the remainder is shipped to Hobaken, Belgium.

Fluorspar and Barytes are still recovered and sold on, but this is all taking place just outside our area. The once extensive quarrying and mining that took place and created numerous jobs is a thing of the past. Bats now roost in the mines, bugs and birds nest in the quarries.

Hearthstone

A hamlet of this name lies near to Riber and at about the same altitude. The name suggests that hearthstone was produced here but there is no evidence of this, unless it came out of a mine in the yard at Hearthstone Farm. This stone was used as a whitener for hearths, sills and doorsteps of houses and was sold commercially under various brand names: Snow-drift Step Powder and Osowhite Step Powder.(Sowan pp.584-6)

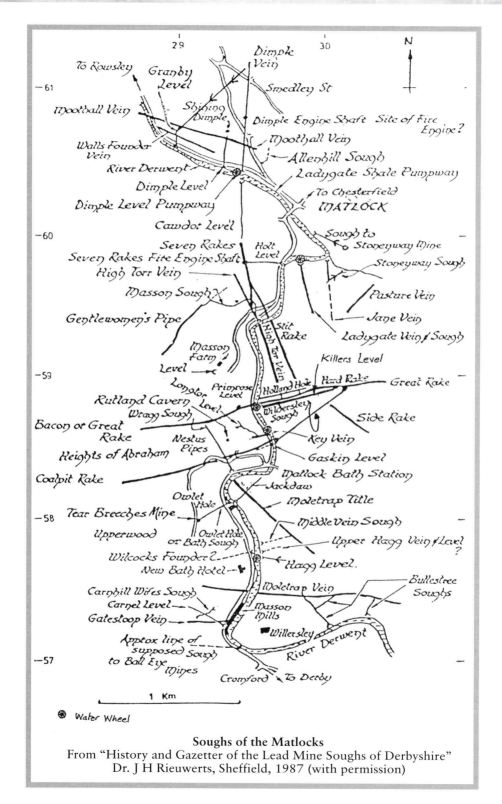

Soughs of the Matlocks
From "History and Gazetter of the Lead Mine Soughs of Derbyshire"
Dr. J H Rieuwerts, Sheffield, 1987 (with permission)

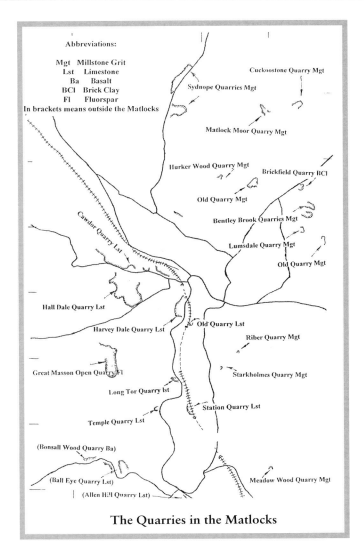

The Quarries in the Matlocks

CAUTION: mines and quarries are dangerous when working and are even more so when abandoned. Do not explore these places without an expert as one of your party. Join a local society such as the Peak District Mines Historical Society which arranges underground trips for its members. Or, visit one of the show "caves" to see what a mine was like underground. The Peak District Mining Museum, Matlock Bath, has some admirable exhibits which explain in detail how the mines were worked and the ore processed, together with Temple Mine where one can have a safe and dry visit to a real mine which was used for the extraction of fluorspar.

NOTE: *The writer is indebted to his valued friends Dr. J H Rieuwerts and Dr. T D Ford OBE for their generous help and advice and permission to quote heavily (unless stated otherwise above) from Dr J H Rieuwerts' seminal work on Derbyshire soughs which is being considerably expanded and updated for a second edition. The reference to early mining is from The Upper Nestus Pipes: An Ancient Lead Mine in the Peak district of Derbyshire by John Barnatt and James Rieuwerts, Peak District Mines Historical Society bulletin, Volume 13, No. 5, Summer 1998, p 51 with additions by the author. The section about the quarries is entirely the author's work.*

Matlock Bath developed as a drinking spa whereas Matlock Bank developed as a bathing spa. The former had a longer life but the latter was hugely successful for about a hundred years. Matlock Bath is newer than Matlock Town having grown out of its use as a spa village. This was not always the case, for the area was rich in lead deposits especially on the commons on the great hill known as Masson. The valley was known as Masson Dale, an expression that fell out of use after Arkwright had built his Masson Mill on an island in the river already occupied by a paper mill. This same site was originally occupied by a duck decoy.

The profusion of trees were planted in the Georgian and Victorian eras following the enclosure of the commons on Masson hillside in 1784, and these obscured the many mine workings and were exploited as pleasure grounds. The warm springs were evident as they produced tufa, which coats everything it washes over with a calcareous layer known as petrifaction and as travertine. This too was exploited by the Victorians. There is now little to be seen, but pieces can be found where the water issues today and as linings for paths and roads. Particularly fine examples of this petrifying can be seen where the water forms fountains and falls such as an area at the bottom of Temple Road, in the Derwent Gardens and the fish pond opposite the inn of that name. It was quarried to provide Victorian gardeners with stone for their grottos and some was exported to the continent. The Old Bath Hotel (now lost), the New Bath Hotel and the Pavilion all stand or stood on banks of this stone.

It is often claimed that the Romans were the first to discover the warm springs at Matlock Bath for which claim there is no evidence. The earliest reference that could be found (1374) was to the area round the springs called Haliwellker or holy well, which suggests that the springs were venerated and were possibly the location of healing springs of which there are many in the country. This could also point to Celtic use for they venerated springs and relied on them for water, not only for day-to-day use but also for curing conditions such as eye troubles and skin problems.(Naylor CD)

However, the first recognition of these springs for the location of a bath for curative purposes was recorded in 1696, when the waters were "discovered". A crude bath house was built of stone slabs and a timber shed cover. The Wolleys of Riber claimed that they had known about and used this spring many years before. This is the bath that later entrepreneurs ascribed to being discovered by the Romans. This is also the site where the Old Bath Hotel was built, now lost.

The rights of the commoners, as opposed to the Lords of the Manor of Matlock Bath, were contested and three counsel were appointed. The Lords had let the land to a George Wragg and his successor Pennell. The opinions of Messrs Abney, Willes and Holden were preserved.(Add. MSS Wolley,

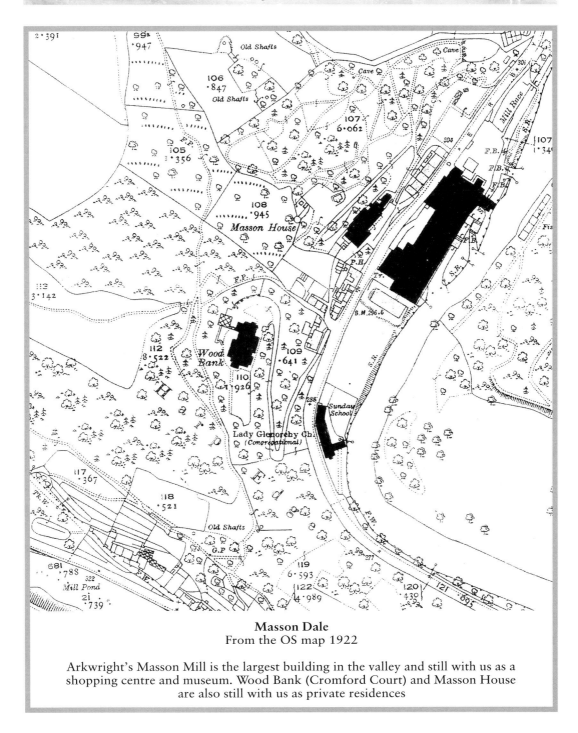

Masson Dale
From the OS map 1922

Arkwright's Masson Mill is the largest building in the valley and still with us as a shopping centre and museum. Wood Bank (Cromford Court) and Masson House are also still with us as private residences

Opposite page: Tufa Bank, Matlock Bath - 1749. The flat area is of tufa where the Pavillion now stands. The waterfall into the river exists. The stooping figures are possibly washer women but might be lead ore washers (Bryan p.121 facing)

6668 ps.347-352) It demonstrated that the Manor of Matlock was extensive with several commons, the freeholders and copyholders having right of common for cattle. From this we learn that one of the commons called Masson had a "ffyne spring of water" let to George Wragg at 2s 6d (12.5p) per annum, which he enlarged, erecting several buildings around it. This caused a dispute as Wragg relet this bath at £50 to £60 per annum, making the copyholders angry! Wragg then increased the rent to the copyholders to £70 per annum, which confirmed the lease, to which was added two acres (0.8 hectares) of land. Pennell bought this lease and erected a new bath house. A Mr Richardson, owner of the "Fountain" (the Hotel Bath) that was attached to the Great Hotel on the South Parade, drew the cases alleging that he also had a claim to rights of common and was used to grazing his cattle on it. The lawyers could not come to a conclusion of the case except one who stated that Richardson might "prostrate" the buildings. This was pursued and we hear no more about this, we can assume therefore that the parties were satisfied.(Bryan ps 90-1).

A traveller notes in 1732 that,
Here are no inhabitants, except a few Groovers. Who dig for lead ore, and whose Hutts not higher than a good Hogstye . . . . . I was up early in the morning . . . when came out one of these Hutts a Woman, I may say, Naked, for I am sure she had no Shift on, at least but a one Piece one. I was surpriz'd at the Impudence of the Woman, and she as much surpriz'd to see me . . .the People laugh's at me, Lord, Sir, says the Landlord, we never mind those things.

The act for the enclosing of the Masson Common is dated 1775-6 the boundary line passing between the Matlocks and Bonsall. Matlock land had an area of 200 acres (81 hectares) which was enclosed and divided between the freeholders and copyholders, the latter as Lords of the manor receiving a 22nd part of the whole "in lieu of compensation for their right of the soil and the getting of *Lapis calaminaris* (calamine) or any other stone thereon." Allotments were also awarded to the rector, hospitals and persons after which all rights of common ceased. The land remained in the King's Field of the Low Peak or the Soke, Wapentake and Hundred of Wirksworth subject to the mining customs. The adjudicator was a Mr Alexander Barker of Edensor (this would have been the original Edensor which stood to the side of today's village of that name.)(Bryan p.92)

A proportion of the miners paid tithe on their lead ore based on the belief that it grew, for only things that grew like cereals and vegetables were subject to tithe. Most miners ignored this imposition, anyone with an iota of common sense could see that the ore could not and did not grow. An inept try by a local incumbent, the Rev. John Chappell, Rector of Matlock to compel the miners to pay tithe failed. The matter was not clear, for some continued until the 18th century paying tithes but it went out of use and the miners were freed from this tax.(Flindall & Hayes p.16)

The development of this site had to await the building of a carriage road from Cromford direct rather than the pack way, which followed the river from

Left: Temple Hotel once an annexe for the Old Bath Hotel, where Lord Byron and Princess (later Queen) Victoria stayed. Upper Towers can be seen at the top of this picture

Right: Matlock Bath from the Old Bath Terrace. Upper and Lower Towers on the Heights of Abraham can be seen as can High Tor in the distance (sans TV tower). The buildings in the right foreground are the stables for the Fishpond Hotel which can be seen bottom left. The stables stand where the Pavilion is now. Note the Landua with two horses on the road.
(Author's collection)

Willersley to Matlock Bridge, used by lead miners. Two of Sir Richard Arkwright's partners, Smith and Pennell paid for the laying of such a road and they had ideas of developing the site.

By 1811, it is evident that this watering place was starting to increase in popularity for it was recognised at this time that the village had its season: from late April to November each year.(Davies p.477). It is strange to note that the season had shortened from Whitsuntide to September/October in each year following the arrival of the railway.(Bryan p.131). An inland spa had been created, and it grew in popularity in direct proportion to the advance of this railway up the valley from Derby to Manchester. It arrived at Matlock Bath on 4 June 1849, when the line was extended from Ambergate to Rowsley. This gave the denizens of Derby, Nottingham, Birmingham and beyond easy access to the area and they arrived in droves, to the delight of the shop keepers and other minor entrepreneurs and to the disgust of those who appreciated the romantic delights of the valley.

By 1879, comments about the area were coming thick and fast, and there were few that were complimentary. One visitor wrote "to assert that Matlock Bath is crowded on Good Friday is really to extenuate circumstances. . . Rudely aroused on the buniferous day from her Winter's rest, Matlock received visitors from half-a-dozen counties."(Badbury p126)

Things were no better by 1903, when it was recorded that Matlock Bath station "let loose callous rowdies, who envy Attila his destructive secret. . . . . The debasing influence of the day tripper is everywhere visible . . . . The shops deck themselves out with vulgarities and banalities to please their patron".(Firth pps 390-392)

The village grew apace to cater for these hordes of mostly day-trippers and now offered public houses, tea shops, ice cream parlours and for the more energetic, the pleasure grounds, petrifying wells and caverns.

Of particular note are the pleasure grounds called "The Heights of Abraham" which opened in c.1800 and are still open. This area on the slopes of Masson Hill offered a visit to a "Roman Mine", a prospect tower – Victoria Tower – and arboreal walks with seats and resting places commanding views unrivalled in this area renowned for such. The name is taken from the heights of the same name at Quebec, Canada and were so named to commemorate James Wolfe's (1727-59) victory on the Plain of Abraham in 1759. He was killed in the action. Apparently the heights at Matlock Bath feature the same heights as those in Canada. These same pleasure grounds undertook a new lease of life when they were taken over in 1976 by Andrew Pugh, who has expanded access to the underground attractions with an outstanding audio-visual display, excellent tea rooms and cable car access.

A second pleasure ground was created in competition with the original one and was called "The

Heights of Jacob", offering two show caves and woodland paths amongst crags. This became part of the Pavilion and the site is now occupied by a pleasure ground aimed at children and called "Gulliver's Kingdom".

In the 19th century the growth of attractions included 14 known show "caves". Most were mines and there were at least four petrifying wells. Now there are none of the latter left, the last one closing within the past 20 years, and much lamented.

Meanwhile two major hotels were built, the Old Bath and the New Bath. The Old Bath is no longer with us but was a considerable building in Victorian Gothic having an annexe at the Temple Hotel. The Old Bath Hotel was demolished in the late 19th century to be rebuilt in the early 20th century. It finally burnt down in 1927, the area it occupied now being a car park where a tufa grotto is all that is left of this enterprise. The Old Bath Hotel superseded the Royal Hotel whose water supply it appropriated. This was the spring referred to as being found in 1689. By 1712 the spring had been captured in a lead lined timber bath of which we have no details. A few years later a stone bath was constructed utilising two new springs, lodging houses were erected and carriage roads made.(Bryan p 202)

The Temple Hotel, which dates from the 1760s, became independent of the Old Bath Hotel after the latter burned down. It certainly has the best views of any hotel in the area if not in the country. During its Victorian heyday it gave shelter to Princess Victoria (later Queen Victoria) who rested here on her visit to Chatsworth House. Lord Byron also stayed here when in pursuit of Mary Chaworth and he scratched a poem on one of the window panes. This pane and the Princess's signature can be seen in a show case at the Hotel.

Defoe tells us that on his visit to these springs,

One of these is secured by a stone wall on every side, by which the water is brought to rise to a due height; and if it is too high there is a sluice to let out as low as you please. It has a house built over it and room within the building to walk round the bath, and so go by steps gradually into it. The water is but milk warm, so that it is not less pleasure to go into than sanative.

Principal Attractions of

MATLOCK
BATH ❧ ❧ ❧

The Heights of Abraham,
The Great Rutland Cavern,

which is brilliantly lighted with gas, and contains Lofty Natural Cavities, large quantities of Fluor and other Spars, and numerous interesting Minerals, Fossil remains, &c.; also

The Victoria Prospect Tower,

commanding the finest views of the far-famed Matlock Scenery.

S. SPRINTHALL, Proprietor.

Tufa Grotto - all that
is left of the Old Bath Hotel

The Lysons tell us that the bath was 17ft (5.2m) long, 20ft (6.1m) wide and 33ft (10.0m) high, with a reading room over it.

A bathing place was created on this site by the Wolleys of Riber being cut out of the "marl" rock.(WMSS 6667, f.318)

The original Old Bath was built by the Rev. Joseph Fearne, rector of Matlock, Benjamin Hayward of Cromford, George Wragg of Matlock, Adam Wolley of Allen Hill, Matlock c.1696 and called Wolley's Well. Later Wragg took it over, taking a lease from the Lords of the Manor by paying a fine of £150 and a rent of six pence (2¹/2p) per annum to each Lord for 99 years, the rent being no mean sum. Wragg appears to have treated this as a serious business proposition building a few small rooms adjoining the bath which were referred to "as a poor convenience to strangers".(Bryan p203)

Smith and Pennell of Nottingham purchased the property for £1,000 in 1745. They built two "large" accommodation blocks and stables, and also a coach road to Matlock Bridge, later to be extended to Cromford.

The New Bath Hotel is still with us and under the same name, having been started shortly after the Old Bath opened. This hotel is fed from a warm water spring at 68°F (20°C) which feeds a basement plunge pool, the outdoor swimming pool, and an ornamental pond that steams in frosty weather. This hotel has an unfortunate 1960s' type of extension otherwise it is a solid, well built Georgian building. In the late 19th and early 20th centuries the water was considered to have medicinal properties and was consumed in large quantities. This water was referred to at that time as being thermal and there was much debate as to why the water was warm. Erasmus Darwin got it right when he suggested that the water came from a depth sufficient to receive its heat from the bowels of the earth, but it is now considered to originate from the Bonsall Fault.

A further use of local warm springs was "The Fountain". These "springs" were both warm and cold and they were separated by driving a tunnel that was dug to intercept Wragg's Sough in 1786, when the first bath house was built. It was demolished in 1881 to be rebuilt and opened on 2 March 1883. It offered the same waters as the two hotels but without the accommodation. This building still exists and is used as an aquarium.

The local authority also tried to cash in and built a pavilion. This is also still with us although its construction was undertaken on the cheap. This had a pump room with a fountain fed from the same water supply that supplied the Old Bath Hotel. The name was changed to the Kursaal in an attempt to increase its number of customers. It was used for public functions and now serves a useful purpose as the home to the Peak District Mining Museum, a Tourism Information Centre and a night club. Originally the stables for the Fish Pond Hotel, the pond in question being to the front side of the pavilion where a fountain of the same water has built up a cone of tufa. The water is home to some exotic fish.

As part of the Victorian expansion, the road was raised above the flood level of the river and named North Parade and the Promenade. Some fine buildings were erected overlooking the road having balconies, the ground floors of which are retail outlets. A "Museum" was built along the Promenade and this is now divided into various outlets finishing with Hodgkinson's Hotel.

The coming of the railway in 1849, opened the doors to visitors who started to arrive in droves and their behaviour was at times appalling. Mill owners would arrange a group booking for their employees and these would disgorge at Matlock Bath station and walk in Indian file to visit the beer houses, petrifying wells and especially the show caves. One can only try to imagine the logistics of getting a party of more than 100 boisterous and tipsy mill workers round the confines of a cave. It is recorded that a party of 5,000 excursionists invaded the valley and locomotives having up to 50 carriages were not unknown. Excursions from as far away as London also arrived. One visitation of 3,600 youths, most under 20 years of age, arrived at Matlock Bath in 1853. They ran rampant and were described as the "very scum and scraping of the factories and streets of Birmingham". Over 50 robberies were recorded; they looted a spar shop and ran over gardens stealing flowers as they went, which were promptly offered for sale to visitors. The police looked on in awe and one assumes they were helpless in the face of this onslaught. However three arrests were made including a ten-year-old boy who was sentenced to be whipped privately. A further assault was from a party of 5,000 steel workers from nearby Sheffield.(Flindall & Hayes pp 20/21)

The thirst of the visitors was slaked by beer from a brewery at Cromford in the mill complex and water from Mary Whittaker's mineral bottling plant, both demolished. Her distinctive bottles can still be found locally having a trade mark cartoon cast upon them of two men sitting at a table. One says, "How's that for a drink?" the other replies "Tremendous!" These screw top bottles were made by Dobson and Nell Limited of Barnsley, South Yorkshire, a town famous for its glass works.

Guides would station themselves at strategic locations offering leaflets to the many visitors, promising untold delights both above and below ground which inevitably led to fighting between these people. The general fee for an underground trip was a shilling (5p). If compared with the average income of 2s 6d (12.5p) per day, earned through hardship and danger by a miner, one can understand their enthusiasm for tourists.

A comment made in 1884 rings true with the writer who could have said exactly the same 60 years later: *In one cavern at least a compulsory fee for admission was followed by a strong appeal for a voluntary one on exit . . . When the party . . . had crept through the narrow entrance and traversed the tortuous path into the interior, the guide . . . throws himself against the only means of egress, and coolly blocks the way whilst his quickly doffed hat is going the round of the company.*(Flindall & Hayes p.20)

The first to be opened was Cumberland Cavern in about 1800, followed by the Rutland Cavern in 1810. The lure of a new fad for "romantic cave scenery" and a new interest in geology quickly encouraged the locals to open nine such caves.(Flindall & Hayes p 19) These operators were contravening the Derbyshire Mineral Courts Act of 1852, by operating in a lead mine without the title being registered and for using a mine for purposes other than lead ore extraction.

At its zenith, the following show caves were available to an unwitting public, each one extolling the virtues of their own show assuring the unsuspecting visitor that his or hers was by far the best in the dale. This also led to a new craze for geological scenery brought about by a renewed interest in the composition of areas such as the Matlock hills.

Common Name	*Also advertised as, and approximate dates*
Angelina's Cavern	An alternative entrance to Speedwell Cavern
Cumberland Cavern	The first to be opened to the public
	1810-1960
Devonshire Cavern	1925-1895
Fern Cave	Associated with Roman Cave
Fluorspar Cavern	1815-1940
Gaskin Mine	Museum Mine 1825-1835
Great Masson Cavern	See Masson Cavern
Great Rutland Cavern	Rutland Cavern 1810-today
High Tor Grotto	1825-1915
Long Tor Cavern	Long Tor Roman Fluor Spar Cavern 1895-1915

	Note the "Roman"!
Masson Cavern	Great Masson Cavern, associated with Rutland Cavern 1875-today
Owlett Hole Mine	Owlett Hole Sough, Victoria Cavern 1885-1905
Roman Cave	1865-today
Rutland Cavern	1810-today
Side Mine	1825-1845
Smedley Cavern	1800-1835
Speedwell Cavern	Royal Speedwell Mine 1820-1940
Stalactitic Cavern	A name only, no trace of it as a mine or show cave.
Temple Mine	1920s' fluorspar mine open today

Prices fell as the century wore on and the Heights of Abraham allowed a party of 3,600 to visit, including Rutland Cavern, for the total sum of £10.

Angelina's – Located at Upperwood and at one time under the control of Angelina, a single entrepreneur who lived in an adjacent hovel. The entrance is now closed off.

Cumberland Cavern – This is considered to be the oldest of the subterranean attractions in the village, having been in the possession of the Smedley family for most of the 19th century and accessed by the public since c.1775. Entrance off The Wapping and links to the Wapping Mine; is now collapsed but accessible from the Wapping Mine for experts only.

Devonshire Cavern – Adam states that this was opened to the public in 1824 but was mined before this date for lead. Up to 1860 it was in the possession of Benjamin Bryan who died the same year, later by a Mrs Chadwick of Lower Towers. Off the Upperwood Road, now dangerous due to many roof falls.

Fern Cave with *Roman Cave* are located on High Tor and are old open lead mining works where one can walk along the sole of the vein with the vein walls each side and open to the sky. These are the only mines in the Matlocks to be scheduled as an ancient monument.

Great Masson Cavern – In the Heights of Abraham it forms an extension to the Rutland Cavern to the north. Now visited as part of a package trip through Rutland Cavern, not to be missed. This was

Original part of the New Bath Hotel to the right with a late extension to the left

originally mined as part of the Old Nestus Pipe Vein. This cavern links with a number of old lead mines in Masson Hill.

High Tor Grotto – This is situated at the foot of High Tor near to the Colour Works. It was famous for the crystallisation, dog tooth spar and the like. At the turn of the 19th century it was in the possession of a Mr J H Cardin, an "intelligent proprietor", who held a teacher's certificate from the South Kensington Science and Art Department, London, in Physiology and Geology. It is now derelict.

Long Tor Grotto or Mine – A disused lead mine believed to have been worked by the Romans originally run by Mrs Whittaker, the same Whittaker as at the Mineral water works close by. Runs as a sough under the A6 from the river bank near to the paint works. The name grotto hardly fits this mine but was for luring tourists.

Owlett Hole Mine – In the grounds once known as the Heights of Jacob and accessed by a footpath that climbs to Upperwood Road from Temple Road. It has some fine crystal formations. It is protected by a strong steel door and is now owned by the Peak District Mines Historical Society Ltd. The lessee at the turn of the 19th century was a Mr Jacob Raynes. This is a worked out pipe vein. On some maps it is referred to as a sough, which it is not.

Roman Cave – see Fern Cave above.

Rutland Cavern – Opened in 1810, this spectacular cavern is located in The Heights of Abraham. A Roman connection is postulated and this may be true. It was originally mined for lead under the title of the Nestus (New Stoce) Mine.(See Chapter 3) At the turn of the 19th century it was in the possession of a Mrs Chadwick.

Speedwell Cavern – Also known as New Speedwell Mine, Pavilion Mine and Royal Mine but originally worked for lead and fluorspar under the name of Tear Breeches Mine and, as tradition would have it, Princess Victoria – later Queen Victoria – visited it during her stay at the Old Bath Hotel nearby. Originally called the New Speedwell Mine it was situated in the Old Pavilion Grounds. It was heavily worked for fluorspar during World War II by the Banks and Barton partnership. It boasted many fine mineral formations until recent times but most of this was robbed. It now forms part of Gulliver's Kingdom. It is very unstable in parts and is dangerous. It links with Fluorspar Cavern.

Temple Pipe Cavern – Originally Temple Mine by which name it is known today, this fluorspar mine was opened in 1922 by a Mr Crowther who abandoned it three years later. In the 1950s it was worked by the Banks and Barton partnership. In 1975 it was cleared out and made safe for visiting by the Peak District Mines Historical Society Ltd and visits can be made by arrangement with the Peak District Mining Museum opposite, in the Pavilion.

The problem with Matlock Bath as a resort is that it attracts many more visitors from late spring to early autumn, and at other times it is quiet with but a few brave visitors. At the time of writing Matlock Bath has became a Mecca for motorcyclists who arrive in numbers at weekends, more on Sunday than Saturday. They park their machines on the road side and meet to talk about their possessions of which they are justifiably proud. They are now a feature of the place; doing no harm, except to themselves, as some race along the A6 south of the Matlocks, the death toll from accidents being frighteningly high.

The petrifying wells open to the public were as follows:

- On the side of the A6 main road opposite Clifton Road. This still exists as a well but has been boarded up for many years. It stands on its own and is painted white.

- On the same road and on the same side as the above, it is represented by a fountain flowing through a mound of tufa. This is not covered and sits at the end of the shops north of the Pavilion. This was possibly the most successful of the wells and was treated to a modern enclosure in the 1960s, now swept away for yet another fish and chip shop. The Royal

Museum owned this well in its heyday and they exhibited its products for sale. The proprietor during these years was a Mr A W Smith.

-   The aquarium boasts a good example of a petrifying well, which can be seen in operation.

It is said that it takes a year before a suitable crust of travertine has accumulated to a saleable degree. The author's memories of these wells dating to World War II was of birds nests, a human skull, eggs, gloves, many pots, coins and anything that the public wished to leave – subject to the scrutiny of the keeper.

There was a period in the 1950/60s when the mines and caves were occupied by young people living in them. They called themselves Troglodites and were known locally as Trogs. Their scruffy appearance caused some controversy and no doubt the visitor numbers started to dwindle because of them. A principal residence was the Royal Cumberland Cavern,

where they revaunched upon society, ate out of tins, smoked hashish and drank out of bottles, breathing the dank air and listened to the dripping of Derbyshire waters on their way to the Petrifying Well, and considered their Karma and the astral plane.

Some were converted by the Jehovah's Witnesses, which latter undertook a survey underground and counted 500 Trogs. A meeting of local villagers banned them from public houses and elsewhere and "No Trespassing" notices became common. They left thereafter never to return, graffiti and rubbish being their only legacy.(Gosling)

A hill like Masson would not be complete without its monster and folk lore would suggest that it had one. Legend, which resides in R L Tongue's *Forgotten folk tales*, has it that a monster dwelt in this cavernous hill in the form of a black dragon no less. Needless to say no-one was safe from this beast, neither man nor woman and the good people of Chesterfield would appear to have been a target for this worm. When the worm became a threat, a youth from Ashover had ploughshares beaten into a large sword by the village blacksmith. Our hero pressed two other youths and a donkey to help him in his quest. They used the donkey to drag the sword along to a place where they wedged the sword into a cleft in a rock to await the arrival of the dragon, which was approaching Chesterfield, laying waste the countryside as he advanced. His hot breath twisted the steeple on the church – and we all thought this was due to badly seasoned timbers! The bells were rung, the sword was spun such that its blades flashed dazzling light reflected from the sun, causing the dragon to fly about in a confused state. The dragon capitulated due to these forces, losing his power and flew over the hills diving into Jugholes, a mine near the top of Salter Lane. There he still lies, still fiery, and that is why the springs in Masson Hill run warm and when his tail twitches we get earthquakes at Winster.(Paulson)

To conclude this chapter, mention must once more be made of the warm springs that are sometimes referred to as being thermal. This is not so. The definition of a thermal spring is when the temperature of the water is higher than the average temperature of the surrounding air throughout the year. This is only the case in two places in Great Britain: at Bath (Roman Aquae Sulis) and at Buxton (Roman Aqua Arnemetiae). However, global warming may deprive even these of their "thermal springs".

MATLOCK & MATLOCK BANK
- THE HYDROPATHIC TOWN

Matlock Bank was preceded by Matlock Town, the original settlement on higher ground than the flood plain of the Derwent and centred round the church of St Giles. Today the town covers all the area round Matlock Bridge at low altitude.

Originally the land was a conventional field system of small enclosed fields, mostly down to arable use. Oats would have been a main crop from which we have the tradition of oat cakes still made by local bakers. One visitor of the 18th century complained of Matlock that it was "all oats, oats, oats and mutton, mutton, mutton" and this was probably near to the truth, lamb as we understand it was not eaten then. The field system expanded south along the hillside of Riber and beyond, up to and including Bow Wood near to Lea Bridge. Lynchets – ridge and furrow working – dating from the 15th century can be seen in some of these fields near to Willersley. This area is still farmed, in the fields left after the landscaping of the early 19th century by the Arkwrights when many trees were planted to make it a sporting estate. Most of these fields are used for beef and lamb. Of these farms, Castle Top is of importance having been modified to make it a shooting lodge and being the birthplace of Allison Uttley the writer.

The river crossing was important, for the bridge carried all the east – west traffic comprising some carts but mostly pack animals. The river was capricious and prone to flooding at short notice, therefore the flat area by the river now occupied by Hall Leys Park would have been a water meadow in winter and good growing land for root vegetables in summer. By the 13th century the bridge had been built, narrower than it is today, for all it had to pass were people, pack animals and narrow carts. Anything bigger had to use the ford at Matlock Bath.

The area remained as royal manors as it had since the time of Domesday, 1086. In 1493 the King's tenants complained to the High Steward of the Manor of Tutbury that,

they ben gretly wronged by Philip Leche esquire that there where they and other Kinges tenauntes ther have in comyn for their catell without interpucion of any man . . and now the said Philip hath closed in the said comyn XI acres and more to the gret hurte et enpoverishing of the said tenauntes

Leche was the then owner of Chatsworth.(Heath p51) In 1629 the tenants bought the manor from the City of London to whom Charles I had sold it the year before and trustees were appointed to run it.

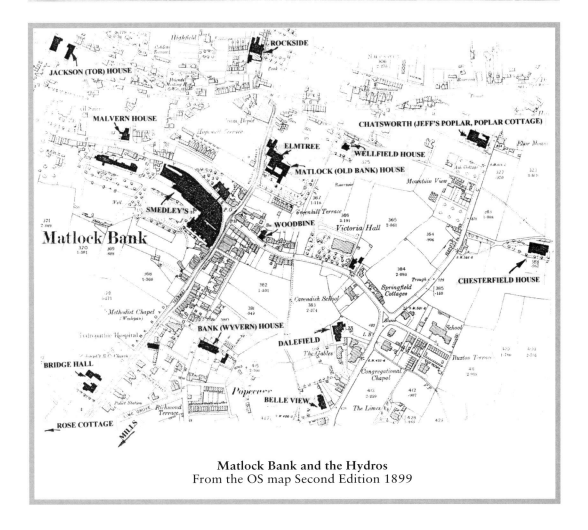

Matlock Bank and the Hydros
From the OS map Second Edition 1899

Matlock Green was always closely associated with Old Matlock town, the latter on the hill, the former near to the Bentley Brook. Matlock Green was located above the flood plain from this brook and was predominantly where the medieval corn mill stood and where the market was held.

Every community of size had its all important water powered corn mill, windmills came later, which would handle oats for rolling, wheat for grinding and animal feed for granulating. It is likely that this stood near to the present day Huntsbridge Mill on the Bentley Brook and was operated by a water wheel. This was to be the first of a string of mills leading to those at Lumsdale.

The enclosure act for Matlock was part of that for Matlock Bath (see Chapter 4) and was at the behest of Peter Nightingale, John Wolley and others, Lords of the Manor in 1780. This extended to a stated 1,500 acres (608 hectares) but a survey showed this to be 1,719 acres (696 hectares). The Lords were to have one twentieth part of the whole with Lumb's Mill and all the buildings, weirs, goits and six acres (2.4 hectares) of land from which they could extract stone for the building and repair of

Opposite page: Smedley's Hydro, Matlock Bank c.1905. The two phases of construction are obvious by the different architectural styles. The lawns are now a car park. The glazed building was the Winter Garden and is still with us (Yeomans)

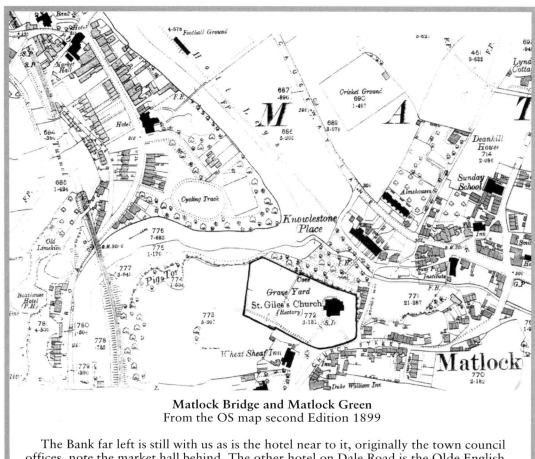

Matlock Bridge and Matlock Green
From the OS map second Edition 1899

The Bank far left is still with us as is the hotel near to it, originally the town council offices, note the market hall behind. The other hotel on Dale Road is the Olde English. The cycling track is evident now built over. In Matlock Green, the Almshouses, Knowlestone Place, Institute (now Tawney House), Hotel (The Red Lion) and Hotel (The Horse Shoe) are all with us still, only the Sunday School has gone

houses, bridges, walls and fences. After the award of allotments all rights of common ceased. This also came under the jurisdiction of Wirksworth as enumerated in Chapter 4.(Bryan p.92) The arbitrator was a Mr John Nuttall.

The cattle market, which was held every two weeks, was where the tyre depot is now and close to Tawney House. A sheep fair was held four times a year and swings were provided for children in an adjoining field. The lack of use completed the closing of these markets in 1941, having been in decline since 1931. The present market, not for cattle or sheep, is now housed in a purpose built building on the Bakewell Road.

This part of Matlock remained an agrarian area until the arrival of John Smedley, who was to revolutionise the Matlocks generally and Matlock Bank in particular. He was born on 12 June 1803, the son of Thomas Smedley, worsted spinner and hosier of Wirksworth. He took over his father's business and appeared to have improved it, for in 1818 he rented Lea Mills then owned by the Nightingale family. Sadly the business had problems and in 1823 it failed. John borrowed a little capital and restarted the business. He prospered by adapting the stocking frame to handle wool, but too much work and long hours took their toll and he suffered a breakdown in his health whilst on his honeymoon in 1846. The nature of his illness is a mystery. Some claim that he had had a fever, others that he had a nervous breakdown. This latter has more credibility when one examines his behaviour hereafter. He went to a hydropathic establishment at Ben Rhydding, Otley, near Keighley, West Yorkshire where he was treated by a Dr Macleod. Here he was cured of his malady and found religion at the same time. He bought an estate near Cheltenham, where he had intended to retire, but returned to Lea having two desires, one to give the world the benefit of his new found medicine and two, to convert the world to his own brand of Methodism. He never disguised his contempt for doctors of medicine and divinity.

He started with his own employees at Lea Mills, subjecting them to preaching and cold water. In return, the workers enjoyed many benefits denied most mill workers at that time. Having conducted his experiments at Lea, he decided to throw his ideas open to the world and bought a small hydropathic institution on Matlock Bank. The principles he used for his patients were based on those then in use at Harrogate and Buxton. This was to become an outstanding success, to the enrichment of both the local community and Smedley himself.

This first establishment was already in business, operated by a Ralph (or Rafe) Davis of Darley Dale who had originally hawked his treatment door to door in the area. He then rented an 11 – roomed house at £12 per annum in c.1851 and installed hydropathic equipment with advice from John Smedley, who bought the house in 1853. As this building soon proved inadequate, he pulled it down and built a larger establishment. This was the origin of the huge establishment he was to build and that is still with us. In 1861 it was forecast that this would become a serious rival to Matlock Bath. It became more than this, it outclassed Matlock Bath completely.

There were two such establishments at this time, Smedley's – this is how it came to be known – and Ralph Davis's new venture, Chesterfield House founded as early as c.1800, which he bought from its current owners.

In 1853, Smedley banned tobacco, snuff, drugs, confectionery, alcohol and over – eating from his establishment and fines were imposed on his patients for minor misdemeanours, such as gentlemen entering the Ladies' Lounge. His emphasis was on water applied externally rather than drunk as at spa resorts and he advocated strenuous exercise as apposed to billiards.(Havin p137) The methods by which the water was applied varied from cold sheets to needle showers and some of the treatments were severe, especially his mustard baths which caused excruciating discomfort to the patient. One is only astonished that this did not kill people. He expanded his ideas by buying a marquee, which he set up in villages up to a radius of 10 miles from Matlock, where he preached sobriety and the gospel. He paid for the building of chapels at Ashover, Birchinwood by Alfreton, Bonsall, Higham and Holloway.

Over the next few years the establishment started by Smedley was constantly expanding, all to his design – one assumes he did not trust architects either – and he also acted as his own clerk of works. At the same time he was personally attending to his clients and the running of what by now was a considerable business. In all this he was ably aided and abetted by his wife – he had married Caroline Ann Howard in 1846 – who took responsibility for all the female patients.

In 1867 he treated 2,000 patients, many having to be turned away and this figure

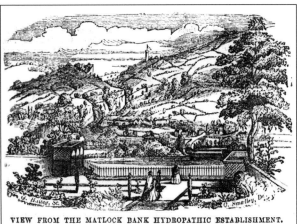

Right: The view of Masson Hill from Smedley's. The Victoria Tower on the Heights of Abraham can be clearly seen and somewhat out of scale. In the foreground is one of the terraces now lost. (Author's Collection)

VIEW FROM THE MATLOCK BANK HYDROPATHIC ESTABLISHMENT.

quickly rose to 2,500 patients per annum. The strain became too great and he engaged a real doctor – in spite of his apathy towards these gentlemen – a Dr William Bell Hunter who took over the medical side of the establishment. In 1875 the "'hydro" was floated as a limited company, of which a Mr R Wildgoose was made the chairman, a post he held until he died in 1900. £30,000 was spent in improving the premises, equal to about £1,500,000 today.

By 1897 he had made a greater fortune with his hydropathic treatments than he had at Lea Mills. In 1901 another block was added on the south side – the original hydro was on the north side – of Smedley Street and the two were connected by a double – decked bridge, still in use. The cost of this extension, which added even more bedrooms, was £11,000 (£550,000 today). The winter gardens were added in 1901 at a cost of £6,000 (£300,000 today). In the trading year of 1900/1 the turnover was £41,584 (an astonishing £2,080,000 in today's money per annum!). A church was built on the site, now lost, where Smedley could preach his own brand of non-conformism and it was in this church that a new generator was housed complete with fuel tank when the hydro was electrically lit. There is no trace of this church to be found.

Smedley's was patronised by the famous such as Sir Thomas Beecham (Orchestral Conductor, 1879-1961), Ivor Novello (Ivor Novello Davis, Welsh composer, 1893-1951), Sir Harry Lauder (Hugh MacLennan, Scottish comedian and singer, 1870-1950), Sir George Robey (George Edward Wade, comedian, 1869-1954), General William Bramwell Booth (son of the founder of the Salvation Army whose mother came from Ashbourne, 1865-1950), Bing Crosby (Harry Lillis, USA film actor and crooner, 1904-77) and allegedly Robert Louis Stevenson (Scottish novelist and poet, 1850-94) wrote *Kidnapped* at the hydro. It was also used for housing cricket teams from abroad.

This would have been the time after Smedley's death when the rules were relaxed and people visited Smedley's for a rest. Alcohol was allowed and dances were held with a resident dance band. Alcohol was consumed even in the austere days of Smedley's rule when men, especially, sneaked out in the evenings to frequent the Gate Inn across the road from the hydro on Bank Road. The landlord must have had a roaring trade.

To give some idea of the scale of this business, the following were placed in cold storage for Christmas Day 1901: geese, turkeys, pheasants, hares, grouse, pigeons, poultry, venison, beef and pork, in total weighing 7,000 lb (3.2 Tonnes). Also there was a "quarter of a ton of butter" (254 kgs), 100 gallons (455 litres) of milk, ten tons of potatoes (10.2 Tonnes).

One cannot fault him for his charity and generosity especially to his workers at Lea Mills. This is a fit memorial for the man's care of others; his other memorial is his house which dominates the sky line like a folly (Riber Castle), of which more elsewhere. It was in his "castle" where he died on 27

The Ascending Douche –
"Now Sir, do sit still".
The Cartoonists had a field day lampooning hydropathy. This is typical of numerous cards sold both locally and elsewhere.
(Author's collection)

The Ascending Douche. "Now Sir, do sit still."

July 1874 at the age of 71 years.

Throughout this Smedley period, many houses were built on Matlock Bank to house his and other hydropathists' employees as well as framework knitters who either worked at home or at Lea Mills.

(Bryan pp 221 – 230 except as noted to the contrary)

The years between the two great wars (1914-1918 and 1939-1946) saw a decline in hydropathy. People were looking elsewhere for their entertainment and medicine, and the requisitioning of Smedley's by the War Department excluded its use by the public during World War II. During the depression of the 1920/30s it became a favourite watering place for retired people especially from the colonial service. The introduction of the National Health Act in 1948 signed the death knell of hydropathy as this act refused to pay for treatment in such establishments. It struggled on until 23 September 1955 when it closed through lack of custom, the last hydro to do so, thus bringing an end to a one time lucrative industry.

However, it was to acquire a new use, as it still is today, the headquarters of Derbyshire County Council. The building was sold in 1956 when it became County Hall (known as the Kremlin to many rate payers!) the opening ceremony being performed by Alderman Charles White, CBE, JP on 28 April 1956. A plaque inside the main doors commemorates this event. Since then the authority has expanded into other buildings in the area and "temporary" premises within the grounds. The tennis courts and bowling greens have been covered in tarmac to create car parking places for both staff and visitors. Some of the original gardens formed from rockeries exist as does the tufa grotto in the old Winter Garden.

Smedley's predilection for stained glass can be seen inside County Hall. A superb window located in the entrance hall off Smedley Street rises through three floors by the grand staircase. The ground floor windows show large figures, the whole being set off by silvery-white Renaissance style canopies. The left window features Hygeia (goddess of health) represented by a single female figure with a serpent and cup. This has the motto *"Mens sana in corpre sano"* which translates as, "a healthy mind in a healthy body".

The central window has the figure of "Truth" seated at the bottom of a well, with a mirror in one hand and a goblet of water in the other. A medallion portrait of John Smedley is above this figure and at the base the motto, *"Magna est veritas et prevalebit"* which translates as "Great is the truth and it will Prevail". The right window has the figure of Esculapius, the Greek God of Medicine with the motto, *"Venienti occurrite morbo"* which translates to "Hasten to meet disease as it comes". The Pool of Bethesda is depicted in the windows on the middle floor. The left shows the figures of Jesus and St. John healing a sick man, an angel is in the right window and in the centre is a group of people beside a pool. The sheep market at Jerusalem forms the background. The upper floor window represents Pure Air, Pure Water and Exercise in the form of three female figures, the bottom panels depict fish and marine animals. The whole is framed in the traditional egg and dart motif and a legend across these windows says, "Welcome the coming, speed the parting guest". (DCC) The bottom of the window gives the birth and death dates of John Smedley as 1804-1875 – these should be 1803-1874.

By 1866 many others had copied Smedley, who it would appear encouraged all of them, often lending ideas without reward. These were:

Bank House Hydro (Wyvern House Hydro)

Founded by Henry Ward in year unknown but closed in 1920. From 1922 to 1983 it was the Ernest Bailey Grammar School and from then on it has been occupied by the Derbyshire County Council Records Department (previously County Archives). Ward was from Manchester and married to a woman from Crich. He employed eight bath men including one Alban Vokius from Kingston-upon-Hull, South Yorkshire. Of note is this new profession of bath man, unique to this industry.

Barton's

Possibly an early name for one of George Barton's hydros: he was involved with many.

Belle View

Founded by the Revd. R Nicholson and a Dr Cash in c.1870 and later run by a Mr and Mrs Allsopp. Probably a casualty of World War II it is now apartments, located at the top of Steep Turnpike at its junction with Chesterfield Road.

Bridge Hall Hydropathic Establishment, Matlock Bridge

This was run by a Rev. Richard Nicholson a native of Highgate, London and recently of Great Yarmouth, Norfolk who offered the "Smedley Mild Cure." It boasted it was the Hydro nearest to the train station.

   This building became the offices for Matlock Town Council, now the offices for Derbyshire Dales District Council, and still exists, with extensions, on the corner of Bank Road and Imperial Road.

Charles Rowland's

Presumably created by a Charles Rowland of Burton-on-Trent, Staffordshire and recently Coton-in-the-Elms in south Derbyshire. One might assume that this is the same man who founded Rockside, or was this the precurser of Rockside? Was he also the Rowland involved in Matlock House Hydro?

Chatsworth (Jeff's Poplar, Poplar Cottage)

Charles Wood founded this hydro in 1857, which was later run by a Mr Haywood. During World War II it was a service hospital and then the headquarters of C&A Modes, a multiple clothing store. It closed in 1946 to be taken over by Derbyshire County Council for the use of Matlock College. It is located on Chesterfield Road before the junction with Wellington Street.

Chesterfield House Hydro, Matlock Bank

This is the original hydro, predating all others by many years. Chesterfield House was originally a dairy farm built c.1750 now incorporated into the east end of the current building as a kitchen and the rooms above. In c.1800 a Mr and Mrs Ralph (Rafe) Davis bought the building and started hydro-pathic treatments as a cottage industry. Davis's eldest daughter, Harriet, having married a Mr. Richards took the business over, from which time it developed rapidly. There was much expansion under both the father and the daughter, a date stone above the present kitchen reads: "1861 RD AD" the RD clearly refers to Ralph Davis. In c.1900 the Richards sold the establishment to a Mrs Hickling known locally as "the best dressed woman in England", who added the word "hydro" to the title. She added to the west wing a ballroom, front lounge and entrance hall and 18 bedrooms with toilets and bed-rooms on the second and third floors. In Davis's heyday, he employed six male and nine female bathmen and servants.

   A Mr and Mrs John S Kay from Ilkley Hydro, West Yorkshire were employed as managers for an interim period before it went into liquidation, after which it was acquired by Sir Albert Ball and Mrs Margaret Southerns. It became a convalescent home for the military in 1917 until 1921 and from this latter date until 1927 it lay empty. It was bought by the sisters of the Presentation Convent in 1927 who are still in possession.(Brown and Gold ps.16-17) For its life to date see Chapter 12.

Church View

Opened by a Mr W Maycock in 1871 and later in the possession of Henry Ward, it is now a private residence.

Dalefield Hydro, Matlock Bank

This hydro was built in a Gothic and Romanesque style by a Mr Geo. B Barton in 1862. It opened as a hydro in 1881. Along with Mrs Barton, they offered a good cuisine and hot, cold, vapour, Turkish, Russian, electric, needle, douche, spray, rain and other baths! The name was changed later to Lilybank Hydro (qv). This establishment offered lawn tennis, billiards and "entertainments".

Elmtree Hydropathic Establishment

This hydro, dating from 1862, was operated by a Mr William Bramald, who offered the "Mild Water Cure". To give a more personal attention the establishment was limited to 25 guests. The "domestic arrangements" were under the control of a Mrs Higginbotham. It is now apartments.

George Davis's

Probably an early name for one of the many hydros the Davis family was involved with.

Jackson House, (Jackson Tor House), Matlock Bank

This establishment was re-opened after a spell of disuse by a Mr and Mrs George Barton of Dalefield fame and by 1862 it was owned by a Mr Leonard Bramwell of Bakewell and previously of Bridge Hall. After World War II it became a hotel. Several owners have operated here with varying success. At the time of writing, permission is being sought to convert the original building into seven apartments and the 1990 wing into three maisonettes. This building has had mixed fortunes over the years and many owners. Perhaps it will enjoy a new lease of life now.

Jeff's Poplar Hydro, Matlock Bank

This opened in 1857 with 200 beds, the name being changed from Jeff's Hydro and later to Chatsworth House Hydro. This latter association is in name only with the Duke of Devonshire's seat higher up the valley – thus adding a certain cachet?

It boasted a promenade, bowling green and tennis courts together with an altitude of 800 ft (244 m). It was advertised as "no better place for gout, sciatica, rheumatism and bronchitis, diseases of the respiratory organs, liver and kidney complaints and nervous debility, over 20% cured." It served as a hospital in both World Wars later becoming part of the Matlock College and now part of Derbyshire County Council's offices.

Joseph Crowder's

A mystery hydro of which no trace could be found, however we do know that Joseph Crowder was Matlock born.

Lilybank Hydro, Matlock Bank

George Barton opened part of this hydro under the name of Dalesfield in 1890 and under his name initially, being changed to Lilybank Hydro in 1906. In 1919 the same Mr and Mrs Kay of Chesterfield House Hydro, using an inheritance left to the latter, formed a company and took this hydro over and became joint managing directors for the next 35 years. They made important additions to this hydro. In 1922 they bought The Gables, an adjoining property, from a Mrs M Wildgoose and incorporated it into the hydro, which in its final years was run by Mr. Kay's niece, Mrs. S Connor. The two buildings were linked by a ballroom in 1923. At its peak this establishment employed seven males and five females.

This hydro had a mixed existence until 1962 when it was purchased by the sisters of the Presentation Convent for use as the Nagle Preparatory School.(see Chapter 12)

In July 1995 the hydro was bought by Mr Jeremy Keck for use as a nursing home, later taken over in October 1999 when it came into the possession of Knights Associates Limited Group of Homes headed by Mr Peter Knights. It is now known as Lilybank Hydro Care Home with the motto, "Caring for you – Caring about you."(Brown and Gold ps. 17/18 MM 04.12.92 In. Litt. Walker 04.12.02)

Malvern House Hydropathic Establishment, Matlock Bank

This is located on the corner of Smedley Street and Smith Road (named after Job Smith) and was founded in 1893 by Job Smith, becoming part of Smedley's in 1918. After World War II, it became a furniture repository for Michael Morris (see chapter 9) after which it became first nurses' then student accommodation and, after Matlock College closed, it became flats and is due to be restored for use as apartments.

Job Smith was of local council fame and the progenitor of the Matlock Tramway of which he became the manager. He was also a Director of the Gas Company, Church Warden of All Saints' Church, Manager of All Saints' School, Chairman of the Matlock Waterworks, Chairman of the Social Institute and Chairman of the High Tor Recreation Grounds. For many years he was the Chairman of the Local Board and the first County Councillor for Matlock. He was apparently a man of high integrity and tireless in his efforts to improve Matlock for the benefit of both residents and visitors.

Manchester House

Became Matlock House Hydro.

Matlock House Hydro, Manchester House,

(Old Bank House) Matlock Bank

Opened in 1863 by a Mr Lee of Manchester – although it is recorded that he was born at Belper – and named Manchester House, it was run by a Mr Rowland with a Miss Wise. It boasted croquet, tennis, pastoral plays, theatricals, *tableaux vivants* (a "living picture" whereby living persons in costume portrayed a motionless picture) and every form of outdoor and indoor games and amusements. It also offered golf and fishing within easy walking distance, walking tours, etc.

Later it was occupied by the Matlock Modern School and of late by the local tax office – which moved to Alfreton – thereafter becoming apartments. It is located high up Bank Road on the right above Smedley Street.

Mills Hydro

This place is a mystery. It was called a hydro and was close to the old police station on Holt Lane. However splendid this sounds it appears to have been a common lodging house favoured by the police for housing vagrants and tramps and who visited the establishment nightly to check on the occupants. It was run by a Mrs Mills from Belton, Leicestershire employing two servants and she charged 4d (2p) per night. It was said that a customer had to put a bed leg in each of his boots to prevent overnight theft. Perhaps it had seen better times?

Oak Tree House

Only the name survives to tell us that there was once a hydro of this name.

Old Bank House

Opened by Jonas Brown of Mansfield, Nottinghamshire and Rose Barton, now part of Rutland Court – see Matlock House. They employed seven male and three female servants, some from as far away as Elgin and Perth, Scotland.

Oldham House Hydro, (Oldham House, Prospect Place, Rockwood) Matlock Bank

Built in c.1890, having 70 bedrooms, for Mr and Mrs Wildgoose (Mrs Wildgoose being the daughter of Thomas Davis – see Prospect Place) it quickly became part of Prospect Place. Later it housed nurses employed at Rockside Hydro. It was sold to the Misses White (one became Mrs Dimmock). It became the Woodland School and later during World War II it was a hospital for the Royal Air Force. Later it became part of the Matlock Training College, to be sold in 1965 to the Evangelical Movement for "Project Missions" as a conference centre. Derbyshire County Council bought it in the 1970s using a third only; it was demolished in 1978/9. Known locally as Wildgoose's Hydro.

Poplar Cottage

Became Jeff's Poplar Cottage

Prospect Place Hydro (Oldham House), Matlock Bank

Opened in 1859 by Thomas Davis of Matlock it amalgamated with Oldham House Hydro.

Ralph Davis's

Only the name tells us that this existed at all, unless it is an early name for South View.

Rockside Hydro, Matlock Bank

Built by a Mr Charles Rowland of Burton-on-Trent in 1862, it was one of the more successful hydros in the area which was heavily altered in 1903-6 by the architects Barry Parker and Raymond Unwin. Of interest are these two architects, both were Derbyshire born and worked according to the Northern Art Workers Guild Union, Unwin being a mining engineer with the Staveley Iron & Coal Company designing houses and amenity buildings. After it closed it became part of the now defunct Matlock College.

Charles Rowland had met John Smedley when he suffered poor health. This converted Rowland to the principles of hydropathy, building his first hydro at Coton-in-the-Elms near Swadlincote in south Derbyshire. Rowland was active in the Matlocks as one of the progenitors of the Cable Tramway up Bank Road, becoming the vice-chairman of the company, and was also the chairman of the Local Board.

At one time the hydro was run by William Atkins who also owned Atkins' Hydro at Darley Dale, now St Elphin's School. He employed a Dr William Moxon LRCP of Knowlestone Place, Matlock Green born at Rugeley, Staffordshire, as a resident physician.

On the outbreak of World War II (2 September 1939) the military walked into the main entrance and told the owners, the Misses Lennie and Lillian Goodwin (cousins, not sisters) to empty the place within 48 hours. All the patients were compensated and sent home and those who lived in were found spaces at Lilybank Hydro. The third in command – the bookkeeper – Marjorie Webster (now Mrs Yeomans) assumed that her job was now redundant. On the following Monday she was visited at home by an adjutant who begged her to return to work at her old job, as she knew of the local services and suppliers.

This she promptly did and worked there for the duration of the war. The building had been turned over to the Royal Air Force as a hospital for those air crew who had suffered from battle fatigue and severe strain. She undertook a stock-take and allocated people to their rooms, managed the telephone exchange, admissions and discharges. As there was no NAAFI, she organised a shop for the sale of luxuries to the patients – mostly cigarettes, the profits going to pay for entertainment – until the NAAFI arrived. The latter organised frequent dances attended by the local girls. The British Red Cross, of which Marjorie was a member, organised a library. A young woman living locally who helped out, was to become famous as Lady Isobel Barnet, a TV celebrity of the 1950s and 1960s. Max Wall was a patient for a time, as was the organist at Westminster Abbey. The neurological side of the premises was run by Sir John McIntyre with help from Wing Commander Gillespie and Squadron Leader Gall.

Above: The garden at Rockside Hydro **Below:** Rockside Hydro. This painting taken from a postcard gives an impression of how spendid this hydro was. The original building is the turreted one in the foreground. At the time of writing it is derelict and in poor condition (Yeomans)

In 1946 it was sold to Derbyshire County Council for the sum of £30,000 to form part of Matlock College. After the college closed it fell into decay, suffering from vandalism and pilfering. At the time of writing there are plans to restore it and convert it into apartments – a fitting rescue bid to be applauded.

Rose Cottage

Little is known about this hydro other than it was an early establishment run by a Mr Richard Freckingham of Matlock and later by Aaron Rigard and located on the Dimple. It then became a private house called Rosegarth and is now called Spa Cottage. The intention was to exploit the Allen Hill Spa at the bottom of the Dimple in an attempt to make Matlock a spa town, a venture which failed. At this time it employed ten men and nine women.

Shepherd's

Little is known about this establishment other than Shepherd was a bath man at Smedleys. There is a possibility that this hydro was absorbed into Matlock House Hydro.

Smedley Hydropathic

Dealt with in some detail elsewhere in this chapter, commonly known as Smedley's.

Smedley Memorial Hospital

Created by Smedley's widow in 1882 as a memorial to her husband it was later to become the town's cottage hospital. It is now a youth hostel belonging to the Youth Hostels Association, opened in 1984.

South View Cottage

Ralph Davis founded this hydro in 1857, its fate and location are not known.

Spa Cottage

A date stone tells us that this was built in 1767.

Spring Villa Hydro

Little is known about this hydro except that it stood close to Victoria Hall on Smedley Street, an area given over to housing.

Stailey House

All there is to remind us of this establishment is its name only.

Stevensons

Established in 1861 by a Mr and Mrs Stevenson who later opened Belle View. As there is no further information to be found one can assume that they left this place to move to Belle View c.1870.

Sycamore House

Thomas Davis may have had something to do with this hydro, a John Dawes of Holloway, Derbyshire ran it c.1885. It was later converted to apartments. It is assumed that this was close to Smedley's.

The Mount

Mentioned in a 1920 guide book and this is all that is known of it.

Tilley's Hydro

A reference can be found to this hydro with a photograph of people playing tennis but no trace of it can be found elsewhere.

Tor House

George Davis founded this hydro in 1858 and by 1902 this was the only Davis left in the business. He used "Mr Smedley's system"

Wellfield House

Joseph Crowder founded this hydro in 1862 to be succeeded by Dr Spencer T Hall. It is now a private residence.

Wildgoose's Hydro

Local name for Oldham House Hydro

Woodbine

The origin of this hydro is obscure other than it was run by a "Professor" Alexander. The premises are believed to form part of a motor repair shop on Smedley Street a few doors from the Gate Inn.
If one was without any qualifications in those days one could call oneself a professor with impunity.

Wyvern House Hydro

This was originally Bank House.

A total of over 40 hydros, and most are or were on Matlock Bank. It is significant how many times the name of Davis and Barton occur. A Thomas Davis was involved to a greater or lesser degree with Oldham House (his daughter), Prospect Place, Sycamore House and Tor House; Ralph (Rafe) Davis with Smedley's, Ralph Davis's, South View Cottage, Chesterfield House; and George Davis with George Davis's and Tor House. The Bartons were involved as George or G B Barton with Dalefield, Lilybank, Jackson House and Barton's!

(6) TRANSPORT

It should be noted on older maps and references that a few highways have changed their names over the 19th century, thus:

Original Name	*Current Name*
Carson Lane	Rutland Street
Dob Lane	Bank Road
Hackney Lane	Smedley Street
Tag Hill	Church Street

The Matlocks were a relatively isolated community from prehistoric times to the beginning of the 19th century. The area was of insufficient importance to warrant a sophisticated infrastructure but not so 2000 years ago.

Roads

Roman

It has been postulated that the Roman road, known as Hereward Street which connected Rocester with Chesterfield, ran through the parish comprising Cromford Hill, a ford at Willersley and climbing up Willersley Lane to the Slack and beyond. This road crosses another Roman road, the Street, which connected Buxton (Aquae Arnemetiae) with Little Chester near Derby (Derventio). Where they crossed near to Carsington was, it is now believed, the old lead mining centre of Lutudarum. Excavations undertaken before the inundation which created Carsington Water seem to verify this.

In 2002, pupils at All Saints School unearthed what may be a Roman road in the school grounds under the guidance of an amateur archaeologist, Tim Page. This lies under the play area at the Hurds Hollow site. This certainly has all the hallmarks of Roman road building, being 2.8 m wide with a 1.0 m deep drain channel each side.(MM 11.08.02)

Packhorse and Ancient Ways

Ancient trackways abound in the area most being based on old routes for miners and agricultural labourers.(See the map) According to Arkle, a trackway once followed Stoney Way, under Lilybank, Henry Road, Smedley Street East, Wellfield Cottage and thence over the moors.(Arkle p.30) It is also believed that a medieval trackway ran from Tansley to Hurst Farm and on to Matlock.

The earliest means of moving goods across country was by the use of the packhorse. These movements, of lead from Derbyshire, salt from the Cheshire Wichs and wool, created a matrix of packhorse routes.

A pack-horse way from Grangemill to Chesterfield passed through Matlock (Bridge), descending the flank of Masson Hill along a road called Salters' Lane suggesting that salt came this way. Before refrigeration, this necessary chemical was used for preserving meat. The Roman army was paid in salt,

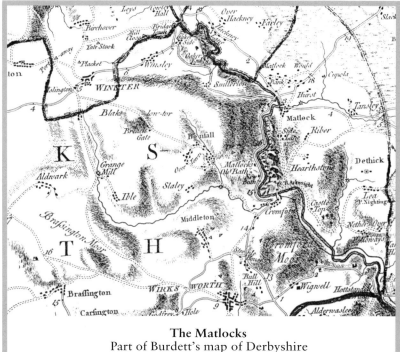

The Matlocks
Part of Burdett's map of Derbyshire

It can be seen that there was a corn mill on the Bentley Brook
(under the word Hurst)
and a lead smelter in Lumbs Dale above Hurst to the right. The
road down the valley from Matlock Bridge to Cromford is shown.
Baileys Mill stands where the corn mill is shown. The road north
towards Rowsley climbs to Hackney via the Dimple

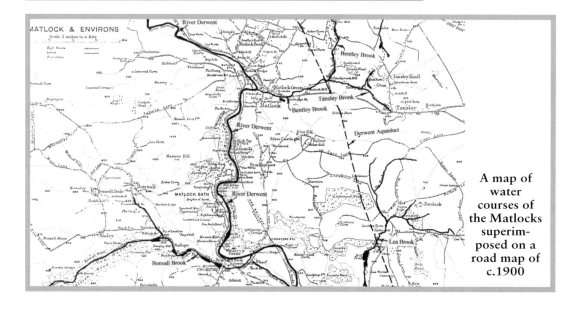

A map of
water
courses of
the Matlocks
superim-
posed on a
road map of
c.1900

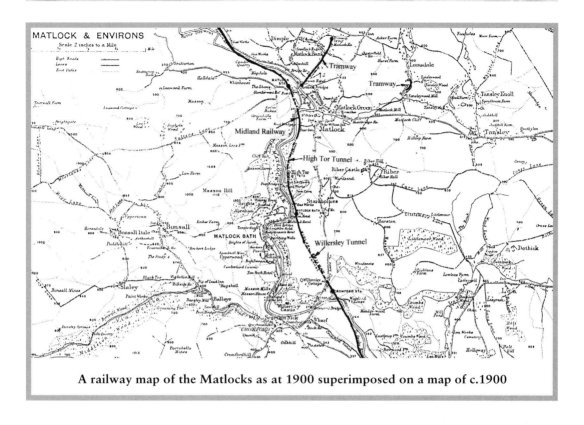

A railway map of the Matlocks as at 1900 superimposed on a map of c.1900

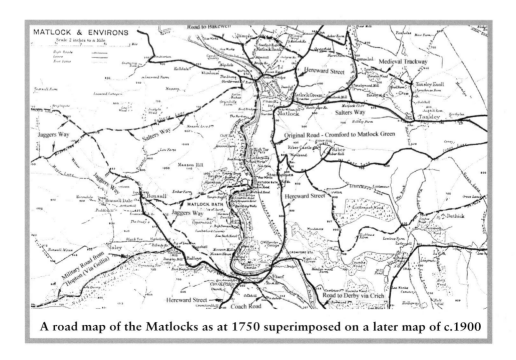

A road map of the Matlocks as at 1750 superimposed on a later map of c.1900

the soldier's salarium, from whence our salary. Another packhorse way followed the Roman Hereward Street linking Rocester with Chesterfield. In these far off times the routes would have crossed the river Derwent by means of fords, later replaced by the bridges we see today at both Matlock Bath and Cromford, both widened later to take wagons. A salter's way also came from the Leek to Bakewell road through Elton and Salters' Lane to Matlock; a lead mine close to this way is named Saltersway Mine.(Dodd & Dodd ps. 92-8)

A horse way for lead was called a Jaggers Way, the driver being known as a Jagger who in the 17th century earned 1s 0d (5p) a day.

Early Roads for Wagons

Before Smith and Pennell built a road to the Old Bath from Cromford and a horse way from this point to Matlock Bridge, the way south was via Starkholmes, Cromford and Wirksworth. This former route along the bank of the Derwent was improved by Arkwright when he cut through the hill at Cromford in Scarthin Nick. It was intended that this should be a tunnel but was not pursued. This cutting was substantially widened in the early 1960s. The road north passed close to the New Bath Hotel, the Old Bath Hotel and thence on a raised bank to Matlock Bridge. This was widened at Masson Mill creating new retaining walls for the houses on the hillside and from the river bank to support the road. There were sacrifices to be made; the Glenorchy Chapel and house, an inn and several houses were taken down as well as a petrol filling station.

The road north to Bakewell from Matlock Bridge was by means of The Dimple and Hurds Hollow.

The route to Alfreton was by means of Causeway Lane which was prone to flooding until it was built up, large stones being used to take the weight of the growing trade from quarries at Tansley and Upper Lumsdale. At this time the area known as Hall Leys was a flood plain and had a reputation for being water logged. The road south from Matlock Bridge, before the new road down the dale, was via Holt Lane.

Just prior to 1900 a "Carrier" Holmes took a covered wagon every Tuesday and Friday to Derby taking a day each way, with a change of horses at Belper. He would divert through Lea or Wirksworth if requested and would also deliver gaming cash to Derby as there was nowhere in the Matlocks at that time for gamblers.

Turnpikes

The first turnpikes were authorised in 1346 by King Edward III and the idea grew to have its apogee in the late 18th and early 19th centuries. Many were abolished in 1772 and finally all were supposedly done away with; however some lived on until 1889.
The turnpikes which came through the Matlocks were:
Nottingham and Newhaven Turnpike: it arrived in the Matlocks via Alfreton and Wessington cross-

Above: A carrier below High Tor. The only means of transporting goods at the time, c. 1850. Note the heavily rutted road (Asdam W 80)

ing Matlock Bridge then on to Snitterton, Wensley, Winster and Pikehall, thence to Newhaven.

Derby to Chapel en le Frith Turnpike: from Derby it proceeded to Whatstandwell, Wirksworth Moor, Cromford, Matlock Bath, Matlock over Matlock Bridge to Bakewell via The Dimple and Hackney Lane, to join the Chapel-en-le-Frith road near Great Longstone.

Cromford Bridge to Langley Mill Turnpike: via Lea, Holloway and Ripley.

Belper to Cromford Turnpike: A private coach road already connected these important mill villages, located higher than the valley bottom to avoid flooding. This was built jointly by Jedediah Strutt of Belper, Charles Hurt of Alderwasley and Richard Arkwright of Cromford for their own use. In 1818 this road was routed at a lower level between these same places and is known today as the A6 Derby to Manchester road.

Chesterfield to Ashbourne Turnpike: This passed through Walton near Chesterfield, Kelstedge near Ashover, East Moor, Matlock Bank and Bridge and on through Matlock Bath, Cromford, Middleton by Wirksworth, Hopton, Carsington, Kniveton to Ashbourne, total distance being 21 miles.

For those wishing to access London and Manchester, from 1814 a coach ran each way daily. Goods and parcels from London were brought by carrier to Matlock by meeting the London wagons at the Tiger Inn, Derby every Monday and Friday.(Bryan p.66)

All routes out of the Matlocks had toll houses except the road to Cromford via Starkholmes, which was free. One assumes that they would not have had the nerve to charge for taking carriages and wagons up the Starkholmes road at Willersley.

The toll houses or bars were at:

- Warm Wells Gate, Matlock Bath now lost but was outside Masson Mill
- Holt Lane, Matlock Dale now lost
- Artists Corner, now represented by Toll House Cottage
- Matlock Bank represented by the Gate Inn
- Darley Dale
- Tansley

The portion of the road from Cromford to Matlock Bath was created by Smith and Pennel through the lost village of Willersley. This was to give access to Pennel's residence by Masson Mill (later to become the home of the incumbent of the Lady Glenorchy Chapel, both lost) and to the Old Bath. The cutting through of Scarthin Nick came later on the instigation of Sir Richard Arkwright, to divert traffic from the view from Willersley Castle. This is also the reason he demolished the lost village of Willersley, which supported a lead smelter where the church of St Mary now stands. Later this road was pushed through to Matlock Bridge and was the origin of the A6 road.

The age of coaching not only brought us the turnpike system but a whole new approach to travel for those who could afford it. These coaches were limited by law on how many passengers they could carry, a law that was blatantly flouted.

Steep Turnpike in Matlock was built as a short cut for coaches from and to Chesterfield. Harley House facing the library was where they kept the cock horse (a blocked up arch indicates where this animal was kept) for attaching to coaches to help the other horses up this steep hill. Passengers had to alight and walk behind the coach. This house was infamous as the site of the "potty murder", see *Wedgwood Benn* in Chapter 9.

Carrier Holmes also kept a cock horse at the bottom of Tag Hill (now part of Church Street) to help coaches and wagons up Starkholmes Road and Lime Tree Road.

On 29 June 1815, a coach was inaugurated and ran from Buxton to Matlock Bath and back, whose main source of passengers travelled from the Rutland Arms at Bakewell to the Old Bath at Matlock. This had a competitor, "a new fast chariot, carrying three inside and six out." This left Smith's Hotel, Matlock at 0830 hrs and arrived at Buxton via Newhaven at 1200 noon. Its return trip included Bakewell and started at 1600 hrs arriving at Matlock at 2000 hrs. This journey today in a motor car takes approximately 40 minutes on much busier roads, but of course much better roads also. The enterprising person who did this was a Timothy Greenwood.(Bryan p. 127)

The following coaches ran up the dale every day:

-   1130 hrs a mail coach from London to Manchester returning at 1400 pm.
-   1400 hrs the "Lord Nelson" from Nottingham to Manchester with another "Lord Nelson" returning at 1500 hrs.
-   1015 hrs the "Lady Nelson" from Nottingham to Manchester, returning at 1200 noon, again there must have been two such coaches.
-   1000-1200 hrs the "Royal Bruce" from London via Nottingham and Derby to Manchester returning at 1730 hrs.
-   The "Peveril of the Peak" adopted the same route and times as the "Royal Bruce."
-   0900 hrs and 1700 hrs the "Peak Ranger" from the Greyhound Hotel, Cromford through the Matlocks, Bakewell and Ashford in the Water to Buxton.
-   0900 hrs the "Star" from Birmingham via Tamworth, Derby, Belper to Sheffield, returning via Baslow and Bakewell at 1645 hrs.
-   1000 hrs the "Star" from Sheffield returning from Birmingham via Lichfield and Burton-upon-Trent at 1600 hrs.
-   1000 hrs the "Quicksilver" using the same route as the "Star" but in reverse. Returning at 1600 hrs.

Modern Roads

Causeway Lane was probably built in the 1830s to handle the stone from the quarries at Tansley and Lumbsdale and later flour from Bailey's Mills. It was said that as it had to cross a water meadow, part of Hall Leys, the causeway was built of blocks of stone "as big as pianos" to carry the weights of the laden wagons or drugs as they were called.

When the present Bakewell Road was laid, crushed limestone was used blinded with limestone dust, rolled out. When wet this surface became muddy and when dry it was dusty. This white mud, which soiled everything it came into contact with, was scraped off with a special tool in winter.

Whilst the horse held sway, there was a thriving business in hiring carriages and the like. The leading firm for this was Furniss, having taken over the premises (costing £2,030 to build) from Allen, on Bakewell Road.(Arkle p.6) Furniss was famous for his teams of matching piebald and skew-bald horses. Their first motor vehicle was a Belsize taxi and the first omnibus was a Clyde 14-seater charabanc from Glasgow, having solid tyres and a top speed of 12 mph (19 km/hr). It was in this bus that they

Church Street, note the old cottages extreme right possibly 17th century

undertook a day trip to London! How they achieved this is a mystery. The passengers did have to alight up hills as they did with horse drawn carriages. This vehicle ended its life as a lorry. Taxi cabs were also run by an Alf Wood.(Arkle p.15)

The first garage in Matlock Bath was William's Garage of 1905. He had hire cars and ran the first charabanc between Matlock Bath and Matlock Bank calling them "Spa Buses". By 1910, everyone was changing from horses to buses and by 1914 the army had requisitioned most of the horses for World War I.

Carrier Holmes of Matlock Town, already referred to, was an unofficial carrier of urgent messages for John Smedley, who would ride down from Riber Castle and throw them into the front lawn of Holmes's cottage on Tag Hill, part of Church Street now.

Hand and Sons, adjacent to the Gate Inn on Bank Road/Smedley Street crossing hired out four-in-hand charabancs, close and open carriages, landaus with rubber tyres and dog carts. The first omnibus in the Matlocks was run by Hand and Son running to Matlock Bath and Cromford, being a Fiat known locally as the "toast rack" due to the hard lath seats.

The appearance of the motor car changed the area for ever as it did everywhere else. Local wags used to divert drivers, who enquired of the route to Bakewell, up Bank Road and along Smedley Street, waiting to see how far they could climb Bank Road before stalling. The first motor car in the Matlocks was paraded on 27 April 1900 by its proud new owner, Dr Marie Orme the resident physician at Rockside Hydro, this was steam powered.(Arkle p14) The first assent, after many tries, of Bank Road by motor bicycle was in 1907 and it caused great excitement and rejoicing.

Imperial Road was laid by a Jim Shaw in c.1895 for the building of residences for the better off. Dale Road was finally finished with tarmacadam in 1921.

The main London to Manchester Road the A6, is now de-trunked if there is such a word, the arrival of the M6 motorway and to a lesser extent the M1 motorway have rendered it a local thoroughfare only. This road has been widened at Scarthin Nick and by Masson Mill, but the road builders are thwarted by the confines of the valley. There are possibly exciting times ahead for it has been mooted that a tunnel be cut from Cawdor Quarry to Harveydale Quarry thus by-passing Matlock Bridge. Also the prospect of a relief road from Dale Road to Bakewell Road is to go ahead, the writer just hopes to live long enough to see these miracles of engineering undertaken.

Canal

This runs and terminates in the adjoining parish of Cromford but is included briefly to record its effect on the Matlocks. The construction of the Cromford Canal had a profound effect on the area for it opened up trade into and out of the area. This canal was opened in 1782 and had a length of 14.5 miles (23.3 km), joining the Nottingham Canal at Langley Bridge in the County of Nottinghamshire. It carried stone, lead, cotton thread, hay and straw, etc out and brought coal, textiles, pottery, and tiles in, thus opening up all sorts of opportunities to local trades.

Railways

Prior to 1849, Matlockians had to travel to Ambergate to access the North Midland Railway, an omnibus connected this station with Matlock Bath four times a day – the fare being 1s 6d (7.5p) each way including luggage . The North Midland Railway ran from Derby with connections to London via Birmingham and Rugby.(Bryan p.128)

The Manchester, Buxton, Matlock and Midland Junction Railway arrived from Ambergate to Rowsley being opened on 4 June 1849 with the intention of connecting to the Midland Railway. The opening was celebrated with a luncheon held at the Old Bath Hotel presided over by the vice-chairman, Henry Tootal; the Duke of Devonshire being represented by Joseph Paxton, not yet knighted. This railway reached Manchester in 1867. From this day on it was possible to go by train from St Pancras Station in London to Piccadilly Station in Manchester.

Left: High Tor and Matlock Bath Station. This is incorrectly titled "High Tor and Railway Station, Matlock". Note the locomotive with five carriages leaving the station for Cromford. The carriages with two horses is heading for the bridge over the river Derwent. C.1850 (Author's collection)

Initially there were six trains each way on weekdays and two at weekends. This opened the door to day visitors from Nottingham, Derby, Sheffield and Manchester and the number of trains was to increase, especially at weekends. The through trains to Manchester would run along the valley at frightening speed. All other trains stopped at Matlock Bridge as the station was known, disgorging the passengers who had booked in to one of the many hydros. Several boys would wait on these trains looking for luggage to carry for small tips and guiding people to the waiting carriages or the tramway. The scene at Matlock Bath would be as busy, with the day trippers invading the village from Derby and Manchester direct, and those who had changed trains from as far afield as Sheffield, Birmingham and Nottingham. Similarly the local residents could get a day excursion to Manchester for 1s 6d (7.5p). The journey took under an hour.

There is something about railways that not only draws on nostalgic memories, in spite of the soot and smoke, but seems to breed a new type of character. Matlock had them and two in particular. One was the bus driver from Smedley's Hydro known as "Lord" Fred Byron who would not be fazed by high ranking visitors and would not move until he had finished his apple. The other was Joe Wright an awesome individual who was a guard and who always wore a flower in his button-hole and would not put up with any nonsense from the pupils who caught his train to Belper to attend the Strutt School.(Arkle p.11) Similarly pupils caught the train in the opposite direction to attend the Lady Manners School at Bakewell, Allison Uttley writes of this daily journey from Cromford.

There were three stations in the parish, Matlock Bridge (now Matlock), Matlock Bath and Cromford. Within living memory, Matlock station was kept clean and decorated with many flowers and employed approximately 40 persons. Matlock Bath station was built in a Swiss Chalet style, numbering several buildings, of which only two survive, one of these is now the "Whistle Stop Centre". Cromford Station and the Station Master's house were designed in the "French style" by G H Stokes, nephew of Sir Joseph Paxton. The house is now a private residence and the single station building is a retreat for a scout troop.

Over the years this line has changed hands several times thus:

MBM&MJR	Manchester, Buxton, Matlock and Midland Junction Railway
MR	Midland Railway
LMS	London Midland and Scottish Railway
BR(M)	British Rail (Midland)
CT	Central Trains

Midland Railway became the London Midland and Scottish Railway on 1 January 1923. The London Midland and Scottish Railway became British Rail (Midland) on 1 January 1948.

The age of many railways came to an end with the closures by the infamous Dr Richard Beeching (later Baron Beeching), chairman of the British Railways Board 1963-65, which put an end to many rural lines including, in 1968, the one from Matlock north to Buxton except for mineral traffic. The line was kept from Derby to Matlock, which had additional encouragement by the arrival of the cable cars at Matlock Bath.

A group of enthusiasts took over the abandoned rail bed from Matlock to Rowsley in 1975 and have put it back into use, running passenger trains, both steam and diesel hauled on most Sundays and many Saturdays with some weekday services, and many specials covering such as "The Warring Forties", Santa Specials, Halloween Ghost Train and Vintage Traction weekends. The company is now quoted on the stock exchange as Peak Rail plc. The old Matlock Station ticket office is a book and souvenir shop and The Palatine Restaurant, operating in a dining coach is popular with visitors. The dream is to extend the line to Buxton with connections to Manchester, a large project for a small provincial company but help may be at hand at the time of writing, as the government is proposing to reopen this line. Perhaps we will be able to travel from Derby to Manchester by rail again soon? http://www.peakrail.co.uk/index.htm   MM 21.11.02

Tramway

What a wonderful asset this would be today had it survived!

The originator of the idea was a Mr Job Smith of Malvern House hydro fame, as early as 1862 after he had seen something similar at San Francisco, USA. He returned to Matlock in 1868 and made contact with John Smedley to discuss the idea but nothing came of it. The idea was raised again in 1885 when Sir George Newnes showed considerable interest for he had been responsible for the Cliff railway at Lynton, Devon.

Sir George offered to finance the tramway but it was felt that locals should have a stake in it. A limited company was formed having as directors, Sir George Newnes, Robert Wildgoose, Job Smith,

Above: Crown Square, Matlock Bridge. There are five horse drawn vehicles and a single tramcar. The tram terminus is central to the picture and the clock tells us that this photograph was taken at 11.07 am. The bicycle wheel at the far left tells us that cycles could be bought and possibly hired from here and the sign above it proclaims that Pratts Spirits are available here. The barber's pole on the extreme right is attached to a building which with others was demolished to create the Hall Leys Park Head (Yeomans)

Charles Rowland, Dr W Bell Hunter, Charles Hill and G Croydon Marks CE. (CE = Civil Engineer)

The engine house and depot were built first at the top of Rutland Street and still exists. The stone came from the Bentley Brook quarries. Rails and a cable were laid down Rutland Street and Bank Road with the bottom terminus at Crown Square. The roads were not wide enough to accommodate two lines, one line was therefore installed with passing places.

The tramway was opened with considerable ceremony and toast drinking on 28 March 1893 and operated for over 34 years closing on 30 September 1927. There was much heated debate about this closure but the ratepayers had to be protected from the losses, which ran at £1,000 per annum at this time; a considerable amount of money for a small provincial council to have to subsidise. (Fay) Petrol buses took over the gap left by this closure.

Two steam engines were installed on a run and standby basis, which drove a large fly wheel which operated the cable. These engines were steam driven by means of a Lancashire type steam boiler to be replaced with gas engines on the arrival of the cheaper gas. The cable was laid in a road trench and the trams worked as a balance, one up and one down with a drum at the bottom of the hill. These open top trams had 31 seats and were provided with grabs, which the driver engaged onto the cable and disengaged when stopping. As the standard fare was 2d (1p) uphill and one penny (0.5p) down hill it was quickly dubbed "Tuppence up, penny down." There was a single decked third car with side facing seats, which was not popular as the passengers were piled together at the lower end when on the Bank Road hill.

In 1898, Newnes bought out the other shareholders and presented it to the people of Matlock. The price he had to pay was £20,000 (£500,000 today).

In 1899 Robert Wildgoose gifted the clock on the shelter complete with clock tower at the Crown Square terminus. This shelter still complete with clock can be seen relocated in Hall Leys Park. This clock presented a challenge to anyone who thought he could run from Crown Square to Matlock Green in the time that the clock took to chime 12. This was only achieved once by a Mr W R Bradbury and a friend before the World War I. This shelter was also a meeting place for people and an unofficial betting shop. The main part of the actual shelter is now in Hall Leys Park. It had stained glass windows and brass door handles, nothing was spared in making this shelter an example for all such shelters.(Arkle 2/3)

The tramway was popular with visitors to Smedley's Hydro and to the local residents on Matlock Bank when shopping at Matlock Bridge. As the trams ran at 5 miles per hour (8 km/hr), it was easy for little boys to hop on when the conductor was distracted and hop off again when he saw what was happening. There was an unofficial agreement that telegraph boys could ride free when on duty.

The tramway finished work at 9.00 pm every night except when it was kept running to take advantage of the cinema audiences when the films had finished. The only halt other than the termini was at Smedley Street for the Hydros – Smedley's in particular. It was the steepest tramway occupying a street in the world at a gradient of 1:5 (18.2%).

The Crown Square shelter now in Hall Leys Park and the engine house at the top of Rutland Street are all that are left of this tramway. The stained glass panels from the shelter are now at the National Tramway Museum, Crich, as is one of the three tramcars. The other two were placed on Sandy Lane and Dogs Farm.

Rivers and Streams

Derwent

This river is included in this section as it has presented problems for the road system locally (and still does) for two reasons; congestion at bridges for road traffic and flooding. The latter problem has been overcome but not the former. Also it is more than likely that the Romans floated their lead ingots down the river to the Trent and on to the Humber.

It has always been a capricious river with a long history of flooding the surrounding land, well into the late 20th century. The name "Causeway" Lane, Matlock tells us that this road was built up above the flood plain. This capriciousness is due to the molten snow and springs in and near the valley, not forgetting the numerous lead mine soughs, letting free vast quantities of water after heavy rain, and particularly after the snow melts on the high ground to the north of the county. Particularly bad years were the first week of October 1881, followed by further inundations in March and October of the following year, mid November 1890 and the end of December 1901.(Bryan p.79-84).

In the last century the river rose to new heights, see the markers by the footbridge in Hall Leys Park, which show the dates of floods in 1961 and 1965. The 1901 and 1931 floods caused major disruptions in Matlock Bridge by rising to several feet above Crown Square. The former flood occurred on 29 December after heavy snow; the latter occurred on Friday, 4 September causing damage estimated at £30,000 (£500,000 today). The flood of 1931 started with heavy rain followed by the opening of the flood gates at Howden Dam.(MM 06.06.02)

The last flood was in 1965, after which major works were carried out in 1983-4 to the river bank where a flume was created above Matlock Bridge and downstream the river bed was excavated below High Tor with sluice gates between.

There is one recorded instance of the river freezing over, in January 1895, due to exceptionally cold weather, with snow drifts up to 8 ft (2.44m) high. The river was frozen over from Artists' Corner to the ferry upstream of the weir near to Masson Mill such that on Sunday, 10 February 1895 people were walking on it.

This river has always been famous for its trout. The last two otters were killed in 1888, as they were considered a menace to the fish.

Crossing the river

Cromford Bridge

The first crossings of the river Derwent in the Matlocks were fords where Matlock Bath bridge to the station and Cromford Bridge now stand. This must have made the journey more hazardous for pedestrians and horses. So much were these crossings feared that the ford at Cromford had a chapel complete with a squint, which housed an oil lamp to guide the travellers across through the water. If one looks into the clear water of the river in line with this chapel the bed of the ford can still be seen. A priest would take offerings from the traveller in the hope of a safe journey. This ford was replaced by a bridge in the 15th century. Half of this bridge is in the parish of Matlock.

Matlock Bridge was built in the 16th century and widened in 1903-4, the original bridge is the downstream half. It is possible to see the two bridges by looking upstream from the bank of the river in Hall Leys Park. The widening had been demonstrated as necessary by the traffic having to queue to cross it, comprising wagons, pack and other horses and pedestrians. From 1874 there was much arguing over costs and liabilities for payment to widen this bridge. It was finally agreed that the cost would be met by the County Council paying £3,700 and the Matlock Council £500, paid for by an increase in the rate of 6d (2.5p) in the pound.(Bryan 96-101)

Cromford Bridge, which is partly in Matlock parish was maintained by the county from Easter 1700 and was intended for pedestrian and horse traffic only. The earliest reference to this bridge is in the will of one Richard Smyth, vicar of Wirksworth, who died in 1504. In 1524, Thomas Blackwell of Wirksworth bequeathed "a fodder of lead to the chapel at Cromford towards its maintenance of Divine service." It is recorded that a visitor to the chapel in 1753 recorded a window with the Talbot Arms on it, the Talbots being one time Lords of the Manor. It was used for two dwellings and Richard

Arkwright had these demolished and removed. Carved on the parapet of this bridge, but not in its original place, is "THE LEAP OF MR B H MARE 1697". This purportedly refers to a time when a Benjamin Heywood of Cromford Bridge House nearby, rode his horse over the wall and into the river, both being unscathed. This creates a mystery, as the only Benjamin Heywood to be found in the records died in 1696, less than a week old. This bridge is unique in that when it was widened a different configuration of arching was used such that one side is pointed and the original side is rounded.

Matlock Bath Bridge

This is also of stone and was built by the railway company to give access to its station at Matlock Bath, opening for traffic in 1849. As referred to elsewhere this is probably the location of the ford in Mestesford.

Bentley Brook

This is a tributary of the Derwent, which it joins at Hall Leys Park. The brook supported numerous mills and supplied at least one bleaching works in its short length as it cascaded down the slopes from the moors, levelling out near to Matlock Green. It has numerous mill ponds created by damming the stream and many footbridges to give access to the mills and houses particularly at Matlock Green.

Footbridges

A suspension bridge spanned the river Derwent near to Artists Corner, it was taken away in the latter half of the 20th century as being beyond economic repair. The abutments still exist and the original access is blocked off for safety. This bridge was opened in May 1903.(Bryan p.137)

Hall Leys Park Bridge is of wrought iron lattice construction with timber planking and connects the park with Dale Road via Derwent Avenue. The current footbridge here dates from the 1920s.

The Jubilee Bridge at Matlock Bath commemorates Queen Victoria's jubilee of 1897, connecting North Parade, Matlock Bath with the bandstand. A steel lattice girder bridge connects to the Via Gellia Colour Works and the base station for the cable cars.

Matlock Bath has a new bridge that replaced an older one which connects the riverside gardens to the Lover's Walks.

The railway crosses the river by means of a bridge under Pic Tor.

Ferries

Ferries have been in use on the river until recent date, the most important of which was one that crossed the river opposite the Boathouse Inn, hence its name. It linked Matlock Dale with Matlock Town. This was replaced by a footbridge in the autumn of 1872, to be washed away in a flood in February 1921. A more robust bridge of iron was erected with a footway at a higher level a year later at a cost of £240 for the ironwork; the Misses Askew paid for the piers.

A further ferry was located near to Artists Corner to serve the same purpose as the above mentioned and a third was located near to the Pavilion at Matlock Bath. None of these exist but at least two of them were operating within living memory. (See Chapter 7, which under markets and fairs refers to a sheep crossing)

$\textcircled{7}$ SERVICES

$\mathbf{M}$ost of the statutory services for the Matlocks arrived, as elsewhere, in the 19th century, being improved in the 20th. Before the arrival of piped water, coal – later piped natural gas – and piped sewage, the locals had to rely on wells and springs, candles and paraffin lamps, soil closets and sheer luck. The conveyance of letters whilst reliable was expensive and policing was a haphazard affair. Today, we cannot imagine what it was like to have to cope without modern services, all piped or cabled to our homes, offices and factories.

Water

This basic and most important commodity used for medicinal purposes is covered in Chapters 4 and 5.

For an area that seemingly appears to be overflowing with water, the piping of it to premises in the Matlocks seems to have been difficult. One reason of course is that the area grew more rapidly than anyone would have dreamed. The problem was finally solved with the introduction of the ambitious Derwent Valley scheme. Prior to 1862 water for the area was derived from a variety of sources including the warm springs.

The first we hear of a piped water supply is when the Matlock Water Company was founded in 1862, and an Act of Parliament authorised the raising of capital, comprising £4,000 with a borrowing of £1,000, to undertake the works. This was piped from the Wold Spring and was fed into a reservoir on Hackney Lane, 12 yds square (120 m). This supply was gauged at 113,385 gallons daily (515,450 litres/day) in March and 90,000 gallons daily (409,140 litres/day) in winter, which was normally sufficient but with the advent of the hydropathic institutions and the influx of visitors it proved to be inadequate.(Bryan p.59&169)

A further Act of Parliament was sought to allow the tapping of four springs, which yielded 10,000 gallons a day (45,460 litres/day) at a cost of £4,300. The new reservoir was delayed until 1883 – completed three years later – costing £2,658 and having a capacity of 500,000 gallons (2,273,000 litres).(Bryan p.59-60&187)

In 1893 an auxiliary supply was laid on from Brown's Spring near to the High Peak Junction on the main road. This lies behind an iron door on the roadside of the A6 and yielded 150,000 gallons a day (68,190 litres/day). As this lay on land owned by Mr F C Arkwright, his wife had the honour of turning the tap on and drinking the first glassful of water, which she pronounced to be excellent – followed by a supper at the Devonshire Arms Hotel. The engineer for this scheme was a Mr W H Radford of Nottingham and was carried out by Mr William Jaffrey as the surveyor to the Local Board.

However, still more water was required and in 1893 a dowser named John Mullins of John Mullins & Sons, Waterworks Engineers of Bath, was contracted to search for a supply. He was taken to the high ground north of the Chesterfield road a mile or so from the Duke of Wellington Inn. Using a twig, he located a place and headings were driven at an altitude of 1,000 feet (305m).

In March of 1893, a further bill from Parliament was required to allow the Water Company to raise more capital of £5,000 by issuing £10 shares. This exhausted their capital raising powers and the company entered into negotiations with the Matlock Urban District Council who agreed to pay £18,550 for it. After a difficult passing of an act when the Matlock Bath Council made certain objections, the bill was agreed; it also included £2,000 for the creation of council offices and other minor matters. The deal was finalised on 1 July 1898 when the company was wound up.(Bryan p.60-1) (Mullins)

Late in 1890, steps were taken to increase the supply when a contractor from Pendleton, Lancashire was employed to make a boring which took eight months to reach water at a depth of 207 ft (63m). The water rose in the bore to a depth of 38 ft (11.6m) from surface at 800 ft ASL (244m). Pumps were installed and turned on, on 24 July 1901. By November of that year, the Wolds spring was running out, one wonders if the two are connected geologically?(Bryan p.62&187/8)

By 1929 the situation was a little more rational. The various sources were as follows:

Matlock Bridge and Bank (Matlock Urban District Council)

The main supply was from springs intercepted by a trench 10ft (3m) long at Palethorpe Farm, Matlock Moor – 250 yds (8m) southwest of Matlock Moor Farm at an altitude of 840 ft (256m) ASL, and from a spring at The Wolds – 550 yds (168m) northeast of The Wolds and 870 ft. (265m) ASL. Three wells and a bore 700 yds (640m) southeast of the farm were held as a reserve, the yields being 200,000 gallons per day (909,000 litres) from the springs and 15,000 gallons per day (68,200 litres) from the bore hole. This latter supply runs by gravity to a reservoir at The Wolds.(Stephens p.56, 30)

There was also a bore 900 yds (823m) south east of Cuckoostone House at an altitude of 800 ft (244m).(Stephens p.103)

Matlock Bath

This village obtained its water from springs on Cromford Moor. The consumption of the thermal spring water within the village had given rise to "Derbyshire Neck" see Chapter 1. By using the Cromford Moor springs this problem was solved forever.

The Cromford Moor spring at 402 ft (122.5m) ASL produced 91,500 gallons per day (416,000 litres/day) with a hardness of 1.4ph. The lower parts of the village were fed by gravity from Birch Wood Spring, Railway End, Cromford, keeping a 4 in (100 mm) main at full bore.(Stephens p.47, 57) The Willow Well 1400 yds (1,280m) west by north of High Peak Junction, Cromford at 530 ft (161.5m) ASL supplied 40,000 gallons per day (181,800 litres/day) to parts of Matlock Bath.(Stephens p.48)

Although partly dealt with in Chapter 4, given below are details of the three main "thermal" springs in the village:

New Bath Hotel – supplies a plunge pool, outside swimming pool and ornamental ponds.

Royal Hotel (now gone) had its own supply and also fed the Pump Room in the Pavilion, the pump is now located in the Information Centre in the same building. The water can be heard running under the grotto on the car park off Temple Road and also feeds a waterfall and ornamental pond at the bottom of Temple Road.

Thermal Swimming Baths, now the Aquarium, has its own supply from Wragg Sough.(Stephens p.72)

These do not conform to the rules for describing thermal waters but they do provide the lime deposits much exploited but no longer for petrifaction and tufa.

Riber, Starkholmes, Hearthstone and High Leas

They all relied on local springs, Riber Castle from a well in its own grounds. It lies 3200 yds (2.9 km) north west of the Castle and the well is approximately 80 ft (24m) deep and the water was raised by a wind pump discharging into a tank.(Stephens p.103) The tradition that Riber Castle was abandoned due to a lack of water is not true.

Originally Starkholmes took its supply from a roadside spring at approximately 550 ft (168m) ASL. Those who fetched their water by hand, and it was customarily the women, knew of its value. A further source was at High Leas Farm, a mile southeast of Starkholmes at an altitude of 720 ft (219m) ASL but was reported as a "mere trickle" in 1929. It supplied the farm only.(Stephens p.57)

The farms and premises at Hearthstone took their supply from a spring 800 yds (732m) south of Riber Castle at an altitude of 810 ft (247m). The catchment for this seems small given its altitude and it must have had a capricious supply.(Stephens p.57)

The large trunk main from the Derwent Valley Scheme which supplies Derby, Nottingham and Leicester runs through, or rather under, Matlock Bank. Some of the spoil from this created Bailey's Tump referred to in Chapter 13; the main is shown on the map of water courses.

Sewage Disposal

A sewage main was installed in 1899 which connected the Matlocks to treatment pits covering 18 acres (7.3 hecatres) lower down the Derwent valley south of Cromford, the main following the west side of the river for much of its length. The capital for this and other works was raised by borrowing £26,000 over 50 years at 3.25%.

Gas

Each council area had its own gas works, Matlock's being located on Bakewell Road and Matlock Bath's close to where the cable car lower terminus is located. These locations were chosen as being close to the station yards in each case to allow for the necessary coal to be imported with ease.

Matlock's original supply was for lighting only. Its origin is from a meeting of the Matlock Bath Company on 9 May 1857 held at the Queen's Head Inn, when it was agreed to borrow £1,000 for the purpose. The shares were priced at £5 each and 100 were taken up at the meeting. A company was formed in 1886 calling itself the Matlock District Gas Company to serve not only Matlock but also Tansley, Wensley, Snitterton and the Darleys. The new company paid the old one the sum of £15,000 in cash and £1,000 in shares. The capital of the company was fixed at £13,000 in £10 shares and £4,000 in debentures.(Bryan p.64)

The consumption was about 100,000 cubic feet a week (28,300m³). By an Act of Parliament of 1891, the authorised capital was raised to £26,200 and a maximum price for the gas was fixed at 4s 3d per 1,000 cubic feet (21p/283m³).(Bryan p.64)

Matlock Bath's gas service was the cause of much controversy as the council wished to purchase their portion from the Matlock Council. After much wrangling about cost an arbitrator was appointed and an agreement, albeit a costly one, was made. At the cost of £800 plus, a loan of £20,500 was agreed with Cardiff Corporation for 50 years at 3% pa with a further loan of £3,777 to meet the parliamentary costs! By 1901, three years after the idea was mooted, a separate gas works was established near to where the base station of the cable car is now located.(Bryan p.184-86) This scheme was ambitious to the degree that they piped gas as far as the Rutland Cavern on the Heights of Abraham to provide illumination.

(Note: For those interested in all the machinations in this matter, Bryan has covered it in comprehensive detail in pages 184-186 of his book.[see references])

In 1852 attempts were made to form a company to provide hydrogen gas for illumination, the provider was called the Matlock Gas Light and Coke Company, an unusual name given that the by-product from the manufacture of hydrogen does not include coke. This was initially for Matlock Bath only but the scheme was later designed to include Matlock Bridge and Bank. By 1857 it was found that more capital was needed and from hereon there is no further evidence of the use of hydrogen. The interests of this latter company were absorbed into the original enterprise to supply coal gas.(Bryan p.184/5)

The gas company built their own office premises on Bank Road with the ground floor occupied by their showroom and other users, including Gessy the Stationer hence the soubriquet "Gassy-Gessy Parade."(Arkle p.8) The date 1921 is featured on a date stone.

The statistics of the two original companies are of interest and are listed below:

	Matlock	Matlock Bath
Population supplied approximately	12,500	6,000
Share capital paid up	£47,120	£29,278 loan
Loan capital paid up	£9,750	
Coal carbonised	5,942 tons	2,378 tons
	6,037 tonnes	2,416 tonnes
Gas made (ft^3/annum)	62,752,000	26,825,000
(m^3/yr)	17,758,820	7,591,500
Gas sold (ft3/annum)	58,016,000	25,864,000
(m^3/year)	16,418,500	7,319,500
Consumers	1,943	925
Public Lamps	293	145
Length of mains	21 miles	16 miles
	34 km	26 km
Towns and villages supplied.	Matlock	Matlock Bath
	Matlock Bath	Scarthin

The original Matlock Bridge Post Office

Darley	Cromford
Rowsley	Bonsall
Tansley	Winster

(Gas/Transco ps198/9)

In more recent times, the two supplies were combined into the one at Matlock Bridge. Yet nearer to today the whole system was incorporated into the East Midlands Gas Board, fed from the Sheffield part of the grid, with conversion to natural gas from the North Sea being later provided by converting all users' apparatus. It now forms part of Transco.

Electricity

The Derbyshire and Nottinghamshire Electric Power Company was created in 1902, with the powers to have a capital of £1,800,000 (£90,000,000 today) and borrowing powers of £600,000 (£30,000,000 today). The electricity was generated at Warsop in Nottinghamshire with distributing stations at Matlock, Clay Cross and Wirksworth. The principle was to sell electric power to local authorities who would then resell it to customers at a profit. The scheme was incorporated into the East Midlands Electricity Board, now East Midlands Electricity, who for reasons of security could not, understandably, provide a copy of the supply network.(In Lit EME)

Coal supplies

Until the late 20th century coal was a very important fuel, now mostly taken over by natural gas. Prior to this coal was delivered by rail from the nearby collieries in the Notts/Derbys coal field. Ironically a little coal was found in Masson Hill when mining for lead and Lumsdale when quarrying for stone but not in commercial quantities. The coal was kept in the station yards at Matlock Bridge and Matlock Bath from whence it was distributed to the two gas works, the hydros, factories and households.

The principal coal merchants were the Co-operative Society, W Birch, Statham and Sladen, Tom Wright and F G Dickinson. The coal for Smedley's was originally carried by Model T Ford lorries which when fully laden with a tonne or more made them light on the steering. The lorries travelled in lots of three and four and the drivers used sawdust to fill the tyres if they had a burst one.(Arkle p.16)

Mail

There were sub-post offices at Matlock Bridge and Matlock Green, the local head post office being at Matlock Bath. The post box at Matlock Green still boasts the monogram VR for Queen Victoria who died in 1901! The services offered by them, other than routine post office duties, were money orders, savings banks and telegraph offices, only the latter being no longer with us.

The Matlock Bridge Post Office was located in Holt Lane (a florist today), a George Hodgkinson being the postmaster at the turn of the 19th century. This was relocated on to Bank Road on 1 September 1912 the hours then being 0800-1930 for six days and Sunday morning. The use of vehicles was from 1926/7.(Arkle p.8)

In 1814 a mounted postman journeyed from Bakewell, every day bar Sundays, to Derby calling at Matlock and Wirksworth en-route, returning in the evening of the same day. The lowest rate was 3d (1p) for a distance of 15 miles (24 km) only and for a distance not exceeding 300 miles (483 km) the rate was 10d (5p). This service was not cheap and certainly not for the use of the poor. A penny post was established at Matlock by a saddler, Adam Walker, which was a private undertaking and for short distances only.(Bryan p.65-6)

The mail service for Matlock Bath – carried in the "Royal Mail" coach – was well organised, being the centre for the receipt and despatch of letters and parcels for the area as far as Bakewell and Wirksworth. In c.1840 the post office was in a room at a Miss Shore's house, Woodland Lodge. Mail from the south west came from Derby by coach which carried the mail on to Manchester and beyond, the procedure being reversed later in the day. The post office moved to a house in the middle of Woodland Terrace, later to move to North Parade, opposite and on the same road side as Hodgkinson's Hotel. In recent memory it moved twice to its present location on North Parade.

The clearing point for the mail destined for Matlock and Alfreton at this time was the Peacock Hotel, Oakerthorpe near Alfreton.(Heath, p12)

The main post office is now on Bank Road with sub-post offices at Matlock Green, Smedley Street, Matlock Bath and Scarthin.

Law and Order

Originally Matlock had its stocks recorded by Farey as being in existence in the mid 18th century and they stood in the churchyard outside the west wall of the parish church of St Giles.(Bryan quoting Farey p.120)

Petty Sessions had commenced in 1868 in Matlock, having previously been held under the auspices of Wirksworth whose Petty Sessional Court also covered the Matlocks. The magistrates sat every two weeks in the Town Hall.

The original police station stood on Church Street until a new station with three cells was built on Bank Road, Matlock Bridge in 1893 at a cost of £1,239, in the same location as the existing one. A house was also provided for a resident sergeant or inspector. In 1901 a groom's house, stable and coach-house were built for upgrading the accommodation for the use of a district superintendent who had moved from Wirksworth, an indicator if ever there was one that Matlock was growing in population and importance.(Bryan p.64) An Inspector Kennedy used to drill the constables on New Street every week for an hour between the two great wars.

The Derbyshire Constabulary was established on 17 March 1857 under the County and Borough Act, 1856, with a strength of 156 and a headquarters at Belper, under the control of a magistrate at the quarter sessions. The Chief Constable was a W G Fox and pay was 18s.0d (90p) to £1.18s (£1.90p) per week spending 10-12 hours per day on the beat. From 1893 Matlock was part of the Glossop Division until the latter became a borough and appointed its own force. Then Matlock became part of the Buxton Division on 1 April 1947, when the force amalgamated with Chesterfield and Derby and in 1967 the Derby Borough and County forces amalgamated.

The present police station on Bank Road was built in 1966 with stone from the Lumsdale Quarries, replacing the earlier one on the same site, the stone from the original station being used to build a house at Highfields. The Matlocks remain under the Buxton Division.(In Lit. Chief Constable)

Fire Fighting

The original fire station was based at Bank Hall after it became the Matlock Urban District Council offices. The pump was hand operated and the horses used for drawing this machine had to be rounded up from local fields, often with some difficulty.

This facility was relocated to New Street, opposite the end of Firs Parade, manned by part-time firemen who responded to calls from their homes and work places. In 1958 ten houses were built on Turnpike Close, with two more in 1962, for full-time personnel, with backing from part-time personnel during the day time. This system operates to date with two "watches", red and blue, working 12-hour shifts each, alternating between the two. Night cover is provided by alerting the firemen at home by means of "bleepers".

The present fire station, which was purpose-built in 1960, is on Chesterfield Road. In the early 2000s this one station receives on average 300 calls with 70 emergencies and 60 house fires a year. Apparently chip pans are the biggest problem by far with domestic fires a close second! On top of this they are called on to rescue animals and people from hazardous situations once a week.

They have three appliances, including a Mercedes 4x4 Unimog for difficult access along some of our rough and narrow lanes including access to moorland fires, and two Dennis traditional pumps for most other problems, which are not confined to fires. Rescuing people from cliffs, animals from mine shafts and a rescue from a tower crane are all part of a fireman's lot in the Matlocks.(Dochetry in Lit)

Health

The Matlocks do not boast a hospital, being well provided for by the Lady Whitworth Memorial Hospital at Darley Dale. The Smedley Memorial Hospital was the Matlock cottage hospital, see Chapter 5.

Militia

In 1803, during the time of the Napoleonic Wars, a force of volunteer infantry was raised in the country and maintained for five years. The Matlock, Dethick and Lea Company was raised totalling 60 men. The officers were George Hodgkinson (Captain), John Leedham (Lieutenant), and George Nutthall (Ensign). This corps formed part of the Wirksworth Battalion dominated by the Arkwrights: Charles Arkwright (Lieutenant-Colonel) and Peter Arkwright (Captain).

In 1859, Matlock was made the headquarters for a company of Infantry Rifle Volunteers, later to become F Company of the 2nd Volunteer Battalion of the Sherwood Foresters (Nottinghamshire and Derbyshire Regiment). By the end of the 19th century, the B Troop of the Derbyshire Yeomanry Cavalry had its headquarters in Matlock. Both of these companies supplied soldiers for the front during the second Boer War of 1900-2.

A comradeship grew up between the Matlock Volunteers and their Belgium equivalents, resulting in the latter visiting Matlock on 22 July 1867. This contingent comprised some 25 men led by a Major Stoeffs. They were wined and dined, at one point being supplied with champagne in buckets and pails!

At Castle Top Farm a range was created for rifle practice, of which there is now no trace. A further range was located at Cavendish Fields having butts. The land at the farm was given by an Arkwright and the cost of construction was met by J B Marsden-Smedley.

A branch of the National Rifle Association was created for Matlock Bath and Cromford together in 1902, to allow the riflemen to buy rifles and ammunition cheaply and it also meant that the best shots could be sent to the annual competitions at Bisley.(Bryan p.66-9)

The two world wars are dealt with in Chapter 13.

Charities

The Harrison Almshouses are covered in Chapter 10.

The old charities of the Matlocks were as follows:

St Giles Church

George Spateman, by a will dated 27 March 1647, gave £80 for the use of a school in Matlock parish for the education of poor children and £20 for the poor of the parish. This was used to purchase land at Alfreton in 1650 and later exchanged for a house and 5 acres (2 hectares) in Matlock.

Anthony Wolley, by a will dated 17 July 1668, gave towards the maintenance of a free school at Matlock, £5 per annum in perpetuity, instructing that a piece of land be used for this purpose. In 1790 some property owned by the charity was exchanged for 9 acres (3.6 hectares) of land. In 1828 the school benefited by rents to the value of £45 12s (£45.60) per annum, of which £42 was paid to the head teacher.

William Walker by a will of 1631 gave 10s (50p) per annum paid out of his estate known as Hillock Croft, Matlock to be distributed to the poor for ever.

Thomas Johns by a will of 1667 gave £2 to the poor and bibles to the value of £1 out of his estate on the Jankin Flat, Causeway Lane, Matlock and Dick Lands, Matlock. Up to 1827 these two fields were occupied by Adam Wolley who had been paying £1 per annum for them.

Daniel Clark by a will of 1726 left a rent charge of 10s (50p) to be paid to the poor of Matlock for ever.

In 1828 this was paid in respect of lands held by Wigley Haywood Hodgkinson.

Joshua Bradley, by a will of 1738 gave 10s (50p) per annum to the poor to be paid out of rents from a close called Allcock, Matlock Bank.

Thomas Garratt of Hornsey, South Yorkshire, by a will dated 23 June 1791 gave £100 to be invested in Government stocks, the interest to be paid on St Thomas's Day to 20 poor housekeepers in Matlock not already receiving alms – for ever.

Revd. Francis Gisborne of Staveley by his will of 1818 left to the poor of Matlock for ever £7 3s (£7.15p) secured on public funds. In his lifetime he transferred £16,167 13s 4d (£16,167.67p) in 3% consuls stock, the dividend to be used for the purchase of coarse Yorkshire cloth or flannel for the benefit of the poor in a hundred parishes or chapelries in Derbyshire. He died in 1821 at the age of 89 leaving his property of £60,000 for charitable purposes.(Bryan p.43-5)

Holy Trinity Church, Matlock Bath

Miss Anne Walters of Masson Cottage, deceased 1899, bequeathed to the vicar and churchwardens ten £10 shares in the Belper Gas Company, the value of which was £240 in trust, the interest to be distributed to the poor every Christmas for ever. The available income being £10 per annum.

Edward Greenhough – Tradesman and warden of the parish, deceased 1899, left £25 for the repair fund of the church, to be spent at the warden's discretion.(Bryan p.175/6)

Poor Law

Prior to 1834, the poor were sent to the Ashover House of Industry, whence pauper children were apprenticed to farmers and trades people. This constituted slave labour for they were fed and housed but very few got a wage.

At the inception of the old poor law in 1834, Poor Law Unions were established whereby several parishes collected together to create a shared workhouse. What fears the word workhouse conjured up for the elderly poor; for them it meant the separation of married couples and degradation. The community considered that poverty was the fault of the victim and this was reinforced by the work they were set to do, in this institution made famous by Charles Dickens in his book *Oliver Twist.* Both Matlock and Matlock Bath were part of this union. Matlock had a share in the Bakewell Union and the workhouse is the building now known as Newholme Hospital. As such this building is not too bad in appearance, but what misery once resided here.

Markets and Fairs

Anciently there was a market at Matlock but this is beyond the memory of most records. In 1880 it was proposed to hold a cattle market every two weeks, which proposal was accepted by the Local Board and the first market was held on Monday, 13 December the same year. The market was held at Matlock Green and was very well attended. It was focused on an area currently occupied by Matlock Green Petrol Filling Station. A brass plate was produced at this first market, which read, "Tolls for the use of the Lord of the Manor granted by King Charles II in 1661." This has never been authenticated.

A general market, including butter, was inaugurated in a Market Hall in June 1881 and located off Holt Lane where the Conservative Club now is. This hall was replaced, for it is recorded that in May 1867 a new one had started, being provided by investors. The building took 13 months and it was of Continental Gothic in style. The hall held 12 shops in a gloomy environment. An assembly room was built above this hall with a capacity of 500 seated persons. The architect was W Hall of Northampton who employed a W White Jnr to carve the Darley white stone on the front.

In 1887 the Local Board tried to buy the market tolls from the Lords of the Manor. This came to nothing as it was not legal so to do. By October of the same year it was decided to provide a market house as a location for the holding of markets.

The market today does not include cattle or sheep, these generally go to Bakewell for sale. The present market hall, built at the end of Somerfield Supermarket, is open for the sale of fruit with vegetables and a butcher on all days apart from Sunday, with other stalls on the main market days of Tuesday and Friday –plus a flea market on Saturday. The cattle market was held on Mondays from 1881 to 1941 in line with Bakewell.

The old fairs were held on 25 February, 9 May, 16 July, 24 October for the sale of sheep and cattle. By 1900, a further market day on 2 April was established, the one in July being abandoned. At these fairs steers, pigs, sheep and horses were sold and the children could enjoy swing boats and merry-go-rounds. This fun fair still visits Matlock Bridge in September before moving on to the famous Goose Fair at Nottingham.(Bryan ps.57/8)

In 1920 the market moved outside to be held in the grounds of the Railway Hotel, the publican of which was Horace Holmes. It moved to its present location in 1922. By 1926 the 40 stalls were not fully occupied and Horace Holmes took over the job of organising it and, later in his life, shared the responsibility with his son William Horace Holmes, a noted musician who took full control in 1946. The market during World War II had to stop trading on the customary evenings of Tuesdays and Fridays due to the blackout restrictions. After the war, the market was refurbished at a cost of £1,800 and in 1952 the council bought it by compulsory purchase to redevelop the site as a bus station. Horace Jnr leased the

The Ship Loads

land back for the purpose of continuing with the market. Traders paid 10d and 1s.0d per foot for the 33 tubular stalls with roofs and lighting and these were in use on Tuesdays and Thursdays again, with a charity allowed a free stall each week. He sold the Railway Inn in 1958 and retired to the coast in 1974, dying in 1999 at the age of 93. Horace also helped to print the *Matlock Mercury* in the 1930s and was President of Matlock Town Football Club in 1954.(MM 01.08.02)

Whilst looking at markets the sheep wash must not be overlooked. In an area that produces many sheep, the traditional sheep wash was an important asset for most villages. Most of the evidence for these is now lost. The famous one at Ashford-in-the-Water, complete with pound, can still be seen and is operated once a year to show visitors how it was done. Julie Bunting tells us that there was one in the river Derwent opposite the present day Somerfield supermarket and it can be assumed that there was once one in the Bentley Brook near to the sheep market at Matlock Green. This was important before the introduction of sheep "dip". The shepherd, with help, would immerse the sheep in the water and agitate the fleece to ensure that the tics and dirt were removed. The latter ensured a clean fleece when sheared.(PA 26.08.02) Also see Chapter 5 for more about markets.

It is also worth mentioning the ancient language for counting sheep, probably descended from the Celts. When counting to 20, the shepherd's numbering went:

ain, tain, tethera, fethera, fimp
sethera, lethera, hovera, dovera, dick
ain dick, tain dick, tether dick, fether dick, bumfy,
ain bumfy, tain bumfy, tether bumfy, fether bumfy, kicky.

The writer can recall hearing this used in the High Peak, and "ain" was pronounced yan and "tain" – tan.

Where the railway bridge crosses Dale Road is a small garden where a plaque tells us that this was the "Ship Loads" which refers to a Shiplode, an ancient name for a sheep crossing, which was here until the 19th century.(PA 26.08.02)

Every market had its pinfold for stray animals and Matlock's was where the electricity company sub-station is located near to the Alms Houses on Matlock Green.

Agencies for social welfare

These are listed in alphabetical order.

Citizens Advice Bureau (CAB)

This ever helpful organisation (how did we manage before their arrival?) was founded in Matlock in December 1964, the first chairperson being Harold Fletcher, the then managing director of Derbyshire Stone. An Evelyn Skenfield was the first organiser of the bureau, which opened to the public in the spring of 1965, using a room in the Imperial Road Methodist Chapel as it then was. Prior to becoming the organiser she had acted as secretary to the chairman.

In the 1970s, the then government began to invest in the bureau and a paid helper was appointed in each branch. Evelyn in spite of being over 70 years of age accepted this post, looking for a successor at the same time. Evelyn retired in March 1977 when her successor took over. She remained on the management committee until 1982. Her just reward for this was the MBE given to her in 1978. Evelyn did not marry until she was in her seventies but sadly she died on 15 February 2002 at the wonderful age of 96. She was the driving force behind this organisation and she saw it established as an important and to some an essential resort in times when problems occur.

They now operate from an address on Bank Road, Matlock.(MM 07.03.02) In July 2002 this branch amalgamated with others to create the Mid-Derbyshire Citizens Advice Bureau. This covers all the branches in the Derbyshire Dales and Amber Valley districts. With funding from the local authorities the new organisation has started to "out reach" by holding sessions at local villages, thus giving access to everyone in the area. Others are forming alliances with this new organisation such as the High Peaks and Dales PCT and the New Opportunities Fund. At the same time they were also awarded a Quality Mark from the Community Legal Services, with a view to contracting legal work funded by this service.(MM 18.07.02)

Womens' Royal Voluntary Service

This esteemed organisation was active in the Matlocks notably for providing "meals on wheels" for the elderly and infirm, much of the cooking being undertaken in members' homes. In September 2002 it was decided that a private company, Apetito's Food Selection with Wiltshire Farm Foods, might do a better job of this with a more varied and extensive choice, thus rendering the WRVS redundant.(MM 26.09.02)

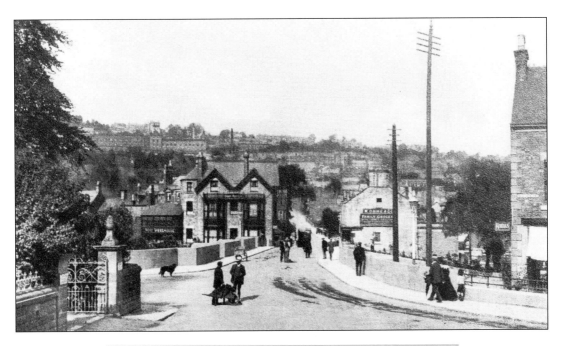

Matlock Bridge from Dale Road post 1904 after it was widened
(Derbyshire County Council, Libraries and Heritage)

⑧ LEISURE ACTIVITIES

The Matlocks are lacking in facilities for leisure time activities, which may come as a surprise to visitors who seem beleaguered by attractions, most of which are ignored by the local residents. At the time of writing there is no cinema, theatre, youth club, bingo parlour or any other place of entertainment except for the swimming pool.

The Matlocks are rich in clubs and societies who have to meet in rented rooms. Significantly there is an enthusiastic amateur theatre group who enact excellent plays for the public but not in a theatre proper. There are rooms rented on a permanent basis for certain clubs but these appeal to the older residents and the young are all but forgotten.

Things may change in the future but for the time being:

Sports

Athletics

An athletics track once occupied the land behind Evans the jewellers on Dale Road, the site now occupied by Derwent Avenue. The surface was finished with tarmacadam and was as wide as the Broad Walk in Hall Leys Park. Brass Band competitions may have been held here.

Football (Soccer and Rugby)

Matlock Rugby Club
Founded in 1926 using goal posts from Riber Castle School and re-erected at Spout Farm Tansley, for practice only. In 1928 a Dr Sparks and a Mr K Kiddy formed the Old Baileans RFC with a pitch at Cromford Meadows. On the closure of the Ernest Bailey Grammar School, the club continued as Matlock (Baileans) RUFC in 1982.

They have three senior teams, Matlock 1st XI, 2nd XI and 3rd XI with "Mini/Midi" teams for 7-11 years old and 12-19 years old respectively.
www.matlockrugby.com

There is also:

Matlock Colts Rugby Club.

Matlock Baileans First XI (for women)

Matlock Town Football Club
This club, as Matlock Football Club, originally played on Hall Leys Park until 1911 when they moved across Causeway Lane to the present pitch. There was a small stand on the park and the stewards used to raise a canvas screen along Causeway Lane to prevent free viewing from passers by.

Prior to World War II the team had to draw players from the coal mines nearby as they could not muster local enthusiasts. Occasionally Chesterfield Rovers used the pitch for their games. However, in 1946 it re-formed to make it the Matlock Town Football Club.

Known as the Gladiators since 1980, being a reference to the supposed local occupation by the

Romans, the tune the "Entry of the Gladiators" is played on the public address system when the team march onto the pitch. This club is unique in that it enjoys the benefit of its own pitch with spectator provision and flood lighting.

Their successes (and failures) since 1946 have been:

1961	Rejoined the reformed Midland League
1961-2	Midland League Champions
1968-9	Midland League Champions again (on goal average)
1969-70	Joined Northern Premier League
1974-75	Football Association Trophy Winners
1993-4	Northern Premier League runner-up (on goal difference)
1992-3	Three points deducted
1996	Relegated to Division One
2001-2	One point deducted

www.fchd.btinternet.co.uk/MATLOCK.HTM

There are and were the following football clubs:

Matlock Junior Football Club
This has played from the 1920s.

Matlock Cavendish Rovers
This team played at Cavendish Fields at the end of Cavendish Road. They have been playing since at least 1920.

At the time of writing the following clubs appear to be active:
Matlock United Under 15 Club
Matlock United Under 14 Club
Matlock United Bees 11/12 Club
Matlock United Devils Under 11 Club
Matlock United Missiles Under 10 Club
Matlock United Aztecs Under 9 Club
Matlock Fifth XI Club
Matlock United Hornets
Matlock Town Junior Football Club, Cavendish Park

Cricket

Matlock Cricket Club
This club, like the Football Club, played on Hall Leys and also like the Football club moved across Causeway Lane to a new pitch adjoining the Gladiators where they still play. They built a stand in the 1920s.

This area was also used for horse racing, horse trotting and athletics.

Matlock Youth Cricket Club
Matlock Bath Ladies' Cricket Team
In existence from at least the 1930s.

Water Sports

Swimming
The Matlocks, true to their tradition of water usage, have been well endowed with facilities for swimming.

Victoria Hall had a swimming pool and the New Bath Hotel has a plunge bath and an outside swimming pool, all fed from springs.

The Lido on Imperial Road was opened in 1938 by the then Carnival Queen, Lilian Knowles, and was open to the elements. This was built at a cost of £90,000 on what was the town rubbish tip. The water was notorious for being cold in all seasons. The users wore special woollen bathing suits made by Smedleys of Lea Mills and a café sold food and drinks, hopefully hot ones.

In 1972 it was roofed over and now boasts a learners' pool and a gymnasium all of which are popular with locals and visitors alike.(MM 15.08.02, 12.09.02)

Matlock and District Swimming Club
(Meets at the pool above)

Angling

The Matlocks, having a fast flowing river of clear water, had to be associated with angling. Trout have been fished from time immemorial as well as salmon and whilst the trout is plentiful along with grayling, the salmon is a rare visitor.

Coarse fishermen are rewarded with barbell, perch, eels, gudgeon, minnows and loaches. The problem of pollution from sewage has been overcome since the installation of a sewage main and treatment works.

The Matlock and Cromford Angling Association dating from 1884 had control over the river from the north parish boundary to the south boundary and a mile beyond. It was customary to add fresh young trout to the water to increase the stock. One instance in 1902 saw 30,000 trout fry imported from the Solway Fishery Company added to the river. A hatchery was maintained above the weir at Masson Mill.(Bryant p.86)
Local angling clubs are:

Matlock Angling Club

Matlock and District Angling Club

Robin Hood Sea Angling Club

Canoeing

Matlock Canoe Polo Club
Once part of Matlock Canoe Club and formed in 1984, it trains in the swimming pool at Matlock but they have been known to train in local rivers and canals. The team competes throughout Britain and Europe and they won the National Division 3 North Championship in 1999-2000.
http://www.matlock-polo.fsnet.co.uk/mcpclub.html

Golf

A golf club – a limited company – was founded in May, 1902 and was located between Upperwood and Ember Farm, Matlock Bath. It was opened by the Honourable Victor Cavendish MP on 23 May

Swimming Pool, New Bath Hotel, Matlock Bath. c. 1936
(Derbyshire County Council, Libraries and Heritage)

Masson Mill, Matlock Bath with Allotments where the extention was built
(now a multi-storey car park). c.1910
The glimpse of a roof bottom right is of the now lost Glenorchy Chapel
(Derbyshire County Council, Libraries and Heritage)

1903. This was a short-lived venture possibly due to its distance from the hydropathic institutions and poor access.

This idea was revived in 1906, when it was decided to open a club on Chesterfield Road where it still is. It was first mooted by H Challand, manager at Smedley's who wanted somewhere for his clients to play. The course opened fully in 1907 with an exhibition match by the number one professional of the world, Harry Boden. The first president was the Honourable Victor Cavendish, later to become the Duke of Devonshire. The present Duke opened the new club house in 1967.

The course has 18 holes and is Par 69 with 5,900 yards (5.39 km) playing length.(Kay In Lit 12.12.02)

Hockey

Hockey is popular in the area with clubs named Baileans First to Fifth XIs.

Matlock Junior Hockey Club

Matlock Old Baileans Ladies Hockey Club

Winter Sports

Whilst there is no record of skiing down Bank Road, there is a reference to tobogganing down Steep Turnpike with the culprits tying their sledges to the tram to take them up Bank Road.(Arkle p.19)

Athletics

Mention is made elsewhere about the race against the clock on the tramway shelter to Matlock Green within the time it took to chime twelve. This was won before World War I by a Mr W R Bradbury.

A track existed behind Evans the Jewellers which was used for athletics, cycle racing, etc.

Cavendish Fields have facilities now.

Cavendish Field Sports Association

They seek to improve the sports facilities at Cavendish Fields by trying to raise money from the Football Foundation in the sum of £300,000 and they need to raise £100,000 from elsewhere. Cavendish Fields host approximately 100 games of football with over 40 teams every two months in season; the number of players using the facilities every weekend is 248. They aim to provide four mini-soccer pitches, four full-size pitches, two junior pitches, and an all weather pitch. The president is Roger Taylor, the chairman is Martyn Moss and the patrons are the Duke of Devonshire and Patrick McLoughlin MP.(Newsletter 11.02)

Matlock Athletics Club

Martial Arts

Matlock Aikido Club	*Derwent Jiu Jitsu Club*
Matlock Karati School	*Kick Boxing*
Derbyshire Panthers Kick Boxing Club	*Tai Kwan-do Club*
Tai Chi Chuan Eternal Spring Tai Chi	

Other sports

Derwent Bowmen Junior Archery Club

Matlock Park Bowls Club

Matlock Cycling Club

Derwent Mountaineering Group

Matlock and District Rifle Club

Derbyshire Dales Group of Rifle Associations

Cinema

The Matlocks enjoyed three cinemas in the earlier half of the 20th century, all now consigned to history.

The first films in the Matlocks were shown at the Victoria Hall (q.v.)

The Ritz

This was originally known as the Cinema House and commonly known as the New Picture House. Sited on the corner of the Causeway and Steep Turnpike at Matlock, it opened in 1922 boasting a "first class orchestra" and a "Café and Lounge" (also Cinema House Café) together with a 22 ft (6.7 m) stage and five dressing rooms.(Franklin p117/8) It showed films until 1999 when it fell empty until 2002. It was then converted into a shopping precinct and offices, and given a badly needed face lift. This unusual building has a local stone front with conventional brick sides and rear, all cement rendered, which had become shabby of late, but is now much improved with the adaptations mentioned. A feature of the Ritz in the 1920s is that the proprietor also offered acts between the films and a good orchestra.

Matlock Picture Palace

Commonly known as the Old Picture House it was more commonly known as the "Laugh and Scratch"!

Situated on Dale Road, Matlock it is now occupied by an estate agent after having been used as an electrical retailers, amongst other things. This purpose built cinema dates from 1913 and a resident pianist sometimes played here, helped out by a violinist and a drummer.

From 1938, a Herbert Siddons did impressions (not impersonations!) of Gracie Fields, starting at the age of 14. He had to wear male evening dress and "Gracie" received a fee of £4 for every performance.(Franklin p57) A prankster, Roy Beech, used to drag a coin attached to a piece of thread so that it tinkled along the cinema queue. This made the patrons stoop to search for the money they believed they had dropped, causing chaos at the same time. (Franklin p96)

One man recalls, as a curious boy, seeing the inside of the projection room where he was,

shown the old carbon arc projectors, and was amazed at the mercury rectifier – a great big glass bowl contained mercury, which somehow converted AC to DC to give an arc. What I remembered most was seeing the electricity dancing about on the top of this bowl, like something from a Frankenstein movie. (Franklin p122)

Matlock Bath Cinema

The Matlock Bath Pavilion had a cinema, amongst its other attractions, which operated from 1910 to the 1930s. Between the two great wars of the 20th century, the local inhabitants had the pleasure of seeing themselves perform in a film about Henry VIII which had been shot locally using villagers as extras.(Franklin p117)

No doubt certain of these cinemas were "flea pits" to the locals but their double rear seats were a haven for young lovers. Not quite the same as today's multiplex cinemas, the nearest of which is at Chesterfield.

Victoria Hall

This fine building, now lost, stood amidst the Paton and Baldwin factory on Smedley Street East.

The first film to be seen in the Matlocks was shown here, the projector being lit by acetylene and hand cranked.(Arkle p.20) The hall was in use from 1895 to 1915 as a pavilion with gardens. The pavilion could accommodate 700 persons and the grounds occupied 3.5 acres (1.4 hectares). The site offered a swimming pool, roller skating, tennis courts, bowling green, dancing, fencing, concerts, plays and public meetings. Brass band contests were held here including a visit from the famous Black Dyke Mills Band.

River Entertainments.

Venetian Nights

An Italian, Remo Tinti, settled in the Matlocks in the 1890s where he married a local girl. In 1897, as part of the celebrations of Queen Victoria's Diamond Jubilee, he created the Venetian Nights. The idea was to recreate the decorated boats used by the Venetians in their annual festival. This has endured ever since and is a now accompanied by illuminations and firework displays. The boats are fully lit and they are rowed downstream in the dark, along the river at Matlock Bath.

The illuminations can be seen during the month from the third Saturday in August to the third Saturday in September. Firework displays are an additional feature along with entertainment from bands, singing groups and dancing groups from both Britain and as far away as the Ukraine. To cater for the large crowds a "park and ride" system is operated.

Raft Race

This is almost as popular with the public as the Venetian Nights, for on average it attracts 10,000 spectators and has been an institution in the Matlocks since 1962. The public are free to enter a decorated boat or raft for a race from Matlock Bridge at Hall Leys Park, to Cromford Meadows, a distance of 3.5 miles (5.6 km). This takes place on Boxing Day (26 December) each year and is well worth watching, and well worth entering for the younger people. The way the rafts are decorated varies from a sitting room scene complete with television to a fire engine complete with crew. For individuals bath tubs, barrels and the like are used. The Derbyshire Association of Sub-aqua Clubs, who organise the event, have members as marshals together with experienced canoeists stationed at places which could prove dangerous such as the weir at Masson Mill. An average of 60 "rafts" take part and in 2002, £2,000 was collected for the Royal National Lifeboats Institution along with diving related causes.(Reflections January, 2003)

Boating

Boats could and still can be hired on the river. It is alarming to recall that there were two places where boats could be hired at Matlock Bridge, opposite the Boat Inn and behind the Old English Hotel. The oarsman would need to be strong and skilful to control a boat in these waters. Apart from the strong current there were the additional hazards of negotiating the bridge and the area at the confluence of the river with Bentley Brook.

Civic Organisations

Matlock Civic Association

This was formed in 1980/81 to monitor proposals for changes in the Matlock area in the absence, at that time, of a Town Council since 1974. The concern that caused this to come into being was the proposed building of a supermarket (Somerfields) with Market and Bus Station on Bakewell Road, Matlock, together with an objection to the idea of a fly-over highway to divert traffic from Matlock Bridge, to be constructed from Dale Road to Causeway Lane, the route being by Pic Tor and over Hall Leys Park.

They have been busy since with the following projects:

- Restoring the Shiplodes, Dale Road, Matlock
- Creation of a memorial garden to commemorate the millennium and Princes Diana, at the foot of the Dimple opposite Allen Hill Spa.
- Several litter bins of quality.
- Several timber bench seats.
- Tree planting, eg, a Lime Tree on Lime Tree Road.
- Bulb planting along Bakewell Road in the grass verges.
- Restoration of the war memorials at Pic Tor and Starkholmes along with the provision of a flower vase each.
- Advocacy of the pedestrianisation of Matlock Bridge.
- Opposition to a housing development in the Convent Fields between the Presentation Convent and Asker Lane.

This organisation is now part of the Arkwright Society of Cromford.(Parker In Lit 02.12.02)

Political Clubs

The Conservative Club

Originally known as the Working Men's Club, it was inaugurated on 29 June 1888, by Messrs F C Arkwright of Cromford and R W M Nesfield of Bakewell with assistance from the ex-MP for North Derbyshire. The meetings were originally held in premises near to the original Post Office on Holt Lane but due to a larger than anticipated membership they had to move to larger premises on Crown Square in January 1897. This time the club was opened by Victor Cavendish MP on 30 November 1897.(Bryan p.70) It now has new premises on Holt Lane, Matlock Bridge.

The Liberal Club

This club predated the Conservative Club, opening on 1 July 1880 when 30-40 members were enrolled. It was officially opened on 18 November 1880 when 150 members were addressed by Lord Edward Cavendish, MP and J F Cheetham MP. The premises were located over a shop on Dale Road. The first President was Edward Miller Wass of Lea, the lead merchant and entrepreneur who rescued Mill Close Mine at Darley Bridge. They shortly moved to the Town Hall.(Bryan p.71) (See Forum Club, its successor.)

United Services Club

This club has permanent rooms over some shops facing Somerfield supermarket. It boasts a bar and billiard room and was intended to be used by ex-members of the three armed forces: The Army, Royal Navy and Royal Air Force.

Clubs for Farmers, Workmen, Wives, etc

Ploughing Association

In 1887, the Matlock and District Ploughing Association was founded and was successful in having J B Marsden-Smedley as President.(Bryan p.78)

Poultry Club

A Harry Fox who kept poultry on Pope Carr, bred high quality birds and had the distinction of being invited to Italy to advise Mussolini on egg production.(Arkle p.30)

Working Men's Club

It would appear that this Working Men's Club was formed separately from the one that became the Conservative Club. This seems to have been a breakaway movement. It was founded 12 years after the formation of the Conservative Club on 1 December, 1900. Within a few days it had enrolled 100 members who met at Prince's Buildings, Crown Square.(Bryan p.78)

Social Club

This organisation occupied premises on the corner of Smedley Street and Rutland Street, Matlock Bank. It was opened for members on New Year's Day 1890. It was open to all and provided amongst other delights: a billiards room and reading room, a smoking room and a play room (what type of play is not made clear!). This club seems to have been popular.(Bryan pp. 238/9)

Matlock Social Institute Company

Having failed to raise enough money to build an institute behind the Post Office on Bank Road, this club started its life in the same year as the above named Social Club, renting premises in Central Buildings on Smedley Street.

Matlock Luncheon Club

This club was founded for ladies only in 1963 and originally met at the Fishpond Hotel, Matlock Bath, later moving to the New Bath Hotel, also at Matlock Bath, where they meet monthly. The first chairperson was Miss Joan Sinar, the then County Archivist; the current chairperson is Anne Brawn. This is a social club which invites speakers to give talks on many subjects.(Brawn In Lit 15.12.02)

Lions Clubs International

This organisation was founded in Chicago, USA in 1917 to encourage local businessmen to improve their local communities. The late Queen Mother introduced the idea to Britain after World War II. Their motto is "We Serve". Matlock Derwent Valley Lions Club was formed in 1979 with help from the Ilkeston branch, the first president being Mr George Prince, together with 21 initial members. In turn the Matlock Lions have overseen the formation of Lions Clubs at Ashbourne and the Derbyshire Dales Club, although the latter have now joined with Matlock.

After meeting at many different places they now collect at the Red Lion at Stonedge every month for a business meeting but they also have an active social life. They raise money and donate it to many national and international causes, too many to mention. The money is raised in a variety of ways such as trolley dashes at a local supermarket, Santa's Grotto at the Matlock Victorian Weekend and sponsored Exercise Bicycle Rides.(Turnbull In Lit 10.12.02)

Whistle Stop Centre

This centre operated by the Derbyshire Wild Life Trust is one of 47 such trusts nationwide. The Whistle Stop Centre occupies one of the old station buildings at Matlock Bath. It boasts a wildlife garden, wildlife gardening exhibition, hands-on activity cart for children, a shop, drinks and snacks.(Brochure)

Matlock Field Club

Founded in 1976 publishing their first newsletter in April of that year.

Matlock and District Hard of Hearing Club

This club dedicated to the deaf and hard of hearing is held at the Imperial Rooms.

Youth Clubs

Youth Hostels Association (YHA)

The YHA had a hostel in the old vicarage in Matlock Bath off Brunswood Road from 1956 to 1983. After the abandonment of the Cottage Hospital on Bank Road (ex Smedley Memorial Hospital) the YHA bought the premises and made it a substitute hostel in 1984.

It was of great benefit to Matlock when the YHA decided to relocate their national headquarters from St. Albans, Hertfordshire into the old Severn-Trent Water building on Dimple Road during the Summer of 2001. The reasons they give for this are of interest:

- To bring the YHA's central administrative and marketing services together rather than the previous three different locations.
- To realise the value of the former headquarters building, the sale of which paid for the cost of purchasing the Matlock site, its refurbishment and the relocation.
- To give them a modern working environment.
- To be closer to their network of hostels.
(Smith In Lit 21.11.02)

Boys' Brigade

This esteemed youth organisation was founded in 1883 by Sir William Alexander Smith in Glasgow, Scotland, to instil self respect and discipline in local boys from the slums. It should be noted that it celebrated its centenary at a large camp at Chatsworth in 1983, hosted by the Matlock company. It has a strong link with non-conformism. Its motto is "Sure and Steadfast" and their emblem is a ship's anchor (Hebrews 6 v19: "Which hope we shall have as an anchor of the soul, both sure and steadfast, and which entereth into that within a veil.") It spread around the world and is still a significant contributor to the welfare of young boys from the ages of 6 to 13 with seniors going on to 19 years of age.

Matlock has its own company founded in 1951, which is attached to the Matlock Methodist and United Reformed Church and is designated as the 1st Matlock Company of the Boys Brigade. This company is the only one in Britain that is not part of a Battalion. It received its colours, it is somewhat militaristic, celebrating its 50th anniversary in 2002 with a mammoth celebration over a weekend.

Tom Pilkington has been the Captain (or skipper) since 1972 and at its zenith it had 55 members, currently about 15 aged 6-13. Members have received the hard earned Queen's Badge eight times since

1972. The annual camp is the highlight of the year and they used to join forces with a Kettering, Northamptonshire company from 1973 to 1995, visiting sites on the east and south coasts of England.(Pilkington In Lit 02.12.02)

The Captains over the years have been:

Cyril Mason
Gordon Ford
Arthur King
Tom Pilkington

Girl's Life Brigade

The female equivalent to the Boy's Brigade, with the same principles, also meets at the same place as the boys and like the Boys Brigade it is a Christian uniformed organisation. It was formed in 1965 by the amalgamation of The Girls' Life Brigade, The Girls' Brigade (Ireland) and The Girls' Guildry.

The 1st Matlock Girls Life Brigade was started at the same premises as the Boys' Brigade in 1940 – they celebrated their 60th anniversary in 2000. The 2nd and 3rd Matlock companies together with the 1st formed the 2nd company, presently comprising 25 girls, three officers and two helpers. They enjoy many pastimes from disco dancing to basic cookery, ten pin bowling to raising money for charities such as the Guide Dogs for the Blind, the Rainbow Hospice trust, the Premature Baby unit at a local hospital and Blue Peter appeals.(Carter In Lit 10.12.02)

Boy Scouts

There are six groups of Matlock Scouts of which the following two are of concern to this book, the others being outside our boundary at Crich, Darley Dale and Wirksworth. The 15th Matlock Group of Boy Scouts was founded in 1957 and is based at Matlock Green. The 5th are based at All Saints church.

Girl Guides

As with the Boy Scouts, there are two companies in the Matlocks, the 5th and the 15th.

2nd Matlock Girls' Brigade	*1st Starkholmes Guides*
1st Matlock Brownies	*2nd Matlock Guides*
Apocalypse Venture Scouts	*Holy Trinity Church Youth Club*
Hurst Farm Youth Club	*Matlock Bath Youth Centre*
St Giles' Church Youth Club	*St Joseph's Youth Club*

Other Organisations

Institute of Advanced Motorists

The Matlock (Derwent and Hope Valley) Advanced Motorists Group teach enhanced driving skills to motorists under the guidance of experts, mostly ex-police drivers. They also offer courses on how to handle winter conditions.

Theatre and music

Music has always had a strong presence in the Matlocks, witness the number of choirs and singers listed below. Of note is Thomas Greatorex born 1758, son of Anthony Greatorex of Riber Hall. For many years he was the organist at Westminster Abbey.

Henry Smith of Matlock has a brass in St Giles' church that states "Divinus, Medicus, Musicus" which tells us that he was a divine, a doctor and a musician. In his will dated 1634, he left all "his books and instruments whatsoever" to his nephew whose name is not known. (Matlock Parish Church Guide)

Matlock Brass Band

This band has been an enduring feature of Matlock for over 150 years. It still exists with its own practice room on Wellington Street, Matlock Bank. It has suffered the occasional relapse but has survived to play another day.

Both Masson Mills and Tansleywood Mills boasted a band in the early 19th century, made up of mill workers, of which little is known. There was a band comprising young men of Matlock and Cromford, who in 1838 relied on collections from the public for a living. They called themselves the Town Brass Band. Its foundation is a little obscure but it must have been before 1860. It was associated with the Volunteer Movement from the founding of the latter and it wore the uniform. In the 1870s a George Knowles (there was a George Knowles who sold musical instruments on Smedley Street at this time) funded the band and it was trained by one of the finest cornet players in the country, Bugle-Major John "Spring" Naylor. Sir Joseph Paxton played the cornet in this band and it was he who designed the uniforms. The band played at the funeral of George Knowles, who whilst he died in Southport, Lancashire chose to be buried in Matlock in January, 1909 aged 70 years.

Some of the players in this band won their moment of glory when they were part of a band that won the National Championship in 1867 at Belle View, Manchester. John Naylor was determined to win this accolade and to do it he fielded musicians from the Chesterfield, Clay Cross and Matlock Bands. They practised very hard, with advice from the director of music from the Crooked Spire church (St. Mary and All Saints) resplendent in the name of Thomas Tallis Trimnell. They also registered a fictitious band called the Matlock Bridge Rifle Band as a diversion. The audience had wind of this "three bands in one" as they called it and made such a rumpus when the band played the test piece that the adjudicators could not hear them. After many false starts the band was told to play on regardless of the din and to everyone's consternation they won. Thereafter the rules were changed whereby a band had to submit the names and addresses of its players beforehand as being the ones who would attend the contest.

It then fell into one of a few lapses, to be revived in 1894 and comprising many of the old band under the baton of a Mr A Holmes (euphonium). By 1903 this band , which went under the name of the Matlock United Prize Band, had won many competitions and was the forerunner of the current band and by this time also, the band comprised mainly new and younger players. At the same time a second band was playing at Matlock Bath under the leadership of a Mr Hilder, "Photographic Artist and Musician", the instruments being bought by subscription. It was named the Matlock Bath Military Band and after many problems it ceased playing in 1901. One can ignore the expression Military Band, this meant that they wore a volunteer type of uniform. The expression United band suggest that it was an amalgamation of existing bands which were not attracting players.

In more recent times the great Fred Slater trained and conducted the band and it enjoyed success under his leadership. His son Murray Slater took over when his father died. And he proved to be as good as his father, alas he died prematurely.

During the 1980s, this band was sponsored by Tarmac, a then large employer locally and they financed a professional director to lead and conduct the band, R J P Kempton, LRAM, retired Director of Music with the Royal Marines.(Naylor Archives)

Theatre

High Tor Players

High Tor Players is a group of accomplished actors and actresses, all amateur, who from time to time field a play, many of which are classics and demanding for the players, who always seem to carry it off professionally. Amongst their vast repertoire can be counted classics such as; Sheridan's *School for Scandal* (1965), Agatha Christie's *The Hollow* (1950s).(Barton pp. 138/9)

Matlock Gilbert and Sullivan Society

Meets at All Saints Church Hall, Smedley Street, Matlock Bank. In 2002 it celebrated its tenth anniversary by staging a production of *The Yeoman of the Guard* staged at the Medway Centre, Bakewell.

Matlock Choir

Rehearses at Farley Congregational Church, Smedley Street.

Dalesman Male Voice Choir

This all male choir has undertaken many concerts in the area. To celebrate Queen Elizabeth's Jubilee they gave a concert on 1 June 2002 at County Hall shared with the Pembroke Male Voice Choir.

The Derbyshire Singers

This is a mixed choir, which since its foundation has achieved a high standard of performance with a widely mixed repertoire. It was originally founded by Gertrude Beresford, a Derbyshire County Adviser and re-formed in 1974 by Joseph Clark as a chamber choir. It has offered over the years a large and often demanding repertoire; to name but a few: Handel's *Messiah*, Verdi's *Requiem*, Paul Patterson's *Magnificat* and David Fanshawe's *African Sanctus*. Their president is Brian Kay, who sometimes conducts, as does Joseph Clark and his wife Lynne Clark. The singers are affiliated to the National Federation of Music Societies and East Midlands Arts.

The Fishpond Choir

This public house in Matlock Bath has established a tradition for music but a recent innovation is its own choir. Under the initial leadership of Lynne Dean the choir is now led by Dana de Wall of South Africa, a classically trained tenor, conductor and composer. This newly founded choir has 35 members at the time of writing and has a large repertoire, ranging from African lullabies to Slavian prayers, Blues to Italian love songs.

Flair Singers

This choir meets at the Presentation Convent, Chesterfield Road, Matlock.

Spotlight Theatre Company

On 21 June 2002 this company joined with the Essential Energy School of Theatre to presented a joint evening of entertainment with songs from *Chess, Joseph* and *Evita*.

Essential Energy School of Theatre

Also see Spotlight Theatre Company.
   This group is directed by Dawn Aldred.

There is also:

Matlock Operatic Society

Matlock Music Society

Social Welfare:

St John Ambulance
This operates from a hut on Edgefold Road.

British Red Cross
The Red Cross in Britain was inaugurated in July 1905 by HM Queen Alexandra. A Derbyshire branch was soon to follow when a Memorandum was signed by Evelyn the Duchess of Devonshire who was appointed president of this new branch.

   During World War I, Derbyshire contributed comforts for the troops. VADs were passed on to the military authorities, a gift of £500 was used to purchase materials, two ambulance motor cars (so-called to distinguish them from the horse drawn type) were donated for use by the Cavalry Division of the Derbyshire Yeomanry and a motor soup kitchen, etc. By 1915, 59,000 articles had been donated plus a 20-bed temporary hospital hut in the grounds of the Derbyshire Royal Infirmary (still in use in the 1960s – author); 613 members were mobilised along with 14 VAD hospitals in the county, having 382 beds; and 50 members were posted overseas. A collection on 21 October 1915 produced donations to the sum of £4,500 and on the same date in 1918, £10,600 was collected.

   Between the two wars, the British Red Cross undertook many activities helping various health agencies and societies. During World War II, Red Cross nurses worked at Willersley Castle which housed evacuated mothers bombed out in London. In the post-war years the society helped out with blood transfusion centres, national hospice reserve and other medical organisations.

   The Derbyshire Branch Headquarters was established at Huntsbridge House, Matlock Green, with a new lecture hall being added two years later.(*75 Years On* by Margery Thompson BEM SRN – courtesy Kay Rowley)

Customs

One of the greatly admired features of our villages and towns is the ancient customs, some of which are unique. The Matlocks have or have had their own customs, most of which are now lapsed.

Matlock Wakes

The annual Wakes is, as with most other communities, linked to the feast day of the Saint which is associated with the Parish Church. In Matlock's case this should be the first Sunday of September but in practice it used to be the Sunday after 8 September. Today the Wakes occupy the second week in September when the schools close for the event. The event was held on Bateman's Park since at least 1885 with the Fairs being held on a piece of land now occupied by Matlock Green Filling Station and originally owned by the Horseshoe Hotel. The dates for this were 25th February, 2nd April, 24th October with a May Fair on the 9th which stretched up the road as far as Matlock Cliff.

The Wakes used to be the signal for the parishioners to clean out their cottages and to whitewash the walls and ceilings. At the same time the adults and the children were provided with new clothes. Dancing with music was enjoyed at this time coupled with much drinking at the local inns, which in the Matlock Bridge area laid on meals to be enjoyed by the revellers. Stalls were set up which sold biscuits, sweets and cakes along with cheap jewellery, toys, etc. Whilst this has died out, fairground amusements have been provided comprising merry-go-rounds, swing boats, shooting galleries, etc. By the end of the 20th century, this gave way to more modern amusements, which vary in character and the thrills they offer.

During these Wakes, the residents would treat themselves to a meal of roast beef and plum pudding; the Starkholmes people went one better and had elderberry instead of plum pudding. At Matlock Bath, Wakes Cake was enjoyed, comprising a sweet cake with currents. Later Matlock Bath joined in with Matlock Bridge to share the festivities.

There used to be a strong connection between the Matlock Bridge community and Proctors the fair ground people, who provided the roundabouts and other amusements driven by the special steam traction engines, which not only provided the motive power for the rides but also generated the electricity to light them.

The community chose a Carnival "King and Queen" who would go about knighting people. They also decorated special floats known as "sprogs", being similar to Chinese "dragons." In the 1920s-30s several attractions were provided including brass band contests, jazz bands and football matches. Amongst the charities to benefit from these events were the Whitworth Hospital, Darley Dale and the Derbyshire Royal Infirmary in Derby. In 1949 the year of the National Health Act, their allegiance changed from hospitals and in that year they sent the handsome sum of £620 to the British Legion. Alas it all ended in the 1950s. Arkle p.23)

In the 18th century, bull baiting was popular. Cock fighting and throwing and dog fighting were still carried over from previous centuries, but fortunately these died out as the 19th century progressed.(Bryan p.110)

Matlock Carnival

The young bloods from the shops on Dale Road started a carnival by decorating their bicycles with flowers, towing trailers behind as they rode along. This was called the "Cysical" carnival and was the precurser of the carnivals of today.

Well Dressings

The Matlocks have a poor record with this local and ancient custom. It appears that it arises like a phoenix from the fire to die out as quickly as it arose. Matlock Bridge attempts the occasional dressing, the favourite site being the Allen Hill Spring at the bottom of Dimple Road. Records are scarce but this location was dressed by the All Saints Brownie Pack in June 1978 under the watchful eye of Dr Doreen "Tottie" Holden.(Naylor & Porter pp. 65/67) This site had a dressing undertaken by the same Brownies under the care of a Deidrie and Trevor Brown of Megdale.

Well dressings were started in Matlock Bath in 1867 when four designs were shown. This was repeated in 1869 but was a dismal affair, for it rained hard and few people came to see it. Another attempt was made on 30 May 1871 when two indifferent dressings were shown.(Bryan p.193)

Plough Sunday

This was celebrated in January each year on the Monday following Epiphany using "plough bullocks", being men harnessed to a plough and paraded around the Parish. Several jesters and harlequins followed, each carrying a bladder at the end of a stick with which they struck the locals. The "bullocks" were decorated with ribbons and paper rosettes. A cash collection was made along the way.

In 1849, fifty or so men paraded the plough with the Matlock Band leading. They started at the Horse and Jockey Inn, visited Matlock Bank, descended to Matlock Bridge, on to Matlock Bath, Cromford and Starkholmes returning to Matlock Bank where a supper was laid on for them. After this supper, a dance was held which went on till dawn. The collection totalled £4. 10s (£4.50).(Bryan p. 111)

Bonfire Night

Matlock Bath celebrated the Gunpowder Plot on 5 November each year until the early 19th century, with a large bonfire and the firing of pistols, small cannons and fireworks. Several weeks preceding this event, the young men collected suitable fuel for this bonfire including raiding the woods for brash. The arrival of the police force put an end to this custom, although it lives on in separate back gardens today.

Part of this custom was the baking of "thor" cakes, a custom which went back beyond memory. These were made of oatmeal sweetened with molasses or treacle, with a little flour and a pinch of salt. They were baked until they were brown and would keep for several days if the hungry children had not consumed them first. Bonfire toffee was also made at this time.(Bryant p.112)

Christmas

It was the custom to dress the houses and the churches with holly, ivy and evergreens such as fir and spruce. This custom is still upheld. A posset cup of ale was drunk on Christmas Eve also – this custom was overtaken by visits to the local public house for a "pint". (Bryant p.112) The local boys at Matlock, Matlock Bath and Starkholmes went guisering from house to house, a custom now lost locally but which is still practised at certain villages elsewhere. It seems to have died out by the First World War. They would perform a simple play, which had to be learned by heart and ran:

Bold Slasher   *I open the door, I enter in,*
I feel my fortune's sure to win;
Whether you stand or whether I fall,
I'll do my duty to please you all.
Room, room, gallants, room!
Stir up the fire, and give us light,
And let us act our noble fight.
If you can't believe those words I say,

Well Dressing. The brownies under the guidance of Dr "Totty" Holden undertook to dress the Allen Hill Spa in June, 1978. Dr Holden, who with her husband John, were local GPs in Matlock for many years. Totty is the adult nearest the dressing (Courtest of Dr D "Totty" Holden)

                                 Let St. George step in and clear the way.

Enter; St.George	*I am St. George, that noble man, that noble champion bold.* With sword and spear I slew the fiery dragon, and won ten thousand pounds in gold More than that, I followed to the castle gates a lady in distress; There came behind a valiant soldier, as hard as he could press, And before anything was said, he nearly cut off my head.
Bold Slasher	*I am that valiant soldier* Bold Slasher is my name, And with my sword and spear I'll make up to thee again.
St. George	*Stand off! Stand off! Thou dirty dog, and let no more be said,* For if thou speak'st again, I'll surely break thy head.
Bold Slasher	*How canst thou break my head? My head is made of iron, my body's made of steel,* My hands and legs of knuckle-bone; no man can make me feel.
St. George	*Can't I?*

Bold Slasher	*No.*

(They fight and St. George strikes Bold Slasher in the stomach. He falls)

St. George	*Doctor!*
Enter Doctor	*Here am I, sir.*
St. George	*How camest thou to be a doctor?*
Doctor	*By my travels, sir.*
St. George	*How far hast thou travelled, sir?*
Doctor	*Through Italy, Sicily, France and Spain,*
	And over the hills and back again.
St George	*What canst thou cure?*
Doctor	*A dead man.*
St. George	*Cure him, then.*

Doctor produces a phial and gives physic to Bold Slasher.

> *Here, Jack, take med'cine from my bottle,*
> *And let it run down thy throttle,*
> *And rise up and fight again.*

Bold Slasher rises, and the play ends)
(Bryan ps.112-4)

The Wishing Stone (or Broad Stone)

This natural stone is located off Wishingstone Lane, off Asker Lane, Matlock and covered with much graffiti. It is believed that those who walked round the stone would have their wishes answered. It is understood that this tradition has not died out.

Dragons

Also see Chapter 4.

There was a belief in dragons in the Matlocks, a common belief throughout the country until modern times. The dread of such mythical creatures was used by parents to frighten their children when they misbehaved, somewhat like the bogey man was. Children were terrified by the threat of dragons that would devour naughty children. How evocative this must have been in the days before street lighting.

If dragons were not sufficient for the purpose, it was believed that wild men dwelt in Hobs Thirst Rocks to the north side of Fin Cop Hill. In Tansley, it was said that fairy elves could be heard squeaking in the damp cavities of rocks where the waterfalls were at Lumsdale. At the turn of the 19th century it was common to inspire children with awe about the female relative of a monster which dwelt at the bottom of the River Derwent called "Iron Teeth and Bloody Bones."(Paulson)

Friendly Societies and similar

Oddfellows Society

This society, originating in Manchester, is strong where mills are found, particularly in Lancashire and Yorkshire. One was founded in Matlock Bath known as the Loyal Devonshire Lodge of Oddfellows, No. 2,966 Manchester Unity. They met in a club room at the Devonshire Hotel. This lodge attracted men from all walks of life and it had a substantial sick and funerals fund.

Freemasons

A Lodge of Freemasons was consecrated on 24 April 1874 and named the Arkwright Lodge No.1495 of Free and Accepted Masons at the New Bath Hotel. The Arkwright coat of arms was used for the lodge emblem. The lodge was consecrated by Bro. Okeover, PGM.(Bryan p.195) The idea had been mooted at this lodge's mother lodge on 2 March, 1874, the Derwent, which met and still meets in Wirksworth. They decided to meet on each Friday after the full moon of each month at the Bath Terrace Hotel (Walker's Hotel).

The first master was the grandson of Sir Richard Arkwright, Commander Augustus Peter Arkwright RN, MP for North Derbyshire, 1868-80 who gifted the lodge furniture. In 1879 the lodge moved to the New Bath Hotel (otherwise known as Mr Tyack's Hotel). In 1936 the lodge moved to the Chatsworth Hydro, then to the Crown Hotel in late 1945 and in January 1964 it moved to the Whitworth Institute, Darley Dale and finally back to the New Bath hotel in October 1981. Masonic symbols can be found in the church of St Giles, Matlock on both ends of a bench pew in the Baptistry.(Spark and Naylor (CaH p.52))

Womens' Institute (WI)

Apart from their meetings, they sell homemade produce along with plants, handmade cards and other crafts in the Imperial Rooms on Friday mornings.

Rotary Club at Matlock – Member Club of Rotary International in the

Association of Britian and Ireland

The first Rotary lunch in Matlock was held on 9 January 1928 at the Queen's Head Hotel under the presidency of Dr E H Chapman. The first subscriptions were two guineas (£2.10) joining fee and the same amount as an annual subscription, paying 2s 9d (15p) including gratuities for lunch. However they had a faltering start with as few as eight members turning up for the meetings when they had promised the "hostess" at least 12 persons paying for their meals. Soon after this crisis the club never looked back. They concentrated on community service: sponsoring the Matlock Chamber of Trade, provided swings and see-saws for children, the district garden competition, formation of the Inner Wheel Club, providing the boating lake and paddling pool in Hall Leys Park etc.

Up to the start of World War II they were involved in numerous contributions to the community including: children's swings at Central Gardens, Smedley Street and sending 20 children who had never seen the sea to the Derbyshire Schools Camping Association camp at Sutton-on-Sea, total cost £23.11s.6d (£23.57^1/2p), an activity they pursued for many years. In 1934 they had moved to the Olde English Hotel.

In 1937 they bought 50 trees, which were planted between Pic Tor and Artists Corner to com-memorate the coronation of King George VI. The war years were lean ones, moving to the Cinema House Café in 1944 and back to the Queens' Head Hotel in 1952 and two years later to Moore's Café. Meanwhile they were busy providing a variety of facilities for local people and organisations.

In 1955 a garden for the blind was created off Olde English Road (by the path to the pedestrian bridge over the river), and recumbent spectacles were provided (for those who could not sit up in hospitals). The following year 147 sacks of clothing and £8,000 was sent to help the refugees from Hungary fleeing from the Russian Army and numerous amounts in funds to local and national causes, too many to list here.

A successful source of income for charitable use are three "wells" located at Hall Leys Park Head, Matlock Bridge, at the bottom of Holme Road, Matlock Bath and on the Heights of Abraham, into which people toss coins in the age old tradition, usually when making a wish. In 1965 they moved to the Temple Hotel via the Ritz Cinema Café where they still meet. (A Broome)

There is also:

Inner Wheel Club of Matlock

Matlock Round Table

This organisation was founded for young men only in Norwich in 1927, originally as part of their Rotary Club, gaining independence in 1929. On 16 July 1935 the inaugural meeting of Matlock Round Table was held at the Cinema House (Ritz Cinema). As the minute books for much of this period are missing it is not possible to record the club's activities, but we do know that in 1940 they were responsible for the inauguration of the Citizens' Advice Bureau, which they administered and staffed. By March 1941 the Table had to close through lack of funds and a gap of 10 years ensued. On 24 January 1951 the Table was re-formed, meeting at the Horse Shoe, Matlock Green from whence it

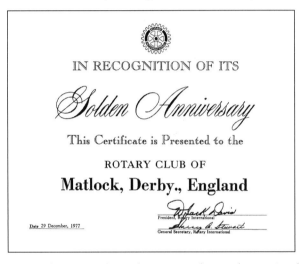

grew in strength, holding its Charter Night at the New Bath Hotel on 2 April 1952.

    Money was subsequently raised for a variety of causes including the East Coast Flood Disaster – £70. There then followed a plethora of activities aimed at helping people and organisations in need, too many to list here, with a few changes of venue.(Dakin)

41 Club

This was created in 1961 for ex-Round Tablers, meeting in a variety of locations both indoor and outdoor.

Forum Club

Formed in 1973 for retired men of any station to meet in the mornings at the Edgefold club – weekly from October to April and monthly from May to July and September – for coffee and a speaker. The origin of this club was the Liberal Club, which met in the Matlock Town Hall where they had a snooker table. They had to resite themselves in June 1965 when the council needed the extra space. It is now non-political. Another club having its roots in the Rotary Club.(In Lit E A "Tod" Dakin 02.02.03)

Ladies Circle

This all female club was originally formed on 4 March 1953 by the wives of Round Tablers.

Tangent Club

This meets at members' homes comprising the wives of ex-Round Tablers.

Inner Wheel

This all female club was founded by the wives of Rotarians in 1946.

Speakers Club

This was originally the Toast Masters' club of which one of their members, Ray Stead, become the National President in 1967.

Royal British Legion

Under the auspices of the Legion, a large gathering of people attend at the war memorial at Hall Leys Park Head on 11 November for a short service and for the laying of wreaths to the fallen of the wars of the 20th century. A procession attends at the memorials at Pic Tor and Matlock Bath from the churches of St Giles and Holy Trinity respectively.

Alas this worthy organisation seems not to appeal to post World War II ex-servicemen. It was founded nationally in 1921 and arrived in Matlock soon after, having 900 or so members originally. However this number fell to 32 members and the Matlock Branch joined with the Darley Dale Branch. At the time of writing the membership stands at 32 and they meet every quarter at the Duke William Matlock Town. Had they had a clubroom, more members might have been attracted.(In Lit E A "Tod" Dakin. 02.02.03)

United Services Club

Formed after World War I, this was intended for all servicemen as a social club, located above some shops on Bakewell Road opposite the supermarket. It is now open to anyone who wishes to join.

Probus Club

Named from **Pro**fessional **Bus**inessmen – for whom it is intended – they meet monthly, except for August, for a lunch and speaker at the Duke William, Matlock Town. This club has its roots in the Rotary Club.(E A "Tod" Dakin In Lit 02.02.03)

Save the Children Fund

Started in Matlock in May 1963 by Mary Greatorex, Chair of the Matlock Urban District Council at the time, Marjorie Yeomans was deputy Chair. The shop was opened in July 1985.

Right: The composite war memorial at Hall Leys Park head with the tram shelter behind relocated from Crown Square

Village Halls

Starkholmes

In June 2002 Starkholmes celebrated the 50th anniversary of their village hall. It is also in this month that Starkholmes holds its gala day, seven days of dance, quiz, treasure hunt, and a pet show, with entertainment provided by a fancy dress parade, stalls selling bric-a-brac and such, tug-of-war, gymnastics, children's races, welly painting, bouncy castle, maypole dancing, face painting and many more activities. A clown is present and the ubiquitous brass band, all with a gala queen in attendance. In this year it was the 53rd anniversary of the gala day when the queen was Sarah Stokes aged 13 years who was crowned by the High Sheriff of the county, Dianne Jeffrey. The queen had a Rosebud and a Pageboy in attendance. The Duke and Duchess of Devonshire gave a sheep for roasting.(PT 07.06.02)

This hall was originally an Army hut for the Canadians during World War II, after which it became the property of the Ministry of Supply. It now has a community use.(Reflections July, 2002)

Societies with animal connections

Matlock Poultry Society

This has had a strong following since its foundation in 1950.

Mid Derbyshire Riding Club

This club is strongly supported by Matlock Rotary Club.

Motoring and Cycling

Institute of Advanced Motoring (IAM)

The Matlock section of this institute meets at Highfields School.

Matlock Motor Club

This recently formed club holds rallies as members of the championships organised by the EMAMC, ANEMMC, EMAM historic and HRCR Historic Road Rally Championship Nocturnal Challenge and HERO Challenge for pre 1960 cars. They are sponsored by AB Motorsport and the club in turn sponsors the Ashgate Hospice, Chesterfield. http://www.matlockmotorclub.co.uk

Matlock Cycling Club

This enthusiastic club has members of all ages who take part in time trials and races as well as leisure rides. Ron Duggins, one time photographer with the *Matlock Mercury*, consistently wins the champion's prize in the over 60s category.

Other clubs and groups

Matlock Camera Club

This club meets at the Gothic Warehouse at Cromford Mill.

Matlock Philatelic Society

Founded in 1972.

Matlock Railway Club

This club meets weekly at the Duke William on Church Street, Matlock Town. They show videos of trains in action with talks about railways. The nostalgia for steam lives on.

Matlock Pre-school Play Group

Meets at 205 Smedley Street, Matlock Bank providing early years' learning for two and a half to 5 year olds. It operates through the Nursery Education Scheme for children from 3 years of age and the playgroup is registered with the Social Services Department and is a member of the Derbyshire County Council Early Years Partnership and is approved by the DfEE and OFSTED.

Organisations with a charitable theme

Matlock and District Talking Newspaper

This organisation provides newspapers and magazines on audio tape for the blind and partially sighted. Every week they record the *Derbyshire Times* with the *Matlock Mercury, Ashbourne News Telegraph, People's Friend* and *Woman's Weekly* and every month *Derbyshire Life and Countryside* and *National Geographic Magazine*. This group was founded in 1978. These are sent free of charge and post free to registered blind persons and those with a visual impairment certified by their Doctor or Ophthalmologist.

This admirable venture is funded entirely by voluntary contributions and is a member of the Talking Newspaper Association of the United Kingdom (TNAUK)

Matlock Hard of Hearing Club

Founded in 1977 by a very deaf lady, Fay Fearn in her home. This group meets every month at the Imperial Rooms having 26 members but has been larger in the past. They used to operate a resources centre for various aids but this has been taken over by the social services locally. The meetings are social in nature and they also organise outings and speakers.(Allen In Lit 16.12.02)

Age Concern Matlock

(This voluntary organisation has no connections with either Age Concern Derbyshire or Age Concern England)

It was started in 1981 with a committee at Cromford and a day centre was established at Cromford Community Centre. The chairman at the time was Mr Bill Linnell and two of the original volunteers are still helping. Other committees formed in Wirksworth and Darley Dale. Cromford and Wirksworth closed but Darley Dale amalgamated with the Matlock branch in 1982.

It operates on Fridays at the Imperial Rooms as a social club for older people, who want to spend a few hours chatting with others and perhaps joining in a short bingo session after lunch. It is directed particularly to those who may find it difficult to get about, as a community bus collects and returns them to their homes.

Volunteers will do shopping – mainly at the local supermarket. A lunch is brought in, which members pay for – chips are very popular! As a way of raising funds, tea or coffee plus biscuits are offered to the general public during the morning. It is quite a popular rendezvous.(K Belcher and M Elson In Litt)

Included under this heading are the following:

Cancer Research Campaign (Matlock and District Branch)

Matlock Hospital League of Friends

Matlock and District Mencap Society

Charity outlets

These are included here as these shops are a meeting place for locals who buy many a bargain from them. The writer has built a sizeable library of which a good proportion is made up of books bought at these places.

Oxfam

The Oxford Committee for Famine Relief has had a shop in Matlock Bridge since 1971 at the same site on Dale Road.

Red Cross

The British Red Cross Society has an outlet on Bank Road, Matlock Bridge, facing Help the Aged's outlet.

Help the Aged

This charity for helping our elderly citizens is also on Bank Road facing the Red Cross outlet.

Sue Ryder

Wife of Sir Leonard Cheshire. The charity shop is in Firs Parade.

Save the Children

Founded in Matlock in 1963. The shop, which opened in 1985, is situated on Bank Road.

Other societies and organisations
not mentioned so far

Matlock Writers' Club	*Dry Stone Walling Association (Derbyshire Branch)*
Matlock Floral Art Society	*Matlock Bridge Club*
Bean Bag Club	*Churches Together in Matlock*
Friends of Tawney House	*Tawney House Arts Society*
Starkholmes Women's Institute	*Matlock Sequence Dancing Club*
Elizabeth Chamberlain School of Dancing	*Womens Royal Volunteer Society (WRVS)*
Hurst Farm Over 60s Club	*Widows Club*
Derbyshire Postal History Society	*Derbyshire Electorial Reform Group*
Matlock Speakers' Club	

UFO Spotting and other phenomena

The sighting of Unidentified Flying Objects in the Matlocks and surrounding areas has now become a pastime for anybody who might believe in them.

As far back as June, 1972 a Charles Chandler of Hurst Farm saw a huge fire ball flash through the sky over Riber. A tanker driver, Douglas Ryder, on his early shift saw the same thing which lasted for at least 30 seconds. He tried, in vain, to follow it using his tanker as a tracking vehicle.(MM 13.06.02)

The number of sightings since has been numerous and most are inexplicable, or, no-one has found a rational explanation for them. The main area of activity would appear to be over the village of Bonsall where some incredible sightings have been made, one being videoed, which caused a sensation and attracted interest from NASA. Television documentary makers have produced programmes about these sightings. We all wait with eager anticipation for the outcome and for officialdom to break their silence in the matter. Activity however has decreased to nothing during the longer days of summer, 2002. Perhaps our visitors feel exposed due to the publicity.

There have been many local explanations: vibrations from quartz veins (there is no quartz in the area), emissions of energy from Ley Lines, hot air balloons (in the night?), aircraft jet engines (confounded by the airports and military, neither of which had aircraft in the area at the time.) We await with bated breath for the next sightings!

A sighting by a pensioner over Causeway Lane, Matlock Bridge described a spectacular array of lights and colours. This was also witnessed by a lady from St. Giles Walk, Matlock Town. The display lasted for 90 minutes from 8.30 pm in August 2001. Other sightings are consistent in that they refer to a triangular shape mostly of an iridescent blue sometimes showing a solid triangle, all with a brighter light in each point of the equilateral triangle.(MM 23.08.01)

Mention should be made of the loud bangs and flashing lights heard and seen many times on the flanks of Masson Hill, dating back before the UFO sightings. These have been ascribed to fireworks, ignited gas from the mines and just plain hoaxing. Or could they be early manifestations of little green men?

This is a list of famous persons who were born, resided in or visited the Matlocks. These are listed alphabetically by surname.

Adelaide, Dowager Queen and widow of William IV

Adelaide visited Matlock Bath on 31 July 1840 in the company of the Duchess of Saxe-Weimar, Earl Howe, Earl and Countess of Sheffield, Earl of Denbigh and others. She rested at the Old Bath Hotel, the village having been tricked out with bunting and flags. The party was rowed down the river and they walked the Lovers' Walks, after which they climbed the Heights of Abraham and on their descent they called at the Devonshire Cavern. After returning to the hotel the event was commemorated by fireworks and a salute of cannon located on the terrace at the Heights of Abraham.(Bryan p.154)

Adam, William (1794?-1873) Curator and geologist

Adam arrived in Matock Bath from Cheltenham in the 1820s at the behest of John Mawe to help in his museum at Matlock Bath, taking over on the decease of the latter in 1829. This was not a success as the business seems to have ceased trading in 1850. The word museum is a misnomer for a curiosity shop which sold many things including: stone and marble ornaments, blue john vases, mineral specimens – mostly local, and "collections" which were sold at 10s (50p) for 50 specimens in a box all labelled, 70 for £1 and 90-100 for £1.10s (£1.50).

He also gave lectures and was for a time the "occasional lecturer to the Yorkshire Mechanics Institutes and to King Edward's Grammar School, Birmingham". He is best known for his epic publication *The Gem of the Peak*, dedicated to the Duke of Devonshire, which went into many editions, the earlier ones being small.

His later years found him in straitened circumstances and an appeal was launched for funds to help to alleviate his distress. *The Times* newspaper printed, "overcome by infirmities and little better than a wreck in mind and body . . . with his aged wife . . . inhabiting a humble cottage at Starkholmes almost in a state of absolute starvation." The sum of £24 was raised, his debts were cleared and he received 6s (30p) per week for as long as the fund allowed.(Adam/Ford)

Allen, John (1794-1867) Poet and scholar

Born at Lea of humble parentage, he was self taught and mastered the English language, arithmetic and verse, all of which he taught at schools locally of his own foundation. He wrote a poem about the Matlocks and his description of the valley is worthy of repeating here.

Mountains lower

> Abrupt; and rocks – rent, rugged, frowning – throw
> Their morning shadows o'er the stream below.
> Stern giants! From the sloping glade ascending,
> They guard the dale – strength, age, and beauty blending.

In winding course the river frets their base,
Adventurous trees their giddy summits grace;
Up their grey forms – pale Ruin's wreath and Time's
Old crown of wine and worth – the ivy climbs,
And richest foliage, like a living soul,
Clings to their sides and feeds on breasts of stone.

A man of such erudition deserves to be remembered as a local hero. He was an accomplished numismatist and helped Charles Hurt Jnr of Alderwasley to date and decipher his collection of coins. Furthermore, he wrote hymn tunes, which were used far outside the county. He married well, a Miss Alsop of Alsop and they settled in Gilderoy House, Matlock Bath.(Bryan ps.139-40)

Bailey family

This family owned the Matlock Cotton Mill generally known as Bailey's. The founding father has a memorial in St Gile's Church which tells us:

In memory of Henry Edwin Bailey, of Matlock who entered into rest on Easter eve, March 31st, 1888 aged 49 years. . . . . . . The clock and chimes in the tower of this church were dedicated Easter, 1889, and were the gift of Mary Ann Bailey, as a memorial of her husband.

F H Bailey is closely connected with the Matlock corn mill near to Hunt's Bridge and whilst it has been converted to apartments along with his fine house, it is still known as "Baileys". The most recent member of this family whose name lived on, founded the Ernest Bailey Grammar School, which occupied the old Hydropathic Memorial Hospital on Bank Road, now a youth hostel.

Bogarde, Dirk (Derek van den Bogaerde 1921-1999) Film Actor

This film actor appeared in many roles, a number of which are now part of the British film heritage. He also wrote his autobiography in several parts, one of which – *Snakes and Ladders* – refers to his time in the Matlocks in October 1943, when he was resident at Smedley's (he refers to it as Matlock Bath Hydro Hotel), where he took a course in APIS (Air Photographic Interpretation Section). He was fond of such devices for he also wrote PGHMTPTC which says "Please God Help Me To Pass This Course". He did!(Bogarde p.80)

Bown, Phoebe (1772-1854) Character

A grave stone in St Giles' churchyard records that:

> Here lies romantic Phoebe
>   Half Ganymede, half Hebe:
> A maid of mutable condition,
>   A jockey, cowherd and musician.

And this is only the beginning! She was also a carpenter, mason and blacksmith. She was "good at fighting, not only with her fists but with an iron bar from her smithy."(Ward-Lock p 53/54)
Hebe was the Goddess of youth and had the power of restoring the aged to youth and beauty, Ganymede was the most beautiful boy ever born and succeeded Hebe in office.(Brewer p 500/593)
Even at the age of 13, she was considered as being an eccentric. One who knew her records:

Her step is more manly than a man's, and can cover forty miles a day. Her voice is more than masculine; with the wind in her favour she can send it a mile. She understands any kind of manual labour, as holding a plough, using a flail; but her chief avocation is breaking horses at a guinea a week (£1.05). She is fond of Milton, Pope and Shakespeare; she is well-taught and performs on many instruments, as the flute, violin, harpsichord, and supports her bass viol in Matlock church.
(WL-M pps 53/54)

The church guide refers to her as being "both jockey, cow-herd and musician." One eye-witness account adds to the above, "The Methodists she swore had borrowed her sacred music."(Bryant p.116)

Her cottage still exists as an outhouse to Dale Cottage, Matlock Dale. At one time she had a little property with a small farm. Her house at Dale Cottage was festooned with various weapons decorating the walls, as she was, strangely for her, frightened of intruders. She wore a man's clothes and there is some doubt about her sex, although one account tells us that she would dress in a petticoat with a blue smock sporting a tall hat. She died on 16 May 1854 aged 85 years and is buried in the church-yard at St Giles' Church.

Byron, George Gordon Byron, 6th Baron Rochdale (1788-1824) Poet

He it was who compared the valley with Switzerland, "There are prospects in Derbyshire as noble as any in Greece or Switzerland" and he should know, he spent much of his life in both countries. "Mad, bad and dangerous to know", his visits to Matlock Bath were undertaken when he was in passionate pursuit of Mary Chaworth of the estate adjacent to his own in Nottinghamshire. She did not share his passion and became bored with him.

She rather cruelly mocked him for having a club foot, which was a source of torment to him, especially when it prevented him from dancing. Moore wrote of Byron's stay at the Old Bath Hotel, Matlock Bath:

In the dances of the evening at Matlock, Miss Chaworth, of course, joined, while her lover sat looking solitary and mortified. It is not impossible, indeed, that the dislike which he always expressed for the amusement may have originated in some bitter pang felt in his youth on seeing 'the lady of his love' led out by others to the gay dance from which he was himself excluded. On the present occasion, the young heiress of Annesley having had for her partner (as often happened at Matlock) some person with whom she was wholly unacquainted, on her resuming her seat, Byron said to her pettishly: 'I hope you like your friend?' The words were scarcely out of his lips when he was accosted by an ungainly Scotch lady, who rather boisterously claimed him as 'cousin', and was outing his pride to the torture with her vulgarity, when he heard the voice of his fair companion, retort archly in his ear: 'I hope you like your friend?'

Cubley, Henry Hadfield (1858-1934) Painter

Tutored by George Turner of Wirksworth and Idridgehay, in his younger years he exhibited three landscapes at the Royal Academy, between 1885 and 1902, of which two were of Matlock Bath.(Fineran pps11-12)

Darwin, Erasmus (1731-1802) Physician and philosopher

The grandfather of Charles Darwin of *Origin of Species* fame knew the Matlocks well but lived at Breadsall Priory near Derby. He was the author of *The Loves of the Plants* based on Matlock Bath and the beginning of this work is given thus:

> *Where as proud Masson rises rude and bleak,*
> And with misshapen turrets rests the Peak,
> Old Matlock gapes with marble jaws beneath,
> And o'er scar'd Derwent bends his flinty teeth.
> Deep in wide caves, below the dangerous soil,
> Blue sulphurs flame, imprisoned waters boil;
>
> *Condensed on high, in wandering rills they glide*
> From Masson's dome, and burst his sparry side.

He also wrote *The Botanic Garden.*

He was the only medical member of the famous Lunar Society which met monthly in Birmingham to philosophise and whose thoughts influenced the developments of the Industrial Revolution. The other members were the likes of Josiah Wedgwood (potter, the other grandfather of Charles Darwin), John Whitehurst (clockmaker of Derby), Matthew Boulton (foundry owner, Birmingham and partner with James Watt), James Watt (inventor and engineer) and other luminaries.

Dinnigan, Simon R (1968-to date) Classical guitarist

This accomplished guitarist chose to come and live in Matlock, hailing originally from Sheffield. He learned to play when young, being hailed as a child prodigy at the age of nine with his first public performance at the age of eleven. He has performed with the Royal Philharmonic Orchestra, the German State Orchestra, the Balearic Symphony Orchestra and in a tour of 44 days he played in every county in England. He also played before HM Queen Elizabeth II at her private Jubilee party.

He has won many prizes including the Sheffield Junior Young Musician of the Year (1981 and 1982) and second prize in the Domecq International Guitar Competition (1983) when aged only 14. He holds the post of Principal Guitar tutor at Birmingham's Conservatoire of Music. He has made many appearances on both radio and television and he has made several recordings.

Extracts from various reviews tell us much about his precocious talent: "a natural sucessor to Julian Bream", "a modern day virtuoso of demonic powers" and "a world class talent – and a major guitarist for the 21st century". He lives with his wife Nichola who teaches guitar from their home in an old Sunday School on Bank Road, Matlock. (Reflections December, 2002)

Drabble family

They are famous for their connection with the Tansleywood Mill in Lumsdale. Mr T Cooper Drabble was much involved with local politics and was the Matlock representative on the Derbyshire County Council, c.1900. He was responsible for persuading the council to contribute to the widening of Matlock Bridge in January 1896. In the 1890s he served on the School Board as a "neutral", meaning that he had no affiliation and because of this he was elected chairman. At the turn of the 19th century, a member of this family, Walter Drabble, owned in partnership a sawing shed in the station yard at Matlock for cutting blocks of stone.

Frederick Henry Drabble was a mill spinning manager at Lea Mills. In 1889 he leased the Tansleywood Mill from Messrs. F & A K Baines, worsted spinners. Drabble changed to garnetting, the recovery of waste cotton and wool to a "fluff" which was sold as a cheap alternative to spinners to rework. By 1912 he was so successful that he bought the business from the Baines, forming it into a limited company in 1914. He expanded the business over a period of more than 40 years to include garnetting, bleaching, dyeing and drying with the customary warehouse and offices. Frederick Drabble took the

Simon Dinningan

business on after his father Henry retired in 1952. The company drew its work force from as far away as Bonsall, Winster, Higham and beyond.

After World War II, Drabbles had difficulty competing with foreign imports and was taken over by a Yorkshire company. However, it continued under the name of F H Drabble & Sons Limited. It finally closed in July 1999 and the premises would appear to be destined for a new and exciting future.

.For further information about this factory see under "Lumsdale" at the end of Chapter 11.

Elizabeth II, Queen of Great Britain (1926-to date)

Her Majesty the Queen has visited the Matlocks on a few occasions, most notably in May 1992 as part of her Jubilee tour. On arrival in the royal train at Matlock Station she was driven to various locations, escorted by the late Sir Peter Hilton, Lord Lieutenant of the County at that time. She proceeded to St Giles School then visited a well dressing and went on to Carsington to open the new reservoir. This was followed by a "relaxed lunch" at Alton Manor the home of the Sir Peter Hilton. (MM 295.92 PT 28.5.92)

Her heir, Prince Charles and his sister, the Princess Royal, have visited the area, calling at the Peak District Mining Museum in the Pavilion, Matlock Bath.

Latham, John (19th century) Photographer

"Mr Latham begs to inform the Nobilty, Clergy, Gentry, and the Public of the opening of his new portrait studio at Derwent Terrace overlooking the river." So proclaimed John Latham in his advertisement dated 1868. He had been the first resident photographer in the Matlocks since 1862 and the studio referred to was at Taghill Cottage, Matlock. He offered residents and visitors alike portraits and views of local scenes. The arrival of a John Clerk from Bakewell in 1864 threatened John's monopoly so he sought to provide something new and different. He therefore offered "stereocards" which with a viewer gave a three dimensional effect. These proved to be popular and he did a brisk business in this innovation. He produced about 1,500 stereoscopic photographs of scenes from not only the Matlocks but also Alton Towers (a private residence in his day), coastal resorts such as Whitby and Scarborough, Lincoln and Lichfield. Later in his life he became swamped by many other photographers but his early work of a high standard made him a pioneer in what was then a new phenomenon that beguiled the Victorians.
(Reflections May 2001)

Marie Amelie, ex-Queen of France

She came to Matlock Bath on 23 September 1856 in the company of the Duke and Duchess of Nemours, Princess Margeurite, Count d'Eu, Duke of d'Alencon, Duke and Duchess d'Aumale with others. This party stayed at the Old Bath Hotel and enjoyed the attractions of the place.(Bryan p.154)

Michael, Imperial Grand Duke of Russia

Accompanied by Baron Nicholay, General Paskervitch, General Kledivsky, Dr. Offsky and others, arrived at Matlock Bath on 22 July 1818 having travelled from Derby. They visited several local attractions and then departed for Chatsworth.(Bryan 155/6)

Morris, Michael "Micky" (1907-97)

Linguist, Vegetarian, Boxer, Furniture store owner and character Micky is still remembered with great affection in the Matlocks as he sat in his chair on the steps to the old Methodist Chapel, Matlock Bath, which was his furniture repository. Many a lorry driver would sound his horn when passing

always to be greeted by Micky. He was from a Polish Jewish family but born in the Potteries to a poor family. His father relocated the family for some unknown reason to Sheffield in the early 1920s, where he started a small outlet for the sale of socks, vests and the like and Micky learned his future trade this way. He started on his own by walking to the area round Bradwell, Hope and Hathersage extending to Tideswell, Youlgreave, Winster, Darley Dale and Matlock, sleeping rough and toting his wares from a suitcase. It was at this time that he became friendly with Dr Glynn Faithfull, Marianne's father, from whom he learned a love of linguistics and who painted a portrait of Micky's future wife Tess. Glynn gave Micky free lodging in a hut, which was to become the Youth Hostel in Shining Cliff Woods.

In 1936 he married Tess and initially lived at Wirksworth be-

Micky Morris (1907-1997)

fore settling in Northwood Lane, Darley Dale. He started selling small items of furniture from Northwood Lane until the outbreak of war in 1939, when he volunteered to be a physical training instructor in the Army. After being demobilised in 1946 he carried on as before, but extended his activities to a large shed on Chesterfield Road extending yet again to a shop on Dale Road, Matlock and yet later to the old chapel at Matlock Bath. The businesses are now run by his daughter and her husband.

This extraordinary and lovable man could converse in German and recite Baudelaire in perfect French. His kindness and trust in people was legendary. He learned how to box so as to retaliate against school children who bulled him because of his small size.

Newnes, Sir George Kt MP (1851-1910) Publisher and politician

Born at Matlock Bath, the son of the pastor at the Glenorchy Chapel, he was one of the progenitors of the cable tramway at Matlock. He founded *Tit Bits* (1881), the *Strand Magazine* (1891), *Country Life* (1897) and others. He was MP for Newmarket 1885-95.(Crystal p 691)

Pedro, Dom II of Brazil

Pedro, Dom II of Brazil with his Empress arrived at Matlock Bath from Sheffield via Chatsworth and Haddon Hall. They were received by a committee and much public interest and, after staying the night at the New Bath Hotel, they proceeded to Cambridge.(Bryan p.156/7)

Rawlinson, James (1769-1848) Painter

A pupil of George Romney, he was the son of George Rawlinson, an architect of Matlock Bath, who designed some of the better villas there. Erasmus Darwin and William Strutt along with George Washington sat for him. He resided in Derby from 1790 but relocated to Matlock Bath on the death of his father in 1823. He exhibited at the Royal Academy in 1798, and in 1822 he published an album of Derbyshire views. Stained glass by Rawlinson featured in Derby Cathedral but was removed during the building of an extension in the 1970s. Some of his work can be seen in Derby Art Gallery. His daughter Eliza also became an accomplished artist.(Fineran p 23)

Rayner, Louisa (Louise) Ingram (1829-1934) Painter

Born in Matlock Bath she was the daughter of Samuel and Ann Raynor who were both artists. She specialised in oils but changed to watercolours in which she excelled. She was raised in Derby and moved to London c.1866 where she was taught by Niemann and D Roberts. She exhibited at the Royal Academy, 1852-86. She maintained her Matlock connections throughout her life and she died at St Leonard's on Sea, Sussex.

Her parents, Samuel and Anne were also artists and undertook engravings in association with Vallance's Royal Centre Museum, Matlock Bath. Her father exhibited at the Royal Academy 1821-72 and lived off Oxford Street, London 1851-60. They had five daughters – all artists – of which Louisa was the best known.(Fineran p 23)

Ruskin, John (1819-1900) Writer and Art Critic

Ruskin was a frequent visitor to Matlock Bath and seriously thought of settling here, but chose Brantwood near Coniston instead. He changed our views of art and popularised Turner. He waxed eloquent about the Matlocks as this small excerpt from a larger written opinion demonstrates:

The painless accessible turrets of Matlock Tor, the guiltless traceable "Lovers' Walks" by the Derwent, have for me a witchery. The vast Masses, the luxuriant colouring, the mingled associations of great mountain scenery, amaze, excite, overwhelm, or exhaust.

One wonders had he stayed if he would have revised this considerably, having encountered the numerous day trippers, who came later.

Smedley, John (1803-74) Hydropathist and Manufacturer

Smedley created the industry of hydropathy and in consequence created Matlock Bank, for before he came it was a hamlet comprising a few cottagers and farms. When he died he left a successful mill and hydropathic industry, the latter drawing many people to the Matlocks. His life is well covered in Chapter 5.

Thompson, Charles c.1753-c.1812)

Thompson was born in Matlock, some say Bonsall, in the middle of the 18th century and by 6 February 1784 he, with his brother John, were citizens of Utrecht, Netherlands where he was a director of music in the English Church there. It is believed that the brothers worked under Sir Richard Arkwright in one of his Cromford Mills, taking their knowledge to Utrecht where it was put to good use in a new cotton spinning mill founded by Abraham Welsingh and Adriaen Swarkendijk. From this it is believed that the industrial revolution was taken to Europe.

By 1818, Charles had changed direction, becoming the Professor of English at Utrecht University, and by 1824 he was listed as a painter and later as a language master. His landlady's daughter in Utrecht, Eliza – her father was from Hathersage – married a Henry Plater and emigrated to the United States of America, taking several paintings with her, one of which is of Charles Thompson. This now hangs in the Cleveland Museum of Art, incorrectly attributed to the "American School".(PT 21.10.01)

Thurlow, Edward, 1st Baron Thurlow (1731-1806) Lord Chancellor

Whilst staying at the Old Bath Hotel in August 1783 and sitting alone in a room, he was accosted by a would-be card or dice player insisting on a game. The Lord Chancellor refused whereon the stranger made many more offers, all of which were rejected. His Lordship however offered "but if you will go with me into another room, I will propose something that may suit you better." Pen, paper and ink were sought and got, whereon the Chief Judge of the land made out a *mittimus* (an order to commit to jail), which dumbfounded the would-be gambler. In spite of the latter's apologies, he was committed to the County Goal in Derby.(Bryan p.131)

Trippett, William "Bill" (1909-2002) Sportsman

Bill was born in Sheffield and by the time he was 21 years of age he was swimming for England at the first Empire – later the Commonwealth – Games in Hamilton, Canada. A month later he organised a swim for Age Concern at Matlock Lido, which was outdoors at the time. He did much to foster swimming in the area on the grounds of greater safety especially for the young.

Turner, Joseph Mallord William (1775-1851) Artist

Possibly our most famous artist, he visited Matlock Dale in 1828 when he produced his "Matlock Sketchbook". He came at the suggestion of his friend and inspiration, fellow artist James Holworthy who had settled in Hathersage in 1824. On a previous visit in 1794 he undertook a sketch of High Tor Mine now in the Turner Collection at the Clore Gallery, London.(Gage pps 42/246)

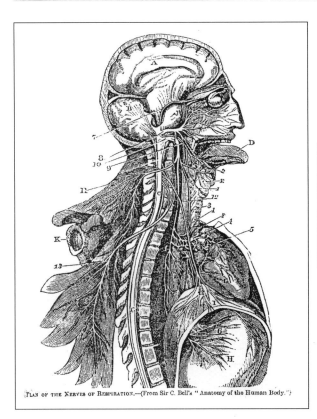

PLAN OF THE NERVES OF RESPIRATION.—(From Sir C. Bell's " Anatomy of the Human Body.")

A typical illustration from Practical Hydropathy by John Smedley 1868. This typifies the lengths that this man would go to, to preach his gospel of hydropathic treatment. It is titled "The Nerves of Respiration." (Practical Hydropathy by John Smedley, 6th Edition, 1863)

Uttley, Alison (1884-1976) Authoress

Born Alice Taylor at Castle Top Farm, she recalled when she caught the train every school day to go to Lady Manners School, Bakewell. In 1903 she read for a degree at Manchester University, one of the first women to do so. In 1928 she began writing her autobiography *The Country Child* about her life in Cromford. This was followed by a series of children's books in the Little Grey Rabbit series, including *The Squirrel, the Hare and the Little Grey Rabbit*. Most of her prodigious output was written after her husband had taken his own life, and she had the sadness of living to see her own son die this way also.

Victoria (1819-1900) Queen of Great Britain

The Queen who gave us the name of an era visited Matlock Bath and stayed at the Old Bath Hotel and took walks in the grounds visiting the caves. On one occasion, when she was still Princess Victoria, on 22 October 1832 she visited a petrifying well. She arrived from Chatsworth in the company of the Duke of Devonshire and the houses in the dale were decked out in garlands. After her visit she continued to Belper to visit the Strutt mills.(Bryan p.152)

Queen Victoria's Diamond Jubilee of 1897 was celebrated enthusiastically by the Matlocks with much street decoration, fetes, parties and the like. This party cost the ratepayer £40, equivalent to a penny rate.(Bryan p.158)

Wedgwood-Benn, Anthony (Tony) (1925-present) Politician

Mr Benn's great-grandfather, Pastor Julius Benn, when 56 years of age, visited Matlock with a view to assisting his 28-year-old son William to recover from a nervous breakdown, placing reliance on the healing properties of the air, water and scenery of the area. They had lodged with Mary and George Marchant and all seemed well until the father and his son failed to appear for breakfast one Sunday morning. When Mr Marchant returned from chapel at lunchtime, he gained access to their room to find the father had been bludgeoned to death with a chamber pot and the son had a cut on his throat.

A doctor was called who pronounced the father dead and stitched the wound on the son's throat. A coroner's jury gave a verdict of unlawful killing. William was then tried in a criminal court but was not fit enough to enter a plea and he was freed to the care of his wife of three months, Florence Nicholson. They went to live in India. Their daughter Margaret, who took the family name of Rutherford, became a much loved actress of recent memory. This event was known as the "Chamber Pot Murder".(Reflections, March, 2002)

Wesley John (1703-91) Evangelist and founder of Methodism

He visited the Matlocks only once, on Monday, 27 July 1761, when he called at Matlock Bath. His diary tells us:
Many of our friends were come from various parts. At six I preached standing under the hollow of a rock, on one side a small plain, on the other side of which was a tall mountain. There were many well-dressed hearers this being the high season, and all of them behaved well; but as I walked back, a gentleman-like man asked me, 'why do you talk thus of faith? Stuff, nonsense!' Upon enquiry, I found he was an eminent deist. What, has the plague crept into the Peak of Derbyshire?

Two days later he preached at 5.00 am near to the Bath. One wonders how many people rose from their beds early for this event?

White, Charles Junior (1891-1956) Politician

Son of Charles White, MP, he stood as the Independent Labour Candidate in 1944 for the West Derbyshire Constituency and defeated the Marquis of Hartington. He held the same seat for Labour until 1950. He was the progenitor for buying Smedley's Hydro as offices for Derbyshire County Council who were originally located in Derby City. His father also called Charles, was MP for West Derbyshire.

York, Duchess of, Princess Victoria Mary of Teck, Princess of Wales, Queen of Great Britain (1867-1953) married to George V

In August 1899 she paid a fleeting visit to Matlock Bath when guest of Mr and Lady Catherine Coke at Longford in the county. She alighted from a train at Matlock Bath, and after admiring the scenery they proceeded by a coach, sent from Chatsworth through the Dale, calling at Haddon Hall and returning to Longford.(Bryan p.155)

$\textcircled{10}$ Buildings & Parks

This chapter deals only with the more important buildings excluding churches and chapels which have been dealt with in Chapter 2. Chapter 5 features Hydros and Chapter 12 school buildings.

Town Hall, Matlock Bridge

Matlock Town Hall currently occupies a building which was known as Bridge Hall, a one time hydro (see Chapter 5), it being bought by the Matlock Urban District Council in June 1894 for the sum of £1,750. In August 1896, a plot of land adjoining this new Town Hall was purchased from the Rev. C Wolley-Dod for £350.

A large wing was added in 1899 to provide facilities for the use of the public and an assembly hall was created on the first floor measuring 60 ft (18.3 m) long, 37 ft (11.3 m) wide and 18 ft (5.5 m) high for the use of up to 450 persons, together with a council chamber measuring 28 ft (8.5 m) by 17 ft (5.2 m), having a separate entrance with retiring rooms for magistrates. External balconies were incorporated from which speeches could be made to the public. The work was undertaken by a local builder, Thomas Kneedham, at a cost of £1,630 plus £300 for furnishings.

The Petty Sessions Court occupied the building on 10 October 1900 with the County Court occupying the premises on 14 January 1901, the first sitting being under Judge Smyly.(Bryant p.56) The cost of this work was paid for from the loan which included the new water works, see Chapter 7.

Accommodation was also found within this Town Hall for the fire brigade, yeomanry and telephone exchange the latter being located in the kitchen. This addition can be seen as being the building to the right when facing from Imperial Road, the original Bridge Hall can be seen to the left. The area fronting Imperial Road, now a car park, was a bowling green. The latest addition to the rear of the old Town Hall was built in 1978-9, the architects being Hadfield, Cawkwell, Davidson & Partners of Sheffield.

Parochial Hall, Matlock Green

This hall also named the Institute and Parochial Hall was erected on Matlock Green and opened on 25 October 1897 and could accommodate up to 300 persons. This was largely used for temperance meetings, the Rector's annual parochial meetings and missionary meetings, with a caretaker's house attached. The cost of £1,200 was borne by Mr Bailey. A gymnasium was provided, also a well stocked

Above: The original town hall, note the balcony now built up with its wrought iron balustrade still in position from wence election results were announced

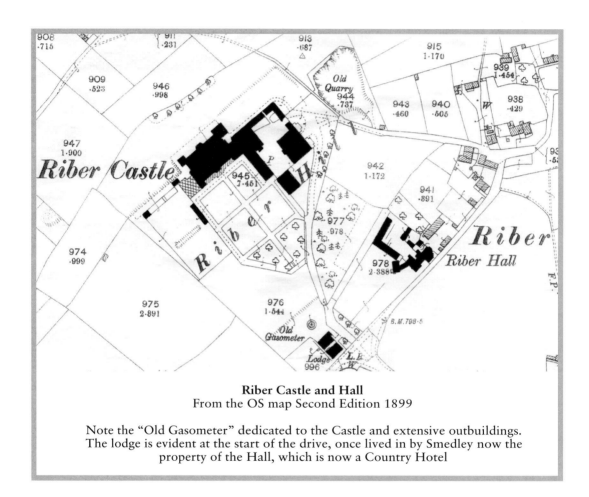

Riber Castle and Hall
From the OS map Second Edition 1899

Note the "Old Gasometer" dedicated to the Castle and extensive outbuildings.
The lodge is evident at the start of the drive, once lived in by Smedley now the
property of the Hall, which is now a Country Hotel

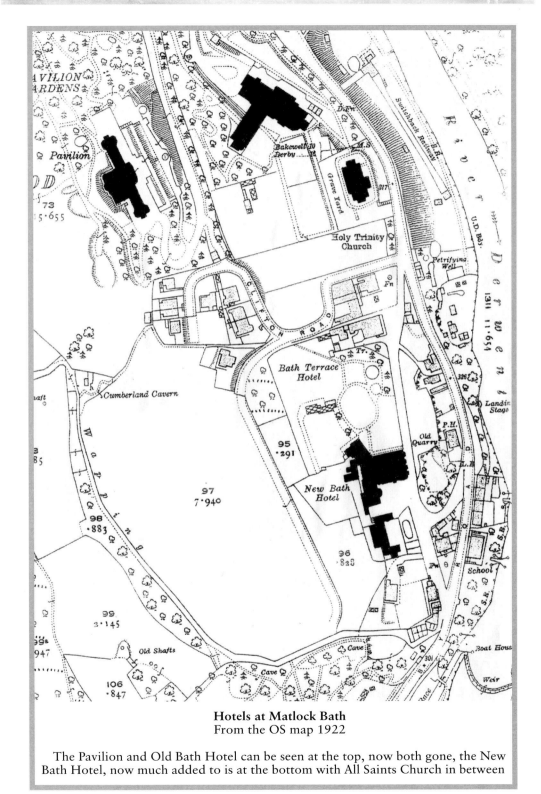

Hotels at Matlock Bath
From the OS map 1922

The Pavilion and Old Bath Hotel can be seen at the top, now both gone, the New Bath Hotel, now much added to is at the bottom with All Saints Church in between

reading room, and refreshments were available.(Bryan p.48) This building with the adjoining house is now known as Tawney House, from the time it became an adult learning centre for the Workers' Educational Association, see Chapter 12.

Almshouses, Matlock Green

The Harrison Almshouses on Causeway Lane at Matlock Green commenced construction on Queen Victoria's Diamond Jubilee Day, 22 June 1897, the foundation stone being laid by Mrs Margaret Harrison, sister of the late Doctor William Harrison MD of Dean Hill House, Matlock. These were intended to "provide rest for the aged poor." They were dedicated by the Right Rev. Dr Were, Suffragan Bishop of Derby on 20 October 1898. There were and are places for six residents. The sum of £8,000 was bestowed on these almshouses of which £5,400 was an endowment, giving an allowance of 6s (30p) per occupant.(Bryan p.73-4)

Parks

Hall Leys Park, Matlock Bridge

The start of this excellent park was the purchase of the land along the river bank and from Crown Square to Knowlstone Place, from a Henry Knowles for the sum of £500 and dedicated for the use of the public forever as a "promenade and pleasure resort". This took place on 24 June 1989 and, in the September following, this occupancy was extended across the Bentley Brook and over the lands of High Tor Recreation Company, between the river and the Tor, at a rent of 10 guineas (£10.50) per annum. Knowlstone Place "ornamental grounds" were added as a public open space at a cost of £500. The council bought the remaining land in 1908. How far sighted this was by the then council, as the entire park has proved to be a popular amenity and saved from later development.(Bryan p.74) The bandstand and café date from 1914.

The park also boasts a miniature railway 110 yds (100 m) long having a diesel locomotive of 4.5 HP (3.36 kW) with three carriages which can carry a total of 36 passengers. There are 10 motor boats for hire on the pond having 1.5 HP (1.1 kW) engines and glass reinforced plastic hulls.

This park hosted the celebrations for Queen Elizabeth II Golden Jubilee on 4 June 2002 with horse drawn traps from Red House Stable Museum, Darley Dale, the Matlock Brass Band in attendance, a procession of cars including a De-Loren   once used as a "Time Machine" in the film "Back to the Future" and one of Lewis Jackson's vintage cars. Radio Peak 107 provided entertainment for 3,000 people.(MM 06.06.02)

Originally there was a row of shops from Matlock Bridge towards Crown Square, which were demolished in 1926 to create the park head.

Knowlstone Place, Matlock Bridge. These houses date from the 1700s and can be seen today including the obelisk. Riber Hill is in the background.
C.1850 (Author's Collection)

Smith's Gardens, Matlock Bank

This plot of land of 3.5 acres (1.4 hectares) was acquired by the council in 1893 for which the sum of £1,750 was paid to the owner, a Mr R Farnsworth. A company was formed to administer this having a share capital of £6,000 in £1 shares.

A pavilion was designed by James Turner, capable of holding 700 persons with a swimming bath measuring 59 ft (18 m) long and 23 ft (7 m) wide. A contract was entered into for the building of this in the sum of £2,904 3s (£2,904.15). By the time of the annual general meeting of the company, on 28 February 1895, only £2,300 had been subscribed which had paid for the site. The building had risen to the first floor level when they ran out of money. However, bankruptcy was averted by the injection of more capital and the finished park and building were opened by the Honourable Victor Cavendish, MP in June 1896. Sadly the company was in financial difficulties and by May 1901 the company was running at a loss and the mortgagee of a loan of £2,250 foreclosed.(Bryan p.241/2) This area was where Paton and Baldwins built their factory and the building became Victoria Hall, all swept away for housing in the late 1990s.

Smedley Street Park, Matlock Bank

This land originally known as the Allcock, was bought by the council in October 1889 for the sum of £203 4s 8d (£203.24). The council had to borrow £910 for this park, including the cost of the roads, drainage and channelling, repayable in part in 50 years and part in 23 years.(Bryan p.76)

Heights of Abraham, Matlock Bath

This is Matlock's oldest pleasure ground and is a private operation. It comprises fine deciduous woodland on a steep hill known as the Heights of Abraham, see Chapter 4. The access footpaths originate at two gate houses where a fee is charged, whence the visitor has to climb the hillside to the Upper Tower terrace. From there possibly the finest view of the county can be enjoyed. Close by is the Victoria Tower, whereon is inscribed "Victoria Stand. 1884. J.P." The initials refer to John Pechell the then owner of the site.(Bryant p.148)

Of more recent date the grounds were taken over by Andrew Pugh, who cleaned up the area and made the place more consumer friendly. Later he installed a cable car from the east bank of the river Derwent to the Upper Tower terrace, along with an interpretive centre and offered trips round the caverns. The advent of the cable cars to the grounds was a major contribution not only for the visitors to the Heights but to the other traders in the area. The base station is on the site of the old gasworks, the upper station is near to the Victoria Tower. The sheer courage required to undertake this venture was daunting, for the cables had to straddle the river Derwent and a main road. The owner, who spearheaded this venture, is to be commended for all the later attractions on this site as well as the cable cars, which has made him an expert in such matters. He later advised on the building of the London Eye, opened for the Queen's Jubilee of 2002. This cable way has a unique device, a "helipoma", a one person machine which is suspended on the cable. By the use of a rotating fan which acts as a brake, the helipoma lets a person down the cable for inspection purposes, but only for the courageous.(Pugh In Lit 06.11.02) A tea room provides snacks and drinks.

Heights of Jacob (Gullivers Kingdom), Matlock Bath

This area of hillside was originally known as the Heights of Jacob by the owner at that time, a Mr Jacob. This was in direct competition with the Heights of Abraham, complete with caverns. It was not a success and, after years of dereliction, the area was taken over by a Mr Philips who turned it into a visitor attraction called Gulliver's Kingdom. Its name suggests the theme of the park where meals and drinks may also be obtained.

A company was formed in 1882, having a capital of £12,000 raised as £18,000 in £1 shares. With this they purchased 16 acres (6.5 hectares) of land including an area known as the Romantic Rocks upon which was erected a considerable pavilion with landscaped gardens. The first sod was cut on 14 July 1882, the foundation stone of the pavilion was laid on 5 May 1883 by Sir Abraham Woodiwiss of Derby, and the building opened on 28 July 1884 by Lord Edward Cavendish MP. The architect was a Mr John Nuttall and a Mr F Speed laid out the grounds. The grounds were and still are covered by trees, all once being in the ownership of a Mr Walter M. Shore Evans. Alas, this company was not successful and at a meeting of shareholders on 2 February 1889 it was agreed to wind it up, whereon the property passed to a private individual.

This pavilion was taken down during World War II and supposedly put into store for rebuilding later. All trace of this has been lost, presumably into the steel melting furnaces in Sheffield. It must have been an impressive sight, having a frontage of 228 ft (69.5 m) embracing a concert hall 90 ft (278.4 m) long and 60 ft (18.3 m) wide. It also had two promenade annexes 60 ft (18.3 m) long and 24 ft (7.3 m) wide, a refreshment room and a reading room. A band played here during the season. It could seat 800 persons.

High Tor Pleasure Ground, Matlock Bridge

This comprises the grounds occupied by High Tor and is accessed from both the riverside and from Starkholmes. There is a tea room at the summit from which superb views can be had. The Roman and Fern Caves referred to in Chapter 4 are near to the tea room. This land was owned by the Arkwrights who granted a lease in 1822 to the High Tor Recreation Grounds Company Ltd, of which an Arkwright was a director.

Promenade, Matlock Bath

A free public park was mooted in 1873 to be situated on the west bank of the river from the Midland Hotel to a point 300 yds (274 m) south. It opened in 1874 and was used to commemorate the Jubilee of Queen Victoria in 1887. The promenade was then extended to the front of the Fountain Baths. The wooded and rocky slopes on the opposite bank were granted by lease at the same time from F C Arkwright. A wrought iron bridge of 85 ft (26 m) span was erected on stone piers, being positioned on 14 June 1887, and a commemorative banquet was held at the New Bath Hotel on 10 January 1888.(Bryan p. 191) This is known as the Memorial Gardens now that the village war memorial is located within it.

Derwent Gardens, Matlock Bath

This extensive park that runs from the present day pavilion south along the river bank was originally an area of land called Orchard Holme. At the turn of the 20th century it offered rides on a switchback, a large timber structure which was a huge success with visitors. It was said that on a good day the owner, a Mr Buxton, took his takings home in a wheelbarrow. A tufa grotto can be seen, the outflow from the New Bath Hotel, which has built up to such an extent that one can walk behind the waterfall thus created.

Batemans's Park

This small park stood where the Somerfield supermarket now stands. It was so named after a John Bateman who was the publican of the Railway Hotel who owned it. The original Crown Hotel stood on this area. The wakes were also held here from 1885. This park was also used by Sanger's Circus.

Sparrow Park

This wooded park stood opposite the town hall on Imperial Road facing the present post office. It was so named because of the profusion of sparrows who lived here. It was a popular area for courting couples. Most of this park area is occupied by the swimming pool and a hardware multiple. It was originally the town rubbish tip.

Allen Hill Park, Matlock Bridge

This small park at the foot of the Dimple, Matlock Bridge boasts a chalybeate sough, which drains water out of Allen Hill. The portal has the inscription "Allen Hill, Spore Restored 1824". This park was part of the original garden to a residence of one of the Wolleys. This sough is the "well" which is occasionally dressed by the Brownies. In 1893 a report was drawn up with a view to exploiting this water as the basis of a considerable spa facility but nothing came of it. They were certainly thinking in grandiose terms for they had already named it the Royal Matlock Spa. It was once boasted that this was the best naturally occurring chalybeate water in the country and it was said that it "effected cures and was eagerly sought if it were properly available to the public". At one time the locals collected this water, rich in iron hence the sinter deposits at its mouth, and was drunk by them as a tonic. It was also said that it was good for eye problems, but this is said of almost any such water. Pools of this type of water are found on Matlock Moor, therefore people have linked these together assuming that the moorland water feeds the spa. This is very unlikely as the water drains from shale that has iron oxides in its make up. Readers are urged not to try drinking this water. Not only would it be unpalatable it could be dangerous depending on what detritus has been discarded here.

Across the road to this park is an even smaller park created in 2000 to commemorate the millennium and as a memorial to Princess Diana. A wild thyme garden, between Wellington Road and Cavendish Road, was opened by the Duke of Devonshire on 12 October 2002 in the presence of Patrick McLoughlin MP, Barrie Tipping (Mayor of Matlock) and Rina Jones (founder of the Wild Thyme Group). At the same ceremony the group was presented with the East Midlands in Bloom Judges' Prize. The group is now raising funds to buy a Henry Moore inspired sculpture designed by pupils at Highfields School.(MM 17.10.2002)

Happy Valley

This unofficial park is half way up Steep Turnpike on the left, a steeply wooded area where children used to play. It is now disused except as a sanctuary for wild life.(Arkle p.30)

Bird Sanctuary, Matlock Bridge

In the spring of 1899, the lower slopes of the High Tor towards the river were declared a bird sanctuary by the secretary of the High Tor Recreation Grounds Company who, at the same time, acquired the shooting rights to enable them to ban shooting. The one time residents of "The Rocks" opposite were influential in this, having worked for the preservation of the local bird life.(Bryan p.76-7)

Bird Decoy, Matlock Bath

A large bird decoy was located on the river near to Masson Mill and was a useful source of fresh meat. Its original date is unknown but one can assume that it was very old. It seems to have vanished when Arkwright built Masson Mill.

Hotels and Inns

Old Bath Hotel, Matlock Bath

This stood where the car park is located off Temple Road. Later a pavilion was built – not to be confused with the present pavilion. The latter was a large structure built after the style of a summer palace, it being demolished prior to World War II.

The original "old" bath was funded by the Rev. Joseph Ferne, rector of Matlock, Benjamin Hayward of Cromford, Adam Wolley of Allen Hill, Matlock and George Wragg of Matlock in 1696 and was cut out of the tufa by the Wolleys of Riber and known as "Wolley's Well". By 1712, the bath had been improved by the addition of a lead lined timber container. This was short lived as the bath was soon improved by the construction of a stone lined bath having lodging houses and a carriage access. Two further springs were "discovered" which were led into the bath by means of sluices and the like. This bath measured 33 ft (10 m)) long, 20 ft (6.1 m) wide and 17 ft (5.2 m) high with a reading room over it of the same size.

It then appears to have become the property of George Wragg who took out a 99-year lease at a yearly rental of 6 pence (2.5p), paying a fine of £150. This lease was taken over by Smith and Pennell of Nottingham paying £1,000 for it and building a bath house here.

The original hotel was demolished in 1867, as it had undergone many extensions in a haphazard fashion and it was decided to start afresh. The result was a fine Victorian Gothic style hotel, which became popular. Alas this burnt down in 1927 under suspicious circumstances and the remnants were demolished, never to be rebuilt. The site is now a public car park off Temple Road. (Bryan ps. 202/36)

New Bath Hotel, Matlock Bath

This is on the site of the second warm spring to be exploited and was in competition with the Old Bath Hotel. It was also known for a time as Mr Tyack's New Bath Hotel. It still exists and when the property of Trust House Forte it was one of their Heritage Hotels. It now belongs to the MacDonald Group. As mentioned elsewhere, this hotel is fed with warm spring water which also feeds its indoor plunge pool and an outside swimming pool.

Above: Old Bath Hotel, Matlock Bath. This hotel before it was demolished, 1867 to be rebuilt, then gutted by a fire in 1927 never to be rebuilt (Adam p.47)
Left: New Bath Hotel, Matlock Bath c.1850. This view is still recognisable from the present car park (Adam W p.51)

Royal Hotel, Matlock Bath

This stood below and close to the Old Bath Hotel exploiting the same warm spring. It was demolished many years ago. The idea for this hotel dates from 1866 as a hydropathic establishment but the company ran out of money before it was completed. However, by 1878 this new 100-bed hotel was ready for use. It was then taken over by a new company in June 1882 with a capital of £30,000 in 6,000 shares at £5 each. The building and its contents were purchased for £25,000.(Bryan p.206) It once boasted, as part of its hydropathic facility, a resident doctor and a resident orchestra.

Left top: The Royal Hotel on fire. This rare and dramatic photograph was taken on a long exposure on the night of the fire in 1927. An inadequate ladder can be seen leaning on the portico of the main entrance but little evidence of fire fighting (Yeomans)

Left bottom: The Royal Hotel the day after the fire. A little smoke can be seen rising from the front corner and the main building is roofless. The rear wing appears to have escaped the conflagration, never the less it was all demolished. The level front along with the hotel's platform are both car parks off Temple Road (Yeomans)

Old English Hotel

A fine example of Victorian Gothic architecture, this hotel stands at the corner of Dale Road and Old English Road. This is the second hotel of the same name on this site, the original burned down and the fire fighters were too late to save it; they had to come from Derby no less, and one of the horses died at Belper en route.(Arkle p.37) A landlord in the 20th century, Arthur Wall, could clear a 6 ft (1.8 m) high fence when wearing ordinary clothes.

The Clarence

Originally founded by a Dr Armstrong as a hydro, it was taken over by a Mr R Nicholson, for many years the chaplain and partner with Mrs John Smedley at the Smedley Memorial Hydro where he offered the Smedley Mild Cure. The Clarence had accommodation for 40 guests who could consult Mrs Smedley if they chose.

Hodgkinsons Hotel, Matlock Bath

The premises were bought by Job Hodgkinson, a wine and spirit merchant, in the 1830s but they are much older. The hanging sign and much of the ground floor interior are original from that time. Job Hodgkinson developed both a considerable wine trade and a brewery on the premises, which used the disused lead mines behind the hotel for the storage of wine.

The *Which?* guide for 2003 refers to this hotel as being "of quirky character". http://www.hodgkinsons-hotel.co.uk/ (MM 10.10.02)

Fish Pond Hotel, Matlock Bath

Still with us, this hotel dates from the early 20th century so named after the pond across the road. Of late this hotel has established a reputation for its encouragement of singers and musicians.

Queen's Head

An important inn in its day, it stood at the corner of Snitterton Road and Dale Road opposite the Royal Bank of Scotland. This was recorded as early as 1835. The first Market Hall was located behind this hotel.

Horseshoe Hotel, Matlock Green

This was in the possession of the Evans family for 99 years until it was sold in September 1949. Most property auctions were held here, including the biggest sale ever in the Matlocks, the disposal of the large Arkwright Estate.

George Hotel, Matlock Bath

All that is left of this once fine hotel is the Hodgkinsons Hotel. Originally this hotel occupied all the adjoining premises that front the South Parade, then known as Hotel Parade.

The site was originally in the ownership of George Wragg of Old Bath fame, having acquired it in 1680, his family mortgaging it in 1730 for £307. A Thomas Brentnall of Derby bought it for £500 in 1752. After that date it was acquired by a succession of persons until it was bought by George Vernon of Stone, Staffordshire for £1,900, who erected the hotel in c.1800. Vernon borrowed £4,860 with the hotel and land as security and sold it all in 1805.

The buildings were converted to a variety of uses after 1805: from 1810 by Brown & Son of Derby – spar and marble ornaments; subsequently taken over by Mr. Mawe until he died in 1829; after which it came into the ownership of his widow with Mr Vallance acting as her manager. Mr William Adam was enticed from Cheltenham to care for the business and subsequently became the owner. This building originally boasted an upstairs room 36 ft (11 m) long and 21.5 ft (6.6 m) wide having a bay window which can still be seen today.(Bryan ps.197/8)

A second George Hotel in Matlock Bath is now a shopping centre.

The Crown, Matlock Bridge

This hotel gives Crown Square its name. It boasted stabling and meeting rooms, but of late (1990s) it has been converted and added to, to create retail outlets. A crown can be seen carved on a plaque on the corner front. However, this hotel originated from Bateman's Park further along Bakewell Road where it existed for about 100 years, it being recorded in 1835. When it was in Batemans' Park it was a common lodging house notorious for its tramps and for its dancing bears and monkeys. The landlord at that time, a Mr J Bateman, hence Bateman's Park, fed a bucket of ale to a bear with disastrous results.

The Lindens (Lyndens), Matlock Green

This was a guest house in the 19th century becoming a convalescent home for NALGO (National Association of Local Government Officers). It was here in 1857, where Dante Gabriel Rossetti stayed with Elizabeth Siddall later to become his wife.

High Tor Hotel, Matlock Bath

This was originally built as a house for the son of Cuthbert, Admiral and Baron Collingwood (1750-1810) who took over the Battle of Trafalgar after Nelson was killed on 21 October 1805. It has been claimed that the Admiral himself built and lived in this house. This would have been impossible as it was erected after his death in 1810. His son's name was Henry Salkeld James Collingwood and the house was known as Tor Cottage in his day. It has had a varied history both as a hotel and a home, currently it is a home again. It is of cottage ornate style with a unique, separate servants' hall.

Other Public Houses and Beer Sellers

There were numerous such establishments on Matlock Bank, possibly cashing in on the abstinence imposed at the hydros, especially at Smedley's. The Gate Inn on the opposite corner of Bank Road and Smedley Street to Smedley's did a roaring trade selling disguised bottles of spirits to customers of the hydro. This inn when a hotel also had livery stables with as many as 20 horses at one time.

There were many others such as the "Hole in the Wall" now a cottage, near to the Friends Meeting House with several explanations as to how it got its name.

Arkle tells us that these publicans adopted an assortment of strange nicknames: Cartoil, Crack, Duck Jack, Gammy, Gentleman Bill, Nightsoil, Putty, Ribs, Smack and Tramfat.(Arkle 25) These names are supposed to describe the occupation, personality or otherwise of these people. I will leave it to the reader to imagine why such names were used. Why would anyone get a name Tramfat, unless he greased the cable wheels on the Bank Road tramway?

Hospital

Smedley Memorial Hydropathic Hospital, Matlock Bridge

Built as a memorial to her late husband, Mrs Smedley opened this small hydro in 1882. It later became a cottage hospital and is now a hostel belonging to the Youth Hostels Association, see Chapter 5.

Bath Houses

Hotels

Both the Old and the New Bath Hotels boasted facilities for bathing in the spring water. This is a little contrary to the ethos of the two Matlocks: Matlock Bank for the external application of water to the body and Matlock Bath for drinking the water. Attempts were made to establish hydropathic establishments in Matlock Bath but none succeeded.

The Fountain, Matlock Bath

This commodious establishment opened to the public on 2 March 1883 offering hot baths, which the New and Old Bath Hotels did not offer.(Bryan p.202) This replaced a previous bath which was demolished in 1881 as it was small and confined, and the public tended to shun it.(Bryan p.204) This building is now the Matlock Bath Aquarium.

Houses

There are no great houses in the Matlocks. Whilst the area attracted numerous people for the delights it offered, it did not attract anyone of means who might have built himself a mansion.

Riber Castle, Riber

Built by John Smedley as his palace, it is at the time of writing a ruinous shell with an uncertain future but it serves as a landmark much loved by many. If this ruin is not preserved it will only be a matter of a few years before the structure collapses.

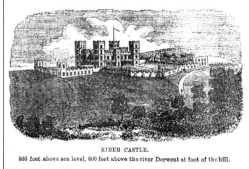

RIBER CASTLE.
860 feet above sea level, 600 feet above the river Derwent at foot of the hill.

It was originally built by John Smedley out of profits from his hydropathic institution on Matlock Bank. He was his own architect, clerk of works, interior decorator and surveyor; this man was daunted by nothing! Prior to starting this he built the lodge to live in temporarily, and it was said that this took four months and a day to be fit to live in. The month in question was February 1862. Whilst the lodge was being built he stayed with George Allen at Riber Hall (qv). The lodge now belongs to Riber Hall.

He then designed an observatory 225 ft (68.8 m) high, which he planned to give to the nation but when advised that it would be unsuitable for the purpose intended, he abandoned the idea. We might have had a more dramatic eye catcher than a pile of collapsing stone?

He then designed the building that we see today. He was obviously aiming to live in the clear "mountain" air of Riber Hill. No expense was spared in the construction and furnishing of this folly, which he duly occupied with his wife. It was said that it cost about £60,000 to build, a more realistic price of £35,000 has been suggested, and even at this latter figure, it was a fortune by any standards. Typical of the man he offered the castle to Queen Victoria as a retreat, which she graciously refused. It boasted its own ice house and a gas holder piped from the Matlock system.

After Smedley's death his widow lived in the castle and, after her death, it was sold to the Anglican, Rev. J W Chippett from Harrogate who established a high-class boys' school (one of two such schools) in the building until 1930. During World War II it was a Ministry of Food store after which it became the property of Matlock Urban District Council, who allowed it to slowly decay; there are other

RIBER ENTRANCE LODGE.

forms of legal vandalism. In 1963 the Hallam family took a lease on the grounds and converted it to the Riber Wildlife Park where they established a reputation for breeding and freeing lynx back into the wild. One notable success was the birth of three jungle kittens, the first at Riber in November 1992. In the year 2000 the lease was called in and the site sold to a developer who sought planning permission to convert the castle into apartments, and build houses in the grounds, fired by a statement from English Heritage in the same year that " Leaving the castle to deteriorate further is not a viable structural option" (February 2000). Their assessment of the cost of stabilising the structure was put at £2,000,000. This caused considerable controversy amongst the people of the Matlocks who are somewhat fond of their ruinous folly. No-one has suggested yet that the most viable solution to the problem is to knock it down!(Bryan ps 246-9 and Developer's brochure, MM 28.11.02)

Sadly, to make way for his castle Smedley removed a cromlech and some of the stones were laid to one side and all were used when broken up for wall building. One cannot help but think, knowing the character of the man, that this edifice of ill taste was built to his own glory, as a showpiece to his self-perceived genius.

Riber Hall, Riber

This house is as near as one can get to a "seat", it being the home of a succession of Wolleys.(see Chapter 1) It was divided into two halves in 1724, one being a residence the other to become a country house hotel owned by Alex Biggin, who has set a standard of excellence in both accommodation and cuisine. He also owns the old gatehouse to Riber Castle. He rescued this fine building and restored it from a state of dereliction in 1970.

BIBER HALL, THE PROPERTY AND RESIDENCE OF MR. GEORGE ALLEN.

One interesting owner of Riber Hall was George Allen (1774-1850), who married an Ann Wolley (1772-1862) from Bonsall of the same family. So contrary to popular opinion, the Wolleys did not vacate the place in 1668 never to return. It was George Allen who gave accommodation to John Smedley, until the lodge to his castle was built. Portraits of the Allen family can be seen on the staircase of the hotel, a gift of the writer. The lodge referred to forms part of the Riber Hall property.

Pevsner called this house "a most felicitous picture".(Pevsner p.308) The initials of two of the Wolleys, GW and MW with the date 1633, are carved over a gable.

Riber Manor House

This was not the manor to the village, the Wolleys owned the manor but resided at Riber Hall. This along with Riber Hall is referred to by Pevsner as "happy surprises, both as the genuine, unselfconscious picturesqueness of minor Elizabethan and early C17 architecture in the county"; one finds it difficult not to agree with him.(Pevsner 308)

Above: Riber Hall. The property of George Allen, who married a Bonsall Wolley. Allen gave succour to his friend John Smedley whilst his "Castle" Gate House was built (Authors Collection)
Opposite top: Riber Castle. As it was then new. With ramparts, look out towers, keeps and battlements it looks every inch a castle. The caption boasts that it is "860" feet above sea level and 600 feet above the River Derwent at the foot of the hill." (Author's Collection)
Opposite bottom: The Lodge to Riber Castle. Lived in by Smedley until his "Castle" was built. It is now part of Riber Hall and the finished building was less ornate than this (By Permission: Derbyshire County Council, Libraries and Heritage)

Willersley Castle

This was built by Sir Richard Arkwright for his own use in 1789-90, of millstone grit from Oakes Quarry, Blakelow Hill, Tansley to designs by William Thomas of London. Due to carelessness by a workman it burned down before he could occupy it. Arkwright had lavished a great deal of money on his mansion particularly on mirrors, he had an obsession with them. His son, also Richard, finished the house using a different architect, Thomas Gardner of Uttoxeter, Staffordshire. The house platform was cut out of the solid limestone along with the cellars and it is said that this alone cost £3,000 in the money of that time. The total cost was estimated at £20,000, which probably includes the rebuilding; insurance as such was hard to come by at that time.

The Honourable John Byng called it "an effort of inconvenient ill Taste" and "It is the house of an overseer surveying his works, not of a gentleman . . . .Sir Richard has honourably made his great fortune: and so let him live in a great cotton mill". Pevsner was kinder, "entirely classical in conception, but romanticised by Battlements" who considered the best feature to be the oval hall, "with galleries on both upper storeys, a skylight." Byng saw the original house of which we know little, perhaps it was of ill taste.

It now enjoys a new lease of life for at the auction of the estate in 1924 it was empty but was bought by the Methodist Guild Holiday organisation, now Christian Guild Holidays, in 1948 and is still in their possession. It was and is noted for its fine trees and in particular a gooseberry tree, which in 1857 measured 30 ft (9m) high with branches spreading 385 ft (111m). It is a Grade II listed building.(Naylor CaH ps 76-7 Pevsner ps. 159/60)

Cromford Bridge House (Bridge House or Bridge Hall)

Near to Cromford Bridge but not to be confused with Bridge House, Matlock Bridge, it is built of carboniferous limestone and millstone grit. It was started in 1642 by Henry Wigley, eighth son of Henry Wigley of Wigwell, Wirksworth Moor, to a Jacobean design. It passed to Millicent Wigley, an heiress of Anthony Wigley in 1684 and then to Samuel, son of John Spateman of Road Nook, who Georgianised it. It was sold to George, third son of Edmund Evans of Winster. His son, by the heiress of Peter Nightingale of Lea Hall, died in 1769 leaving it to a co-heiress who gave it to her son W E Nightingale. It was occupied by another sister, Elizabeth, until she died "very old" in the 1890s. Early in the 19th century it was occupied by the Crompton-Evans family, founders of modern banking.

The house is still a private dwelling, part of which is operated as a nursery school. It is a grade II listed building.(Craven and Stanley p.265)

Cromford Court (Woodbank), Matlock Bath

This very fine building of 1910 stands high off the main A6 road at Matlock Bath. It was built by a Mr Laughton, a barrister, as a residence and as legend has it, a fit and proper place to raise his many daughters whence he intended they should marry into local gentry. He achieved this ambition and bankrupted himself in the process. A vine carved around the main door has each daughter's initials carved upon each leaf, the intention being to add the groom's initials following each marriage.

After Laughton's time, the house had a varied existence, one as a preparatory school. In 1978 the then owner, Mr Dolphin, offered it to the writer for £40,000 including many acres of woodland. In the same year the New Tribes Mission bought it and completely restored the fabric. In 2000, it fell into private hands again.(Naylor CaH p.78)

Masson Lodge, Matlock Bath

Originally occupied by Mrs Charles Clarke JP, second chairman of the Quarter Sessions Court.

Gilderoy House, Matlock Bath

A fine "gentleman's" residence which sits high above Matlock Dale on the slopes of Masson Hill beneath the Heights of Abraham. This house had many and various owners over the years, to mention but a few:

- John Adam
- In the late 19th century it was occupied by a Mr Peters, a German by birth, who had a business in Derby. It was he who sold the land for the bird sanctuary and rescued the land opposite Artists' Corner.
- Today it is divided into two residences, one half of which was the home of Brian Marshall the first head teacher of Highfields School.

Above: Matlock Bath with Gilderoy House
Opposite: Willersley Castle. Built by and for Sir Richard Arkwright but first lived in by his son, Richard Arkwright junior. A fine achievement for a man who started out in life as an apprentice peruke (wig maker and barber) (Author's Collection)

Knowlestone Place, Matlock Green

This fine row of houses was built in lots over a period from 1621 to 1857, thus:

No.3	Derwent House: date stone dated 1621 with 18th-century modifications
No.5	1753 with additional bay of 1772
Nos 7-13	Dated 1857 in Georgian style with some gothic features
No.15	Knowlestone House, early 19th century.

Some of these are now bed and breakfast establishments.(Pevsner p.272)

Other houses at Matlock Green

Swiss Cottages – built to designs by Sir Joseph Paxton in 1839, in the Edensor style. Paxton owned land hereabouts including the old mill. Paxton House and Paxton Tor are not knowingly built or owned by Paxton.(Pevsner p.272)

Artists Corner, Matlock Bridge

This group of houses facing the High Tor are so called as they were a favourite for artists in the Victorian era. They all front the A6 road and amongst them must be the smallest house in the county if not in the entire country. The smallest house in Britain, on the quayside at Conway (Conwy), North Wales is only a little smaller.

Derwent Cottage, Matlock Bridge

This solidly built residence dates from 1820 and sits well, facing the river over the main road. It is said that the eponymous Phoebe Bown organised the building of it. Which should not surprise us but it is known that she lived in an outbuilding here. The present owner believes that she occupied the lean-to against the house end, however evidence points to the building on the road frontage.

Claremont House

Originally built for Charles Rowland who opened Rockside Hydro it probably dates from about the same time, the 1860s. It is now a home for senior citizens.

The Rocks (Rock Villa)

This house sits in a scenic location on St John's Road also built in a cottage ornate style surrounded by an attractive rock garden, hence its name.

Wheatsheaf Inn (later House), Matlock Town

Originally a farmhouse dating from 1681, as a date stone tells us, it has the initials of WSC. It then became an inn and in more recent times a potter, John Whieldon, lived and potted here. It sits overlooking a small green near to St Giles' Church. Mercifully it is little altered and is now a residence and possibly the oldest building in the Matlocks still in use.

Matlock Rectory

This large rectory was brick built in the 18th century.

Station Yard, Matlock Station

The cottage near to the rail station was designed by Sir Joseph Paxton and built in c.1850.

The Shaws, Snitterton Road, Matlock Bridge

Two small houses of 1907-8, are by Parker and Unwin of Rockside Hydro fame, in their Letchworth style. Cawdor Cottage nearby dates from 1898-99.

Commercial Premises

Bank House, Matlock Bridge

This Victorian building, now a bank, is plain in itself. Its greater glory is the extraordinary Grecian access arch overhung by a weeping ash. The modern extension is unfortunate. It is now occupied by the Royal Bank of Scotland and originally by Williams and Glyns Bank.

The fine Grecian portico to the bank at the bottom of the Snitterton Road

Burgons et al

Space does not permit an in-depth look at all the shops that were and are in the Matlocks. As they seem to change in use at regular intervals it would be a time consuming detective story. However there are three which cannot be ignored.

Burgons – occupied premises on what is now the Park Head at Matlock Bridge – they had a trade mark of a black elephant. If the reader cares to stand in the sunken garden at the Park Head a black elephant can be seen at the back of the premises, now occupied by the Derbyshire Building Society, which were later occupied by Burgons, having moved from the Park Head. When this shop was demolished a human skeleton was found in the foundations, it being assumed to have been that of a felon "hanged at the crossroads".

Firs Parade

This ill-conceived and out of character development link road between Causeway Lane and New Street was built in 1964, partly in the gardens which were attached to the present day library.

Museums

The Pavilion, Matlock Bath

Not to be confused with the pavilion referred to under Old Bath Hotel above. It was originally built as a pump room where visitors could imbibe of the same water that fed the Old Bath and Royal Hotels. It is built on a bed of tufa on a site originally occupied by the stables to the Fish Pond Hotel. The Briddons kept 50 horses here at one time. It was early named the Kursaal in an effort to attract more customers. This German word means literally a "cure-saloon" but applied generally to a reception room at a spa.

It has had a varied existence from the offices for the Matlock Bath Urban District Council, to a council store and then a night club. The ground floor is now occupied by the Peak District Mining Museum and a Tourist Information Centre. The story of the museum is covered in Chapter 3.

In the space now occupied by the car park at the side there once stood a timber building where leather gloves were made. This burned down and damaged gloves were found when excavating the floor in the Peak District Mining Museum.

Adam's and Vallance's Museum, Matlock Bath

This building stands on South Parade and originally sold fossils, minerals, spar ornaments and petrified objects. A notice declares this as the Old Museum, which was probably next door, although there is a record that suggests that it occupied the whole row of buildings which also included a hotel.

Right: Glove Factory, Matlock Bath. A rare photograph of the factory front after it had been burned out c.1930. A ladder has been placed to block access (Yeomans)
Above: Glove Factory, Matlock Bath. A photograph of inside this factory the day after the fire. Bundled gloves ready for despatch can be seen far right bottom. This factory stood in the car park next to the Pavilion (Yeomans)

Petrifying Wells, Matlock Bath

All located in Matlock Bath on or near to the A6 road. There were at least four such premises, ignoring the small amateur attempts made by some people, which were short lived and have faded into obscurity.

The biggest of these stood where there is a fountain at the end of some new shops north of the present Pavilion. This was visited by many thousands of people over the years, including the author (several times from 1943 on). The proprietor of this, from its inception in 1844, was a Mr Walker who also operated the boat hire business on the river.

Others stood in locations:

- South-east of All Saints Church run by a Mr Peter Smedley, the building still stands, painted white, on the road side.
- Opposite the National School, run by a Mr Joseph Boden, noted for the large number of horns of deer obtained from Chatsworth Park, this custom ceased in 1868.
- On the slope to the Old Bath Hotel operated by a Mr John Pearson and later by a Mr W Pearson. The skull and horns of a deer was placed in this well on the visit of Princess Victoria (later Queen Victoria) on her visit in October 1832.

Rivers and Streams

Also see Chapter 6.

Rivers are included here as they have for many years been a source of power and of more recent date an amenity enjoyed by anglers and canoe people alike.

River Derwent

The river enters the Matlocks from the north and exits to the south, where it eventually joins the River Trent at Church Wilne. The water is clear and peaty and supports many trout amongst other fish. It plays a significant part in the life of the Matlocks and is responsible for shaping the dale over the millennia.

Its life has not always been benign. Until the 20th century it was prone to flooding, inundating Matlock Bridge to a considerable depth. Fortunately those days are now over, as a flood prevention scheme of the 1980s has put paid to that. However, people still look anxiously from the bridge onto the water when in spate, out of concern that the river might rise too high for comfort.

Floods occurred in 1848, 1852, 1881, 1890, 1960, 1965 – the latter two floods are commemorated at the Hall Leys Park end of the footbridge from Old English Road to the park. These two floods occurred on consecutive days with an interval of five years: Sunday, 8 December 1960 and Thursday, 9 December 1965. It is sobering to look at the height the flood waters achieved, from which one can only imagine the devastation they caused.

Above: Memorial to P.C. Wright, Hall Ley Park - 1911. From Derbyshire Graves. Peter Naylor, Ashbourne 1992. Sketch by Jacqui Truman

The remedial works resulted in the deepening of the river under High Tor and the addition of flumes to the bridge in the 1970s.

It has also claimed many lives:

- 16 January 1852, a Dr James Cumming, surgeon of Buxton but born at Matlock Bath – his mother kept the Old Bath Hotel. He was visiting with his son and hired a boat in spite of a warning about the river's state. The boat was carried away to the Masson weir and it foundered on the rocks on the east side. The doctor then bravely tried to carry his son through the flood to the west bank but both were carried away, the bodies being found 14 days later near the river's junction with Lea Brook. It is said that his widow died as a consequence of this tragedy.(Bryan p.162)
- 11 August 1892 the Vicar of Farnsfield, Nottinghamshire, the Rev. Alexander McKee, had conducted members of the church choir to Matlock Bath. He hired a boat – with four passengers, a young woman and three boys – when it started to run downstream. In spite of a "danger" notice mounted on a buoy, the Reverend tried to bring the boat back to safety. The boat approached the goit to the wheel at Masson mill, he lost an oar but the young woman was able to disembark and wade to the shore. The boat capsized and one of the boys drowned. The Rev. McKee was propelled to the wheel, which was turning, and re-appeared on the downstream side no worse for his adventure.(Bryan ps. 164/5)
- 16 April 1897, a Good Friday, a party of four – two men and two women – hired a boat together with a boatman. They passed the danger signal and the boat was swept backwards over Masson Weir, which was running high. The occupants were thrown out. The body of one woman was found the same night a few hundred yards below the weir, one young man at Willersley the following day, the other young man some three hundred yards (274 metres) from the weir the same day, the remaining young woman was never found. The boatman escaped.(Bryan p.165/6)
- 5 April 1901, a Good Friday, six visitors hired a boat and a boatman. The boat capsized for no apparent reason. Two young men aged 21 and 18 and possibly others were drowned. This tragedy was witnessed by hundreds of visitors who had lined both banks to watch. (Bryan p.166)

Another life this river claimed was due to an act of heroism. In March 1911, PC Arthur Wright had the custody of a 17-year-old girl from Riber, who to escape justice, broke free and leaped into the river. PC Wright tried to save her and he drowned. The crime of which she was accused was the theft of £2.47. PC Wright, who was born at Apperknowle near Unstone, was buried at Dronfield on Thursday, 30 March 1911. A stone stands by the river in Hall Leys Park to commemorate this brave man.(DT 01.04.1911)

Footpaths

One of the great glories of the Matlocks is the footpaths which climb and traverse the hills. In an area renowned for such, those at Matlock Bath in particular are outstanding in that they offer superb views and are easy of access to those with strong legs. A group of notable footpaths are called Lovers' Walks. They are at river level along the east bank of the Derwent from the footbridge, south as far as the wall to Willersley Castle.The Lovers' Walks are a network of attractive woodland walks with fine views up the craggy hill side. This area laid out in 1749 is said to be the oldest public pleasure park in the county, even predating Derby Arboretum, the oldest public park in the country.

Crags and Tors

The Matlocks boast some very fine crags of limestone, which with their trees, provide a dramatic backdrop to the dale. These are on the east bank of the Derwent and are listed below in order, moving south from Matlock Bridge to Willersley:

- Pic Tor – a possible corruption of pig, it is a tradition that a pig market was held here.
- High Tor – this high cliff which rises from the river bank is high indeed and was once a favourite with suicides.
- Lovers' Leap – as there is no smoke without fire one assumes that this might have been the final act of unrequited lovers.
- Hag Rock – a diminutive for hanging rock, that is one with an overhang.
- Wild Cat Tors – is this a distant memory when wild cats actually occupied this area?

On the west bank are the following:

- Romantic Rocks or Dungeon Tors – originally in the grounds of the Heights of Jacob.
- Heights of Abraham, see Chapter 4.

Practicing rock climbing on the cliff below Pic Tor

11 EMPLOYMENT

The oldest industries in the area were agriculture and metal mining but there were others of some importance. At Lumsdale there were bleach works, bone milling, cotton spinning and corn milling; there was a corn mill and a paper mill in the parish most of which was supplanted by the advent of cotton spinning, originating in Cromford, an adjoining parish whose mills spilled over into Masson Dale and encouraged framework knitters in Matlock. There was also a hat making tradition based in the Matlocks, it being especially strong at Cromford and further away at Bradwell.

Lumsdale has been treated as a whole at the end of this chapter.

Agriculture

This would have comprised whatever the farmer could graze or grow in the more fertile valley bottoms as well as the impoverished moorland on the uplands. The story of agriculture was the fight against the acidity of the uplands, brought into use by the clearance of trees and the liming of the soil. The lime kiln was the key to the winning of the upland acidic soil, known as ericaceous soil today. This meant that cattle could be raised as well as the customary sheep. Oats and more recently barley were a favourite crop on this newly won land; we still have oatcakes made and consumed locally as a memento of times past.

Cotton Spinning

Also see Lumsdale at the end of this chapter.

This factory based industry arrived like a whirlwind in 1771 under the auspices of Richard Arkwright (later Sir Richard) of Preston, who built at Cromford the world's first water-powered mill for the spinning of cotton. Not the first mill or the first water spinning mill, these had already been in use for many years prior to Arkwright. What he did achieve was the invention of the factory system. His works are sometimes referred to as the birth of the Industrial Revolution; a dubious accolade given that in the period 1750-1850, many new and epoch making inventions were put into use all of which combined to create the "revolution." This mill was in the possession of Arkwright & Company until 1898 when it was sold to the English Sewing Cotton Company.

There is already a large literature about Arkwright and his works. His principal scene of activity was outside our area in the parish of Cromford, but he did build a large mill, Masson Mill in Masson Dale, Matlock Bath, which still exists and is now a museum and a successful shopping "village." This mill is of brick with stone quoins, with many additions. The original part has Venetian type windows and a cupola for housing a bell. The original timber water wheel has been replaced by a steel wheel, which can still be used to drive electric dynamos.

It is not part of the remit of this book to examine the life of Sir Richard Arkwright, his descendents and his other mills, these have been dealt with comprehensively elsewhere.(Naylor CaH p.54)

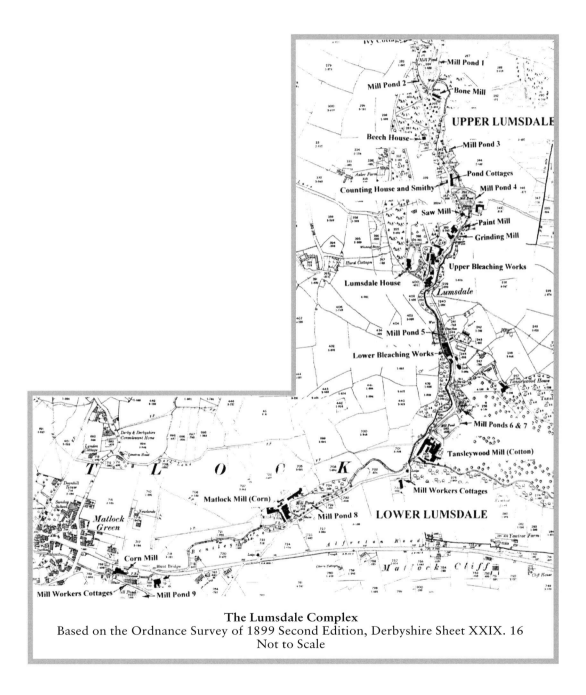

The Lumsdale Complex
Based on the Ordnance Survey of 1899 Second Edition, Derbyshire Sheet XXIX. 16
Not to Scale

Cotton Goods

Framework knitting, invented by the Rev. William Lee, Curate of Calverton in 1589 in the adjoining county of Nottinghamshire, spread throughout the East Midlands. The use of these frames was spread wide in the area with good examples of knitters' lofts in houses in Cromford, all growing rapidly after the arrival of Arkwright's thread. This was a home-based craft undertaken by the men; the women and children worked in the mills. Another home-based cotton product was the manufacture of cotton wick for candles. The Matlocks had a significant number of knitters which formed a lucrative trade.

Paper Manufacture

A paper mill stood near to where Masson Mill was later built. Both Masson Mill and the paper mill were originally on an island in the river. The backward curved weir was built to accommodate the mill wheels and a decoy was located at this place also. This mill was built and operated by George White and Robert Shore, starting work on Christmas Eve 1772. They had the right to water for 21 years with a lease for the land for 99 years at £1 per annum. This would be the date when the south weir at Masson Mill was built.

Robert Shore of Snitterton (the 5th Duke of Devonshire's mine agent at the Ecton Copper Mines, Staffordshire) who had embezzled £1000 and later £500 – for which he was fired and his assets sold off – nonetheless went on to buy the paper mill in question. At this time, George White of Winster (who had operated lead mines at Llwyn Llwyd in Wales in the 1780s) joined him as a partner. White owned the Lumb Smelting Mill near Tansley, which was water-powered from the Bentley Brook. They required water from a height sufficient to drive an overshot water wheel. This was accomplished by driving an adit or sough, the portal being near to the entrance of Cromford Court. A further unconfirmed report suggests that water was taken from Hagg Mine across the river, the water being pumped by a water wheel.

This operated until 1811 but by 1835 this mill was in the possession of a John Skidmore, there were numerous paper makers in Cromford at this time. In 1811, 40 people made brown, blue and white papers using old rope, brown paper, coarse cotton and waste rags. The paper during manufacture was pressed, separated and dried, taking two men to make 10 reams (5,000 sheets) a day. This mill stood where the present day car park to Masson Mill is located. During demolition work in 1955 the foundations of this were found.(Naylor CaH ps. 40/41)

Spinning Angora Wool

The original company, named Derwent Mills, stood on Smedley Street on a site which it shared with Victoria Hall, all swept away for housing. This company was founded in 1911, by a Frederick Samuel James Broome in partnership with a William Else whose mill Broome bought. This original mill stood in the Station Yard at Matlock Bridge. Broome was born in Leicester in 1866 of a Lea family. His grandmother was Agnes Tretheway from Cornwall, daughter of Samuel Tretheway, engineer to Richard Trevithick, who had employed him to build his engines and this activity brought him to Derbyshire. He built the water pressure engine that was raised from Wills Founder Lead Mine, Winster and is now preserved at the Peak District Mining Museum at Matlock Bath. He also built the Leawood Pumping Engine on the Cromford Canal at Wigwell, Cromford. Tretheway's daughter Agnes married a John Broome who became manager of John Smedley's Lea Mills, being a protégé of John Smedley who rated him so highly that he was named as his successor and inheritor. This was not to be as he fell out with Smedley over a religious matter.

The business was founded for the spinning of angora rabbit wool under the brand name of "Furida" and was hugely successful. At the outbreak of World War I, the factory turned to making balaclava helmets, gloves and scarves for the military. In 1931 it was taken over by Paton & Baldwin who during World War II became a satellite of another company for making engineers' taps and dies. Paton and Baldwin also had a satellite mill at Lumsdale.

The Broome family built their residence known as Westlea, at the corner of Chesterfield Road and Asker Lane.(Jackson In Lit 1987)

Cloth Weaving

The outbuildings at Hurst Farm were used for the weaving of cloth on a fairly large scale in the 18th century, the thread coming from a fulling mill in Lumsdale nearby. Tradition has it that a medieval trackway passed by this farm from Tansley continuing on to Matlock Bank.

Ornaments

In an area blessed with attractive minerals it would be expected that these would be worked to make ornaments. Whilst the chief village for this industry was Ashford-in-the-Water, Derby, Bakewell and Matlock Bath undertook their share. Some of this ware was imported from the continent, particularly Belgium and collectors are bedevilled with this as it is virtually impossible to tell our local craft from others.

In Matlock Bath this small industry was started by a Mr Mawe, a mineralogist to whom William Adam was apprenticed c.1820. On the death of Mawe in 1829 a Mr Vallance – who spent 44 years in the marble trade – continued with the management of the business on behalf of the widow for two years when William Adam took the business over. This was the same Adam who wrote *The Gem of the Peak* and he received the patronage of the then Duke of Devonshire. A skilful engraver joined Adam, Edward Bird, who reproduced sketches of moonlit scenes by engraving on to black marble, similar to scraperboard work. A Richard Brown joined Mawe in 1811 and invented a method for sawing marble, using steam engines at his Derby Works. It reached its zenith in 1835 but by the end of the 19th century it was a shadow of its former self.

Local and imported stones were turned by lathes into vases and the like. Use was made of local stone and minerals such as black marble from mines at Ashford-in-the-Water (not a true marble but a dense black limestone which accepts a high polish), Hopton Wood Stone from a quarry near to Rider Point (a grey limestone which accepts a high polish), Blue John (a highly decorative blue and yellow fluorspar from Castleton) and other colourful "marbles" from mines in Derbyshire, such as Duke's red, Rosewood Marble (from a mine in Shacklow Woods near to Sheldon) and a chrinoidal limestone from Ricklow Quarry in Lathkill Dale near to Monyash. The largest source of black marble in Derbyshire was from the Rookery and Arrock Mines, Ashford-in-the-Water, though the quality of the latter was not as good as the former.(Tomlinson J M ps 41-47) (Ford & Rieuwerts ps.94,100,107)

Some beautiful items were produced and many houses boast examples of this work. A favourite was black marble clock cases. Alabaster from Chellaston was also worked into bowls, candlesticks and similar ornaments. For more about Adam see Chapter 9.

Bleaching

The bleaching works was sited at Lumsdale and at the turn of the 19th century was run by Mr Richard Farnsworth and his two sons Messrs. G H and E H Farnsworth. They bleached any cotton cloth from tapes to broadcloth by a process considered to be modern at the time, comprising boiling in a solution of lime and soda, beating, boiling kiers, rewashing and beating and finally into a "Patent Vacuum Bleaching Keir." They served customers as far apart as Nottingham, Leicester, Coventry, Derby, Loughborough and Tamworth. Some of these names suggest that they supplied the lace industry among others.

Flour Milling

The manoral corn mill probably stood on the Bentley Brook where the road to Tansley bridges it (Hunt's Bridge). Of more recent date the Bailey family operated flour mills at Lumbs Dale, their house and mill still stand. Also see Lumsdale at the end of this chapter.

W Evans & Son (Jewellers) Ltd, Dale Road

This business is probably the oldest still operating in Matlock Bridge. The company originated at Wirksworth in 1850, founded by William Evans. In 1893 his son Walter acquired a lock-up shop in Matlock Bridge and a year later had premises built in the current location, this being an empty plot between existing buildings. They have been in the same location for 110 years, their large bracket clock being a local feature. The current owner is David Goward FGA whose paternal great grand-father was the original Walter Evans.

M Wright & Sons (aka Tinker Wright)

This is by far the longest established business in the Matlocks, being founded in 1870 by Michael "Tinker" Wright, who had an outstanding reputation for his skilled craftsmanship both as a general engineer and a tin or white smith. He established his business in the same location as it is today at 96 Smedley Street, Matlock Bank and initially specialised in making small hydropathic baths such as those for the treatment of knees, feet, elbows etc, as well as Sitz baths in both tinned steel and copper. He expanded this business to include general hardware and locksmithing. His son Joseph "Jo" Wright took the business over using the same traditions as his founding father and, in turn, the business passed to Joseph's sons – Leslie who kept the shop, and Maurice who undertook the white smithing. Maurice had the reputation of being the only man in the area at one time who could weld aluminium.

Both Leslie and Maurice retired in 1982. The present owner is Derek Goodall, son-in-law of Leslie and, whilst they no longer undertake smithing, they are ironmongers of some repute with a stock of 100,000 plus items; Derek is still a locksmith in a more sophisticated age than his predecessors. There was a time when this company exported white ware to the world, mostly the colonies, for expatriate Britons who treated themselves with hydropathy. The word "tinker" has dubious connotations but was originally meant for one who repaired kettles, pans, etc.(In Lit Goodall)

Heny, Loveday & Keighly

This firm of solicitors is also well established having been founded in 1902. It was founded by Charles Heny, having taken over the practice of Walter Harris of Matlock and Matlock Bath. Originally this firm was located on Dale Road, later moving into offices above the Matlock and District Gas Company on Bank Road, they were the first tenants in a new building of 1928. At the time of writing the firm is run by Christopher Handforth, Christopher Gale and Richard Roberts assisted by Charles Wildgoose.(MM 18.07.02)

Quarrying

Also see Chapter 3.

Stone was worked in Station Yard using stone from Lumdsale, Tansley, Farley and Ashover. The masons worked outdoors in all weathers suffering from "Masons' Complaint", a form of silicosis, which shortened their lives. Many of the grindstones made here went to Sheffield for the sharpening of cutlery and edge tools, with wood pulp stones travelling to Scandinavia and Switzerland. When work had to stop in the worst weather, the masons were laid off without pay. Local villagers held collections to provide food and soup kitchens for them.

Omya UK Ltd, 112/118 Dale Road, Matlock

Various limestone quarries amalgamated to make a conglomerate named Derbyshire Stone Ltd under the leadership of John Hadfield. They built a corporate headquarters building in Harveydale Quarry (now Derbyshire County Council) and named it John Hadfield House, the entrance of which was flanked by two stone lions rescued from a theatre in Sheffield.

This business was taken over by Tarmac of Wolverhampton who sold it to Croxton & Garry in 1991, a division of Omya UK Ltd. It became Omya, Croxton & Garry and is now known as Omya UK Ltd, a subsidiary of Omya AG, Offringen, Zurich, Switzerland – founded in 1884.(In Lit Elaine Davenport)

Omya at Matlock operate the coatings and adhesives division and is the company's central engineering department. Local works under their control are the Middleton Limestone Mines at Middleton-by-Wirksworth and the Hopton Plant near to the latter.(In Lit Elaine Davenport and www.omya.co.uk)

Lawn Mowers

A firm called Poyser's Patents had premises in the station yard at Matlock Bridge, with a large chimney and originally used as a rag mill. They made lawn mowers and a strange mangle, which would iron clothes without breaking the buttons. They moved to the Dimple in the 1920s. This became the origins of the Qualcast Lawn Mower. The Qualcast company later expanded into malleable castings and in recent times were taken over to become Atco Qualcast part of the Bosch Group.(Arkle p.12)

Salt

At the rear of Dimple House was a building where women were employed to create the twist that contained salt, common in packets of potato crisps years ago. When they expanded to employing twelve women they had to move to larger premises at Scarthin where they earned 3d (1.5 p) per 100 twists.(Arkle p.29)

Noel Wheatcroft & Son

This business of estate agents was founded in 1923 by the person under whose name it operated until 2002, when it was sold to Scargill Mann & Company. Part of the business continued as Matlock Auction Gallery, occupying the Old Picture Palace on Dale Road, Matlock Bridge, where antiques and the like fall under the hammer of Jane Kinnear.(Peak Times 14.06.02) The directors are Richard and Jane Kinnear, and Leon Wheatcroft.(www.wheatcroft-noel.co.uk)

The Two Farmers

Writing in 1964, Francis (Frank) Leo Farmer recalled "I came to Matlock as a boy by pony and trap, from Litton near Tideswell, 1897, to take my first job away from home at the age of 13 years" and so began a double dynasty of successful businessmen.

His acquaintanceship with motor vehicles began at the garage of Guy le Blanc Smith at Matlock Bath, who ran Spa Buses. After service in World War I, Frank returned to a job driving for the Royal Hotel, Matlock Bath, prior to setting up a car hire business with his brother Charlie, c.1921. Their first premises were adjacent to the tram depot at the end of Wellington Street, Matlock Bank. They invested in two vehicles and set on Jim and George Briddon as drivers. Charabancs were next on the shopping list, which were in use seven days a week taking visitors to the hydros on country runs.

They then found a niche in undertaking to handle those who died at the hydros, buying an Austin hearse in c.1930. This entailed delivering the deceased to their home towns all over Britain as well as serving local undertakers such as Greatorex, also still in existence.

By 1933 they had built a new garage on Smedley Street (now part of Derbyshire County Council). Also in the 1930s Charlie Farmer started a different business from a timber shed on their petrol pump forecourt, now Farmers' used car lot. From this shed he would charge accumulators for the public, the only means available for powering the first radios, or wireless as they were then called. This led to the founding of the electrical goods shop on Causeway Lane. Meanwhile Frank had bought a Rolls-Royce motor car for use at weddings and funerals, he dubbed it his "match and despatch" assignments. In 1936/7 Frank expanded into car sales.

At the outbreak of World War II, they had to retrench, selling their Rolls-Royce to Ashover Hydro for £100! Charlie's son John spent five years of the war repairing vehicles at an Army Auxiliary workshop on Bakewell Road, Matlock Bridge. Later they acquired their first agency for Volkswagen, and later still the dealership for the Rootes Group. This expansion led to the building of their workshop off Smith Road on land forming part of Malvern House, then owned by Smedleys. John's son runs the business, which now has the agency for Subaru and Proton cars.

Meanwhile, Charlie had served in World War II as a Warrant Officer in the Royal Army Service Corps from which he learned organisational skills that would help him in running his new business from a shop on Smedley Street. By 1949 he had expanded to a branch shop in Bakewell. In 1956 he bought a shop on Causeway Lane previously a private lending library.

At this time television was coming into its own but in this area the signal varied from poor to impossible. To overcome this, Charlie Farmer erected masts at the high points in the Matlocks linking the signals collected to homes by cable; this must be a very early instance of cable television. The erection of the BBC mast on Stanton Moor overcame this difficulty in 1973. The business grew apace dealing with televisions and white goods and they had to expand into the adjoining premises in 1980, then occupied by Matlock Building Supplies Company. The business is now run by his son Robin Farmer, the white goods department being under the control of Robin's son Jason.(In. Lit. 26.10.02 Jason, Jonathan and Robin Farmer and Julie Bunting 29.11.02) www.cfarmerltd.co.uk

Lumsdale

This valley cut by the Bentley Brook has a wealth of industries both past and present. It is a veritable mine of information which reflects the industrial revolution well. This revolution was firmly placed in the countryside, and this is certainly true of Lumsdale.

Its industries were many and varied from lead smelting to cotton spinning and the author has prepared a map to explain the diversity of these works, which is included in this book. They all relied on the brook for motive power and the water was used for dyeing, bleaching and driving water wheels. The brook runs from Matlock Moor to join the Derwent at Matlock Green and in so doing it falls 371 ft (113 m) from Bentley Bridge – which carries the Matlock to Chesterfield road – to Hunt's Bridge at Matlock Green. However the industrial portion starts just south of the Chesterfield Road and finishes at Hunt's Bridge.

The parish boundary between Matlock and Tansley traces its route down the middle of Bentley Brook along a third of the dale. It was necessary therefore to include the buildings on the Tansley side as this story would be incomplete without them. The following features have been identified following the brook downstream from Upper Lumsdale.

Ivy Cottage

The most northern dwelling prior to 1900 in Upper Lumsdale built in the "Paxton" style – note the windows – it was sold by auction in 1929 for £230, the occupant being a Mrs Crowther who paid £16.8s (£16.40p) per annum rent.

Mill Pond 1

Silted up.

This was one of three such ponds dug to create a store of water for the larger mills downstream – Upper Bleaching Works, Lower Bleaching Works and a Cotton Mill. The piscatorial rights of this pond were let in 1929 to the Sheffield Trout Angling Association at a rental of £12.10s (£12.50) per annum along with the other two ponds mentioned above.

Mill Pond 2

Silted up.

Adjacent to the Mill Pond 1 and fed by a leat, now lost, from the brook upstream of Mill Pond 1. This was dug in the 1780s to serve a Bone Mill.

Bone Mill

Calcined bones were ground here for the pottery industry and for fertilizer. Fed from Mill Pond 2.
Now mostly lost due to quarrying for the masonry.

Beech House

This house was originally two semi-detached cottages known as Beech Cottages. In the sale of 1929 the two cottages fetched £300, a Mrs Kate Saunders and a Mr James Toplis paid £11.4s (£11.20) and £13.8s.8d (£13.42) rent per annum respectively. It was converted into a single residence by the Doctors John and D "Totty" Holden.

Mill Pond 3

Silted up.
Water still crashes over the ruined sluice here.

Pond Cottages

A lead smelter was built here in 1749 by a lease granted to a George Wall and John Twigg – being transferred in 1759 to a Matthew Spark Whitfield, Joseph Boote and Lydia Woodward by Mary and Lydia Twigg executors of the Lumsdale Estate; a John Wall received £200. In June 1762, Whitfield,

Boote and Woodward assigned one half – the northern half – of the smelter to George Norman of Winster with two ore houses, counting house and a smithy adjacent to the cupola. Whitfield was given the other half – the southern half. In May 1770 Norman died leaving his half to his nephews White and Swettenham, also a smelter at Winster. They acquired the other half in May 1771 and sold the lot to a William Longsden of Eyam for £350. The latter sold it to a William Milne of Ashover in June 1790. In 1789 the cupola was converted into five cottages for Watts, Lowe & Co. later to six cottages for workers at the mills downstream. These have recently been renovated unsympathetically using PVC guttering and down pipes,

A "Lummus" Mill is believed to have been near to this site in the use of a Robert Cliffe in 1674 and a Mr Hawley in 1736, who occupied an upper and lower mill in the dale, leased from a Mrs Turner of Bonsall, later to be gifted to the Bonsall School Trustees. One of these was used by a Joseph Whitfield. This was prior to 1774. It was then let to White and Swettenham (see above) who converted the building into a cupola and slag mill, the latter for refining the slag produced whilst smelting to extract as much lead metal as possible. By 1790 both smelters were out of use. This is now ruinous and is known as a Bobbin Mill or Hawley's Shop.

This is probably the mill referred to by Bryan as Lumb's Mill or Lomas's Mill, where "the profits (were) paid to the Lords of the Manor" c.1700. About 80 years later, a twenty-second part of the profits were paid to the Lords of the Manor in return for the use of "all the buildings, weirs, goits (leats), and appertainances, and six acres (2.4 hectares) on which to get stone to repair the buildings, for rebuilding or repairing the houses, bridges, walls, fences, and other works." This suggests more than one mill, possibly including the mills just downstream from the lead smelter. The six acres referred to is most certainly the area known as Bentleybrook Quarries, which had a cartway to the dale.(Bryan ps 11 & 92) The building across the lane was the counting house and smithy now converted into a residence known as "Pine Trees".

The flues were taken a little distance to a chimney, whence the poisonous fumes were ejected to the atmosphere. The long horizontal flue was for condensing the fumes onto the walls for collection later for re-smelting, a common practice. The access door to this flue can still be seen.

Mill Pond 4

Conserved by The Arkwright Society 1983.
The third of the big ponds, also known as Farm Dam. Built in the 1830s it was the last of the ponds to be dug due to an increasing requirement for water for bleaching purposes. A disused quarry lies under the water, consequently this pond is very deep. This pond of clear water is a considerable asset to the area complete with resident mallards, seat benches and a waste basket. The sluice is intact and a waterfall is created from it.

Saw Mill

Conserved by The Arkwright Society
Originally a crushing mill for lead oxides for paint manufacture later to be adapted for sawing timber.
The wheel pit can be seen along with the now dry leats. A byrr grinding stone can be seen beyond this building made from chert, which is found at Bakewell. From here on, a path with steps and handrails has been created by The Arkwright Society to help people to explore this incredible backwater down the steep hill.

Paint Mill

Conserved by The Arkwright Society.
The site of a corn mill dating from the 1600s, this mill was adapted to the grinding of barytes,

which was dried and bagged inside the premises. Barytes was a by-product from lead mining, being a gangue mineral. A grindstone can be seen in this building as can the wheel pit.

Grinding Mill

Conserved by The Arkwright Society
   Also the site of an old corn mill, this was also adapted for grinding minerals found in lead mines, mostly the ochres for paint manufacture. The wheel pit is evident. The Bentley Brook at this point is a crashing waterfall with a drop of about 66 ft (20 m) and is a spectacular sight. It must be the highest waterfall in the county.

Upper Bleaching Works

Used as a plant yard. Originally started as a cotton spinning mill by Watts, Lowe & Co. later to be taken over by Garnet & Farnsworth. The sale of 1929 refers to the water wheel and housing, suggesting that it might have been in use at that time. There was a steam engine here which operated a wagon way on rails to connect with the Lower Bleaching Works. Originally water powered, steam was introduced later.

Lumsdale House

Originally named "Lumsdale". This house boasted an ornamental pond and a swimming pool.

Mill Pond 5

This small mill pond was used as a buffer for guiding the water from the brook and to the wheels of the Lower Bleaching Works.

Lower Bleaching Works

This has been much expanded in the 20th century, some of it out of character. It is now occupied by several small companies. Originally used for spinning cotton by Watts, Lowe & Co and in more recent times part occupied by Paton and Baldwin. The sale particulars in 1929 referred to the wheel and its casing as existing. Originally water powered but steam powered later. This mill connected to the Upper Bleaching Works by means of a wagonway.

Mill Workers' Cottages

There is a single terrace of solid, stone-built cottages which lie behind and overlook the Lower Bleaching Works.

Mill Workers Cottages

A terrace of stone houses built to the standard Arkwright design, now occupied as homes.

Mill Ponds (6 & 7)

Both silted up. These were feeders to the Cotton Mill

Tansleywood Mill (Cotton)

In 1783, Messrs Osgathorpe & Prestwidge entered into a lease from Banks-Hodgkinson of Ashover for a Bump Mill for manufacturing candlewick yarn using flax waste. This venture failed and the business was taken over by a Miss Francis Willoughby in 1792 who sold the site to Sir Joseph Banks – a founder of Kew Botanical Gardens, President of the Royal Society and with Captain Cooke on the *Endeavour* – who let it at a lease of £42 per annum. Cotton spinning was also undertaken from circa 1840. The lease was then taken by a Messrs Thomas & Edward Radford who undertook bleaching, candlewick manufacture and cotton spinning on the site, to be taken over by Messrs Fred & Harry Drabble in 1889 – one time managers at Lea Mills. This new partnership undertook garnetting, the recovery of wool and cotton waste for re-spinning. In 1912 the Drabbles bought the mill and formed a limited company – with the two sons Ernest and Fred as directors – with the idea of undertaking the whole process from garnetting to bleaching, dyeing, drying, warehousing, etc. In 1952 the business was willed to Fred's son Kenneth Drabble.

By this time they employed nearly 400 persons who came from far afield to work in this factory that had an outstanding relationship with its employees. By the 1980s this mill needed 200,000 gallons (90,700 litres) per day of water from the brook and mill ponds. In 1988 it came under the wing of Albert Martin Holdings of Sutton-in-Ashfield, Nottinghamshire who invested £1.5 million pounds in the business. Unhappily it had to close in July 1999. But a new life for it is anticipated, see the Epilogue.

One final note about this mill, it can boast having dyed all the shirts for the Soccer World Cup teams! Water powered originally later to be steam powered. See Chapter 9 for the Drabble family.

Mill Pond 8

This mill pond served Matlock Corn Mill.

Matlock Mill

This mill ground corn and was owned by the Bailey family. See Chapter 9 about the Bailey family.

Mill Pond 9

This feeds another corn mill at Hunts Bridge but the water supply is not from the Bentley Brook.

Corn Mill

This corn mill is in Matlock Green on the site that was most likely where the manorial mill stood. Whilst this was fed by the Bentley Brook originally, it later drew its water from a mill pond where the water level is higher than the brook.

Mill Workers Cottages

A terraced row of very fine cottages, all well kept with front gardens and extension gardens on the opposite side of the brook with a single footbridge for access.

Watts, Lowe & Co

This company were investors, typical of their time. They bought the Lumsdale Estate from the Bound family until Watts, Lowe & Company bought it. These entrepreneurs had investments in Bristol, London and Reading. They went into bankruptcy in 1803, when their interests were taken over by the Garton family who sold it in lots in 1929.

Sources for Lumsdale

Bunting J   *Peak Advertiser*   Volume 20, No. 19   23 September 2002
                          "A new age dawns for Drabbles Mill"

Charlton Christopher   Lumbsdale Tour Notes

Drabble E P   Matlock Field Club, 2nd Report 1972 – Tansley and Lumsdale Mills pp14/15

Holden Dr "Totty"   In Lit. September 2002

Marchant Brookes & Co with Hodgkinson & Son Auctioneers of Matlock

                          Particulars of Sale of the Lumsdale Estate, 6 June 1929

Spencer B   *Reflections*   April 1995 p.26

Willis Dr Lyn   *Bulletin of the Peak District Mines Historical Society*
                          Cupola Lead Smelting Sites in Derbyshire, 1737-1900
                          Volume 4, Part 1 pp105/6

William Twigg (Matlock) LTD

William Twigg began his business career in 1905 and was born in 1881 at Rushley Lodge, near Flash Dam, Matlock.

He was a farmer's son, who developed an interest in second hand plant and machinery and had an eye for a speculative deal.

He borrowed money to buy Slack Quarry, Ashover for his first major purchase and he set up his first office in Station Yard, Matlock, from where he bought, refurbished and resold stone crushers, separators and quarry plant - some being exported to quarries all over the world.

He first moved to Bakewell Road, when he rented premises on the site of the old bus station.

Over the next few years he continued to speculate, always being interested in a deal if he thought he could make a profit. During the 1920's he notably purchased Wingerworth Hall - taking two years to demolish and recycle the material.

He also purchased a North Wales Mine and associated cottages for demolition and recycling.

In the 1930's, he purchased Ilam Hall (now a Youth Hostel), and resold it to Sir Robert McDougall, the flour magnate. Followed by Mill Close Lead Mine, Darley Bridge, one of the largest of its type in the world, to recycle all the machinery and equipment.

His biggest gamble in those early days was when he tendered for and purchased the Manifold Valley Railway - nine miles of track, engines and stations - justified by immerdiate resale to one of the other bidders at a considerable profit.

During the 1920's and 1930's he purchased land on both sides of Bakewell Road enabling the building of the forerunner to today's Dimple Road office and stores and the establishment of today's Steelyard operation.

Harry Allen joined the company in 1934 and was responsible for developing the Engineers Stores on Dimple Road - subsequently marrying William's only daughter Doris. Denis Upton joined the company a little later and worked with William Twigg to develop the steel construction side of the business.

The company erected new quarry buildings and plant all over Derbyshire, and further afield even in Scotland - at Ballidon, Caulden Low, Longcliffe and Perth to name a few.

The company was incorporated as a private limited company in 1946, under the stewardship of directors William Twigg, his wife Florence Twigg, daughter Doris Allen and son-in-law Harry Allen.

In 1958 William Twigg died, leaving his daughter Doris, Harry and Denis Upton who was now a director to continue the development through 1960 - 1980.

Gerald Newton joined the company in 1957, became a director in 1973 and retired in 2002 after more than 40 years service alongside first Harry and then his son David in the Engineers Merchants Division.

David Allen, current managing director and grandson of William Twigg, joined the company in 1968 and worked alongside his father Harry throughout the 1970's, before taking over the reins in the early 1980s.

John Shipman joined the company as a director in 1980, taking over responsibility for Steel and Fabrication in early 1982, and has established the company as a recognised quality steel stockholder and further developed the fabrication division.

The company now employs more than 60 staff and operates as three distinct divisions - Engineers and General Merchants, Steel Stockholders and Structural and Fabrication Engineers - with a customer base of some 3000 accounts mainly in a 30-mile radius of Matlock - but even sending goods to the Falklands.

The company today is very different to that pioneered by William Twigg in 1905, but as it approaches it's 100th anniversary - he would be justifiably proud of his legacy.

The opening of the extension for W Twigg, Bakewell Road 1985. The two men using the bolt cutter to cut a chain are Roy McFarland and Arthur Cox. The others are left to right: Mr & Mrs Allen, Mr & Mrs David Allen and their daughter Nichola (Derbyshire County Council, Libraries and Heritage and Wm Twigg (Matlock) Ltd)

Including Newspapers
The earliest record of a school was for 1647, of which we know little. This was probably a church school endowed by local moneyed people. There is a record of a technical school located on Dale Road, Matlock Bridge, founded in 1891. The students were taught fruit growing, gardening, dress-making, cookery, shorthand, electricity and magnetism, geology, physiography, geometry, building construction, drawing and painting "in all its branches" whichever the students chose to pursue. A broad and generous education! In September 1900 the evening continuation classes of the School Board joined with the technical school, anticipating a government decree of 1902 for the amalgam-ation of all such schools.(Bryan p.72)

The earlier schools suffered from the children being absent for hay making, potato picking and – very local this – bilberry picking, and other farm necessities, a situation not experienced for many years now with the advent of farm machinery.

Matlock Town

The first modern school was one for girls built in 1816, which was enlarged three years later to take boys. This is an early school that foresaw the Education Acts which came later in this century. This school was replaced in 1870 and enlarged nine years later to become the Matlock Town Church of England Primary School.

The old school at Matlock Town, now converted to apartments, was founded from a legacy of George Spateman's, dated 1647, for a Grammar School later to be the Matlock Town Endowed School. By 1817 this legacy was worth £24 per annum, 80% of which was paid to a teacher. In 1870 a new school – referred to above – was built as a consequence of the Elementary School Act of 1870, being enlarged to take 250 pupils in 1889 at a cost of £500. It had accommodation for 50 children.(Bryan p.45-6) This combined school was to become the St Giles Church of England Primary School, which in 1992 moved to new premises higher up Starkholmes Road on the slope of Riber Hill. The original school has been converted into a public house and apartments. This school is now in a new, well-designed building near to the old Charles White School on the slopes of Riber Hill.

Matlock Bath

John Allen (see Chapter 9) founded a "middle class boarding school" in his home at Gilderoy House in the later years of his life c.1840-50.

The National School between the main road and the river was built in 1853, having provision for 200 boys and girls with 70 infants. How did they fit them all in? The master's residence was in the basement almost at river level. It also doubled for the Sunday School associated with Holy Trinity Church.(Bryan p.177) In November 1972 this school moved to a new building at the bottom of Clifton Road, not only changing its surroundings but also its teaching methods.(MM 28.11.02) It is now called the Holy Trinity Church of England (Controlled) Primary School.

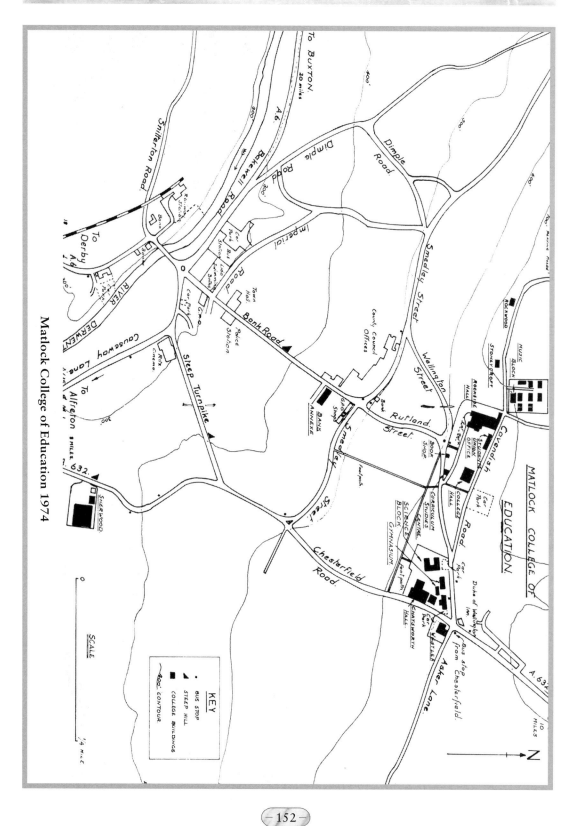

Matlock College of Education 1974

KEY

- BUS STOP
- STEEP HILL
- COLLEGE BUILDINGS
- CONTOUR

SCALE

Matlock Bank

By 1873, the accommodation of the elementary school at Matlock Town was not large enough and it was proposed to build a second school at Matlock Bank. John Smedley led a group of non-conformists with a view to building a school for at least 100 pupils. A poll held on 14 February 1874 was defeated and the venture failed. The matter was revived two years later and a foundation stone was laid by Mrs James Arkwright of Cromford on 6 November 1875. This was a mixed school known then as the Church National School. The site was purchased from the Rev. John Wolley and exists today as the All Saints Church of England (Controlled) School. The building cost £1,000 and opened to pupils on 10 August 1875.

A new classroom block costing £700,000 (compare this with the cost of the original school at £1,000), was officially opened on 27 May 2002 by an ex-caretaker, Eunice Hickman, who had retired from the school after 29 years of service.(MM 30.05.02) This replaced some Terrapin units dating from the 1960s.

At the time of writing a new school is under construction having a six-classroom block all on one site on Dimple Road.

Matlock Green

This was formerly a Congregational Chapel, see Chapter 2. It was named the Matlock National School to be absorbed by the Matlock School Board, opening on 23 September 1896. This school was built at a cost of £5,400.(Bryan ps.240/1) Situated on School Road, it was built in 1897 to take an increase of pupils in the town. It was later renamed the Matlock County Infants, then the Matlock Junior and Infants as two schools, which amalgamated in 1999 to make it the Castle View Primary School.

Ernest Bailey Grammar School

This philanthropic man was the Bailey of Bailey's Flour Mill at Lumsdale. He established his grammar school on New Street, Matlock Bank. This school was founded in 1924 on co-educational lines in a building that had been a hydro. This meant that the local children did not have to travel to either Belper or Bakewell by train every day as Allison Uttley had to.

To gain access to this school one had either to pay or win a much sought after scholarship. This school took pupils up to the School Certificate of Education, later taking them to Matriculation at the age of 16, something the writer remembers well when in Nottingham. The cost of uniforms and sports gear had also to be found. Sports were undertaken on Cromford Meadows. This school boasted an excellent rugby football team, which still exists as Matlock Rugby Club. This school combined with the Charles White School and both moved to the new Highfields School at Lumsdale.

Charles White Secondary School

Named after the local Councillor and Member of Parliament this CLASP building was erected in the 1950s on the slopes of Riber Hill. This combined with Ernest Bailey Grammar School and moved to Highfields School, Lumsdale.

Presentation Convent School

This school is located in the old Chesterfield House Hydro, which was occupied in May 1927 by a Roman Catholic teaching order. Their foundation house was the Presentation Convent, Madras, India, itself founded in January 1842. This is one of 16 such convents with the same root in Madras, of which seven are in India and three were in England but two – Pickering, North Yorkshire and Penzance, Cornwall – united with Matlock.

This came about when Mother Xavier Murphy, Mother General of the Presentation Sisters of south India, whilst visiting Matlock, was asked by the then parish priest of Matlock to make a foundation in Matlock. This she did by transferring the novitiate from Liverpool. The school opened in September 1927 with 25 pupils, increasing to over 100 by 1939. By 1945 it was full to capacity with 157 pupils. Additional temporary classrooms had to be built to cater for the increase in pupils. Permanent buildings with a new chapel were erected in 1956/7, opening in May 1958.

In September 1962 the sisters bought the old Lilybank Hydro, which allowed them to separate the juniors from the seniors, the former transferring to Lilybank, which was named the Nagle Preparatory School –after Nano Nagle (1718-84) the Irish foundress of the Presentation Convent. In 1990 the school at Lilybank was closed, along with the secondary school at Chesterfield House, and St Joseph's Roman Catholic Voluntary Aided School was opened in the grounds of the convent. In December 1993 the convent became a Care Centre.(Brown and Gold ps. 2, 3, 11, 17, 18)

Glenorchy School, Matlock Bath

There was a school room associated with the chapel from the inception of the latter but it was small and inconvenient. Subscriptions were made in 1849 for the building of a larger school room which was duly built and opened on 26 June 1850.(Bryan p.180)

Starkholmes

A National School was built for the children of Starkholmes opening in 1879. A forerunner of this school was a small church school dating from seven years before.

Other short-lived schools

There were a few short-lived schools dotted about Matlock Bank. According to Kelly's Directory there were the following and there were probably more:

Cavendish School, Smedley Street, Matlock Bank

This mixed school was in operation by 1895 and operated by an Edward V W Bynnes-Kingsley. A news report in 1918 reported a "Disgraceful escapade of a gang of Matlock High School Boys" assumed to be from this establishment.

Matlock Garden School

This was located on Rutland Street, Matlock Bank for mixed boarders. In the 1930s it became part of Matlock Modern School.

Woodlands Preparatory School

Located on Cavendish Road, Matlock Bank in the 1940s it soon moved to the old Oldham House Hydro. Father Leroy a Belgian priest lived here and acted as an interpreter for refugees from his mother country during World War II. This was the beginning of the Misses Whites' Woodland School.

Riber Castle

See Chapter 10.

Matlock Teacher Training College.

This college occupied the old Hydros (Rockside and Chatsworth House) with several purpose built premises on Wellington Street. The acquisition of these old hydros is dealt with in Chapter 5. See the map for the complete number of buildings eventually occupied. This college was closed in 1988.

Many teachers received their training in this college and its closure was much lamented. Its role has been taken over by Derby University.

Highfields School, Upper Lumsdale

This newer school took over the role of the following schools:

-   Ernest Bailey Grammar School (New Street Matlock now the County Records Office)
-   Charles White Secondary Modern School (Starkholmes)
-   John Turner School (Darley Dale)

Of these only the first two were within the area covered by this history. After much political wrangling it was decided to establish a new school on the Highfields, Upper Lumsdale to create a single comprehensive school in new buildings on a green field site, although the Ernest Bailey had an annexe here for the years 7 and 8 students. Before the school was finally built an inspirational head teacher, Brian Marshall, was appointed in June 1980 having had experience as a head teacher at the Atherstone School, north Warwickshire with experience at both grammar and comprehensive schools. His first battle was the opposition from the parents of the grammar school pupils wishing to retain the grammar school mystique and the parents of the pupils from the Darley Dale school citing the loss of a focal point for their community. Fortunately, the new head had time before Highfields opened to build bridges, mend fences and visit the schools that would be providing the students of the future.

For the first two years five buildings were used, plus a playing field at Cromford Meadows. These buildings were Ernest Bailey annexe, Charles White, and two of John Turner's – Parkway and Greenaway Lane. This must have been a logistical nightmare. The new head tried to visit every site on every school day as well as his many other duties. By September 1984 everyone had settled down in their new school which took the years 9 and above, with Starkholmes taking years 7 and 8, with approximate pupil populations of 900-1,000 and 500 respectively.

The school is an excellent design by Derbyshire County Architect. It was built by Shand Building of Darley Dale, whose director Barry Whieldon is commemorated by the naming of the Assembly Hall as the Whieldon Hall. He died prematurely before the school was finished. Since those early days the school has developed a reputation second-to-none as an educational establishment with a strong emphasis on music under the tutelage of Joe Clarke, a local musician of note.(In Lit. Marshall and Highfields Mercury 18.09.1992)

Tawney House Adult Education Centre, Matlock Green

The early history of this establishment is covered in Chapter 10. The old institute was taken over as an adult educational centre in 1962 and named Tawney House after Professor R H Tawney. He was a pioneer of the Workers' Educational Association (WEA), who conducted classes in Lancashire and the Potteries in the early 20th century. He was a social philosopher as well as a historian of repute.

The building is run by a Management Committee with representatives from the local authorities, the WEA and at one time from Nottingham University, who operated classes here as part of their extra-mural studies, Department of Adult Education. Over the years Tawney House has offered a vast array of subjects and has been a source for adult learning which is the envy of others.(Tawney House) Adult education is also available from Derby University's presence in the Matlocks as well as local authority organised courses at local schools.

Library

The house currently used as a public library was originally Firs House, which had extensive gardens fronting Causeway Lane and close to Firs Parade of which there is only a remnant left. Originally it was the home of the Else family and later became a surgery for a Dr Hans Fleming who did his rounds in an Errol Johnson motor car.(Arkle p.30) The original stables and hay loft are obvious to the rear of this building.

Newspapers

Matlock Mercury (and West Derbyshire News)

This popular local paper dedicated to the area has been in existence since the late 1940s, when, until October 2000, it was printed at the home of Ella Smith at 24 Bakewell Road. Originally an entertainments guide, it adopted its present form in the mid-1950s. In the late 1970s, Mrs Smith sold the paper to John Uprichard – moving to 4 Firs Parade in October 1999. The paper was taken over by the Derbyshire Times Group of Chesterfield and is now printed by the Halifax Courier. Alas, the original records were destroyed in the floods of 1965.www.matlocktoday.co.uk

Peak Times

This is a sister paper to the *Matlock Mercury*, founded in August 1999, which is delivered weekly and cost free to every household and business premises in the area, from as far apart as Flagg, Hope and Hartington.

Peak Advertiser (Incorporating Peakland Properties)

This paper is published in Bakewell but is included here as it also covers the Matlocks and beyond. This also is delivered weekly and free to households and businesses. It was founded in 1982 and its two great strengths are a listing of local voluntary activities covering every community in which it is delivered and many articles concerning the history of the area, mostly by Julie Bunting.

13 THE TWO WORLD WARS

The two world wars of the 20th century had a profound effect on every community in the British Isles, but there is one fundamental difference between the two – World War I (1914-18) was a soldiers' war, World War II was a peoples' war. The difficulty in writing this chapter is the lack of information. Newspapers were heavily censored and those who took part in the activities described below were bound to silence by the Official Secrets Act.

World War I – The Great War

Matlocks' sons shared in the terrible slaughter in the trenches of WWI and she gave of those sons who never came back, as testified by the war memorials. It is fitting therefore to record these brave soldiers in this book to ensure that they are remembered in print as well as on stone, see Appendix II.

The Derbyshire Branch of the Red Cross provided and maintained a mobile soup kitchen at the front in France. The hydros and a hotel were pressed into use; Rockside Hydro was an auxiliary hospital for servicemen, the Royal Hotel a hospital for Canadian officers. Just prior to this war Evelyn, Duchess of Devonshire, as President of the Derbyshire Branch of the Red Cross, had organised a first aid competition at Rockside Hydro with help from her three daughters.

World War II

The Matlocks were in a strategic position in the second war as it controlled the main road north up the spine of the country, this being the A6 of today. They were close to both Sheffield and Manchester, the former being a major target due to the vital steel industry for which this city is world famous. Also, Buxton had been adopted as the alternative seat of government should London fall to the enemy. Matlock therefore needed to control the A6 for a second reason.

The period of greatest concern was immediately following the evacuation of our troops from Dunkirk, France when Great Britain was anticipating a German invasion. The whole country was put on alert and the Home Guard were prepared to help in preventing or limiting the effects of any invasion. Prior to this the Home Guard were known as the LDV – Local Defence Volunteers and jocularly as Dad's Army.

Regular Army

The regular army manned an anti-aircraft gun located on Bailey's Tump (this was the spoil heap from the mining of the aqueduct for the water main from the Derwent dams to the south), off Asker Lane, established in 1939 and comprised:

-    Four huts housing the messing facilities and barracks with separate latrines
-    Three aircraft spotters with field telephones to a sound locater
-    A mobile sound locater
-    Searchlight, also mobile, which was connected by cables to a petrol generator

- A petrol generator
- Anti-aircraft twin Bren guns
- Range finder
- Ammunition store some distance from the above
- Concrete bunker for protection against attack

Most of the above were protected by sand bags, especially the ammunition store. The establishment had a duty crew of 10 from which it could be assumed that a total of 30 soldiers were needed. The installation did engage the enemy, the last time was when a lone fighter-bomber flew over in February 1945 and let off a burst of machine gun fire. This was the eighth engagement. At other times when the searchlight located aircraft, a message was sent to other similar establishments ringed round Manchester and Sheffield. The establishment was in continuous use from mid-1940 to late 1944.

Home Guard (LDV)

A platoon of the Home Guard patrolled the hills on horseback led by William Smith on a grey horse. He did not marry until he was 52 years of age, his daughter Caroline referred to him as having "a real sergeant-major attitude." They lived at the Red House at Darley Dale, and had to make way for the Auxiliary Territorial Service (ATS) later to be named the Women's Royal Army Corps (WRAC) who occupied it for the rest of the war. It was William Smith who established the well known Red House Stables.(Reflections April 2002)

The Home Guard were equipped with a limited number of Lee Enfield 0.303 rifles and they practised at some butts located at the end of Cavendish Road where the playing fields are now.

The Hydros

The Matlocks were already in use by the forces: Smedley's Hydro was requisitioned as a Military Intelligence Training Centre amongst whose trainees were Evelyn Waugh (Captain Royal Marines – who learned how to interpret aerial photographs here) and Anthony Powell; the Royal Hotel, Matlock Bath was a hospital for Canadian soldiers; Rockside Hydro was an auxiliary hospital for exhausted airmen; Oldham House Hydro was used as a hospital for the Royal Air Force.

Rockside is of particular interest and information is available mostly due to the research undertaken by Eric Taylor when writing his book *Operation Millennium*. He relied on the memories of those who worked there in the early 1940s. He describes the building aptly as a "Dracula-like eyrie". During the Battle of Britain particularly, fought by young fighter pilots and those who flew missions in bombers, the stresses and strains of frequent sorties and the loss of comrades took a heavy toll. Many suffered from combat fatigue and these Non-Commissioned Officers were sent to Rockside for treatment, with a view to getting them fit for flying as quickly as possible. Some were so exhausted that they slept for the first two to three weeks after arrival, some came with facial tics, some were short tempered. In 1942, this hospital handled 859 such patients.

The treatment they received proscribed alcohol and this was banned from the premises. However, some of the airmen bought drink from local hostelries when out exercising. They had to wear an outdoors uniform, still remembered by some in the town, which comprised a bright blue jacket, red tie with a white shirt, much loathed by the patients; it was obvious that they would be recognisable in public.

A fear of having to return to operations or having the epithet of "Lack of Moral Fibre" inscribed on their pay books was very real and must have added to their misery. Alas, at least one would have appeared to have taken his own life. During its life as part of Matlock College, students reported hauntings on the top floor.(PA 09.010.2002 HPN 06.10.1943 In Lit Yeomans)

Air Raid Protection

Air raid shelters made of bricks and concrete were provided for the public as follows:

-   Car park near to the bridge
-   Gardens, now a car park behind the Olde English Hotel
-   An area which is now the bus station

Numerous households had their own Anderson shelters in their gardens or Morrison shelters in their homes. An Anderson shelter consisted of corrugated arches laid in an excavated depression with the spoil heaped up the sides and over the top. The only alternatives to these shelters were the communal ones built of brick walls and flat reinforced concrete roofs. These proved to be almost useless for they could not survive a direct hit from the smallest shell, they were more of a morale booster. (The writer recalls with anguish when one of these shelters fell on him when a bomb dropped a half mile away, making him a war casualty at the age of seven!) The Anderson shelters collected surface water, they were damp, cold and miserable.

Morrison shelters were steel rod cages which were placed in the house into which the family would crawl and sit like hens in an undersized coop. These shelters were named after their instigators but after a while most people stayed at home in their beds.

Matlock Bank with Rockside Hydro top right

Ground Station Zero

Ground Station Zero was a scheme to halt the enemy should they advance north toward Sheffield and Manchester, and to protect Buxton. The theory was that the enemy would use established routes, one of which was the A6, others were the A1 and A5. An imaginary line was drawn across the country as a target for stopping troops from advancing. Matlock played a major part in this and the evidence of it is only just coming to light. This concept was to have secret locations reporting on local events and manned by trained men in groups. No two groups knew each other so that in the event of capture they could not be forced into betraying their colleagues. This group were known as "Ground Station Zero".

They stored ammunition and weapons in Masson Cavern, Jug Holes Mine and to the rear of the old Town Hall – where the new extension is located; mortar and spigot mortar bombs disguised under a heap of scrap iron. Petrol and ammunition were concealed under a pile of wood fuel at the end of the swimming baths, the rear entrance to the bus station occupies this area. A mounting for a light machine gun was located where Alldays is now. The Royal Observer Corp provided back-up, having bunkers at High Ordish near Ashover and Brassington where the brick tower still exists.

The hub for all this activity, "Ground Zero", was a terraced house disguised as Topliss the Tailor, (Burton House) 156, Smedley Street. This house was fitted out on every one of its four floors including the cellar and attic. Jug Holes was also a rendezvous point as well as an arms cache. Those who volunteered for Ground Station Zero duties were picked for their fitness, intelligence and energy. (Attwater)

Matlock under attack

On 4 March 1945 the pilot of a German fighter, said to have been annoyed by the searchlight and anti-aircraft crew at Asker Lane, decided to seek revenge on the peaceful citizens of Matlock. He flew low over the town presumably by following Bakewell Road and Causeway Lane, firing his cannons as he passed over the area three or four times. He was aiming at the buildings and whilst he caused little damage to people, he did frighten a few and caused minor damage to St Giles' Church, two chapels, a public house and a mill. The local press were not allowed to name these premises but evidence still exists in the form of two depressions in the lower part of the gable of C Farmer Ltd's shop on Causeway Lane where it faces the Ritz Centre. The damage to the church was more significant as a shell blew out 100 panes of glass in a window near to the altar, with a second shell piercing the roof, whence it settled into one of the pipes of a disused organ. The public house was hit seven times, including a wall close to where the publican was lying in bed, setting fire to his bed clothes, his wife beating out the flames with her hands! A soldier home on leave and also in bed, witnessed a shell bursting just above his head. He escaped without a scratch. Above a shop in the town centre a woman, and her daughter with her baby nearly lost their lives when a shell passed through the room they were in and penetrated a wall, landing in a bathroom. There were further near misses. Several shops lost their plate glass windows and one shell hit a tree in Hall Leys Park.(PA 26.08.2001)

Volunteer support

Dene Hill House, Matlock Green was the headquarters of the Air Raid Precautions (ARP – later Civil Defence) Unit being protected by anti-bomb blast measures. This would have been protected by the Home Guard if an invasion had taken place. It was also arranged that the bridges over which the railway ran and the tunnels through which it passed would have been blown and blocked when an invasion took place.

The Matlocks during Warship week, 21 to 28 February 1943 adopted *HMS Anthony*. Matlock also has an Air Training Corps, the 140th Matlock Squadron, located on Hurst Rise.

Opposite page: Ground Station Zero **Below:** Anti-Aircraft Establishment, Asker Lane, Matlock. As it appeared in 1940. Sketch by Peter F Attwater. June 1997, but retitled. Reproduced with permission

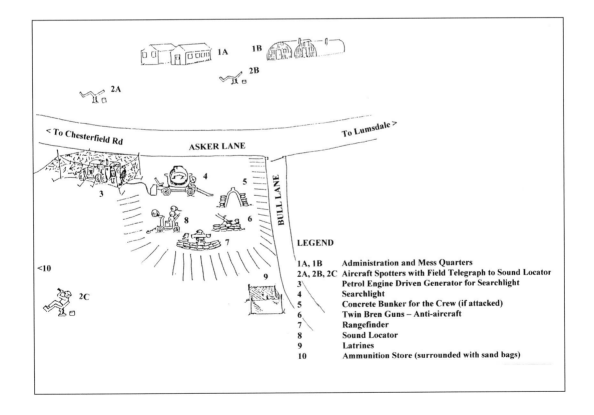

LEGEND

1A, 1B	Administration and Mess Quarters
2A, 2B, 2C	Aircraft Spotters with Field Telegraph to Sound Locator
3	Petrol Engine Driven Generator for Searchlight
4	Searchlight
5	Concrete Bunker for the Crew (if attacked)
6	Twin Bren Guns – Anti-aircraft
7	Rangefinder
8	Sound Locator
9	Latrines
10	Ammunition Store (surrounded with sand bags)

14 LOCAL GOVERNMENT

In the earliest days in the Matlocks, the Lords of the Manor dealt with everything, often in a haphazard way, some conscientiously others not so. This is covered in Chapter I. We had to wait until the 19th century before we had a formalised local government for the Matlocks.

The inhabitants of Matlock Bath had its boundaries settled as a local Government District under the Local Government Act 1858 with effect from 9 November 1861. Matlock made the same claim after a vote by ratepayers nine days later, whereupon they applied for a mandamus (a writ from a higher court to a lower one) to stop Matlock Bath becoming self-governing. One suspects jealousy to be the motive, for Matlock thought itself superior to its now smaller neighbour.

Section 14 of the 1858 Act applied to places whose boundaries were agreed with the Secretary of State, and it was argued that Matlock Bath could not adopt the act unless the parish of Matlock refused to do so. As the boundaries had been defined in the previous order they had remained as previously settled. Matlock Bath struck out this clause by common consent. An order was confirmed to let Scarthin into the Matlock Bath parish, it having been left out before. On 1 April 1874 the Matlock Urban District Council joined with the Matlock Bath Urban District Council – including Bonsall and Cromford – to become the new Matlock Urban District Council. These councils had already been incorporated into the new West Derbyshire District Council the day before.

The Derbyshire County Council issued an order on 10 August 1894 for the two parishes: Matlock – and Matlock Bath with Scarthin – to be separate parishes of Matlock and Matlock Bath. This led to the purchase of Bridge Hall by the Matlock Urban District Council, paying the sum of £1,750. This then became, and still is, the Town Hall.(Bryan ps. 55/6) Matlock Bath became its own Urban District Council whose offices were located in the Pavilion.

At some undetermined time, but possibly in 1937, the old Matlock Bath Urban District Council joined with the Matlock Urban District Council which latter was made redundant when the West Derbyshire District Council was formed on 19 March, 1974, later to become Derbyshire Dales District Council on 1 January, 1987. The new West Derbyshire District Council was formed a few months in advance of the demise of the Matlock Urban District Council, spanning the years of 1973 and 1974.

See Appendix IV for lists of the mayors and chairpersons up to 2003.

(15) EPILOGUE

Had this book been written two years or so hence, it would have recorded great changes to the Matlocks. There are exciting proposals afoot to make better use of the area known as Cawdor Quarry. As it is currently understood (February, 2003) the changes to take place are:

- the building of a new supermarket by Sainsburys Ltd
- the creation of parking spaces for motor cars and omnibuses
- the building of 432 houses with suitable infrastructure
- the creation of a new market area
- the creation of a new bus station

The developer will be Groveholt Limited with Sainsbury's.(MM 28.11.2002)

Coupled with this is a proposal to drive a relief road from Bakewell Road to Dale Road, with the closing of the bridge which would be pedestrianised. An alternative idea is to make this one-way for traffic westwards. A more ambitious proposal has been made for the driving of a road tunnel from the Cawdor Quarry through the lower slopes of Masson Hill to emerge in Harveydale Quarry.

There is talk of rejuvenating the town of Matlock, addressing such concerns as a lack of sports facilities, a community centre, a theatre, and the encouragement of "high tech" industries to form a "silicon valley." One can only applaud the idea to make Firs Parade a covered shopping precinct, this ugly street should never have been allowed in its present form. (Jillings p.12/13)

August 2002 saw the application by the local authority for funding for an English Heritage Regeneration Scheme aimed at improving the retail outlets in the Dale Road and Matlock Bridge Conservation Area. An investment of £198,000 is expected to be spent over three years from April 2003. This should create an improvement to the shops in the area, which have suffered from a motley selection of shop front designs most out of keeping with the area.

Matlock Town Football Club have, as I write, launched an appeal for £200,000 for a new stadium, giving themselves two years in which to do it. One can only wish them well for such a large and ambitious project for what is a small provincial club.(MM 15.08.02)

A scheme starts in 2003, to last for five years, to restore Hall Leys Park, Pic Tor, Derwent Gardens, High Tor and the Lovers' Walks with a new footbridge across the Bentley Brook to connect Pic Tor with the Park. A new broad walk will connect Derwent Gardens with the A6 towards Masson Mill, with a footpath through the grounds of Willersley Castle to give access to the Cromford Mill complex. The total cost has been estimated at £3,600,000 with £2,600,000 from the Lottery Heritage Fund.(DM Autumn/Winter, 2002/3)

A long overdue arts facility looks as if it might be getting the go-ahead centred on Chatsworth Hall and linked with Highfields School. The cost of this is put at £1,000,000 and originates from the Derbyshire Dales Arena for Performing Arts (DDAPA).

It is mooted to convert Drabbles Mill at Lower Lumsdale into a "cyber" village having dwellings, with 70 workroom facilities along with a 26 work spaces, a communal office facility, village store, a smithy, bistro, a village green and stable block "to give priority to people and aesthetics – not cars." A heritage trail and a Joseph Banks Exhibition Centre are also proposed. Alas, the planners are wavering over this.(PA 23.09.02)

Peak Rail should be obtaining leave to use the existing rail station and could well connect with a new proposed service from Derby to Manchester.

The future of Riber Castle is the cause of much controversy with a proposal to turn it into flats and the building of houses in the grounds. The preservation of this "folly" is without question., It is the additional properties and the effect on traffic management which is causing the complaints, except that the villagers of Riber would rather it not happen at all. One assumes the only alternative to this building is to demolish it, as it would cost a huge sum to preserve it and is it worthy of preservation?

Closer links with Matlock's twin town in France, Eaubonne, will benefit both towns and create links with the townspeople in both, particularly the children. It is a fitting partner as the name stands for Good Water. Eaubonne is 20 miles north-west of Paris and is a little larger than Matlock. The twinning was first mooted by the then new Matlock Town Council in 1983 and brought into fruition in 1992.

It has also been suggested that the Matlocks could trade on their spa connections. Derbyshire Dales is still one of the ten members of the British Spa Federation – originally there were 220 spa towns in England alone – and with the increase in health related breaks, a future could lie in this area of alternative medicine. It was reported in March 2002 that spa tourism generates an incredible £1.4bn a year for the English economy. However, three quarters of Britons take health breaks abroad, could they be tempted to come to the Matlocks? Buxton is currently spending £15.5m on a new project to this end. The answer must be yes, but we have to make it attractive enough to tempt them to come.(MM 07.03.02)

The new World Heritage Site runs along the Derwent valley from the Old Silk Mill in Derby at its southern end to Masson Mill at Matlock Bath at its northern end. It is pleasant to know that we rank along with the Pyramids, the Grand Canyon and Stonehenge.

There is no doubt that the Matlocks will continue to be invaded by multitudes of day visitors and holiday makers. This is possibly the most exciting time in which to live in the Matlocks and the author earnestly hopes to live long enough to see it all happen and enjoy it. The controversial comments are the author's only and there is no one else to blame for them.

Matlock College, Chatsworth Hall, June, 1988. Originally the Chatsworth House Hydro
(Derbyshire County Council, Libraries and Heritage)

Matlock Bridge c.1750 looking downstream of the river. The buildings on the left were swept away to create the Hall Leys Park Head. (Derbyshire County Council, Libraries Heritage)

Matlock Dale c.1750 looking downstream of the river. Note the traveller and packhorse
with mine adit at water level with High Tor above.
(Derbyshire County Council, Libraries & Heritage)

Matlock Bath from the top of Holme Road, c.1800. Museum Parade and the Old Bath Hotel
are evident. (Derbyshire County Council, Libraries & Heritage)

Wild Cat Tor and the New Bath Hotel, note the couple in regency clothes. C. 1800.
(Derbyshire County Council, Libraries & Heritage)

A Mysterious picture of Matlock Bath with High Tor to the left and Masson Hill (too steep sided)
in the middle. This print has no date. (Derbyshire County Council, Libraries & Heritage)

High Tor and the river Derwent, a well executed and dramatic sketch, no date.
(Derbyshire County Council, Libraries & Heritage)

Appendix 1

Incumbents Of The Church Of England

St Giles', Matlock Town – Rectors

1300	Walter de Fodringay	Died
1315	Ralph de Ergom	Resigned
1316	Robert de Brydelington	
1328	Richard Bargrave	
1332	Michael de Hayelton	Son of John de Hayelton
1361	Henry de Witham	or Wichiner
1366	Hugh Hykeling	Exchanged with his successor for the preceptorship of Crediton, Devon
1372	William de Loundey	
1373	Laurence de Sundrish	An acolyte [1] admitted "in persona Henry de Foston."
1380	John de Asseburne	
1387	Richard de Stepull	
1409	John Tekyll	Died
1423	Robert Conyngham	Exchanged with his successor for Brailsford, Derbys.
1435	William Egge	Died
1435	William Lowthe	
1459	Henry Anse	
1467	Oliver Dynham. MA	
1482	Thomas Reynald	Died
1497-1504	James Basford. BL	or Beresforde, resigned 1504
1536	Thomas Lyllylowe	Died
1545	Robert Horne	
1554	Edmund Wyld	
1564	Christopher Grange	
1580	Peter Hart	
1603-1612	John Sheraton (Searson)	
1617	Henry Smith	Died 1640
1640	William Thorpe	For two years.
1645	Thomas Shelmerdine	Ejected for Nonconformity, 1662
1662	John Chappell	
1688	Joseph Fearn. MA	Died 1716
1717	Thomas Hinkesman	Died 1738 – also Vicar of Chesterfield
1739	Charles Cartwright	Exchanged for Charborough,[2] Notts. 1753
1753	Benjamin Burrow MA	Died 1779
1780	George Holcombe DD	Died
1836	William Job Charlton Stanton	
1839	William Roylance Melville	Died
1887	James William Kewley	
1923	Alban Urling-Smith	
1949	Charles Henry Ferris	

1957 James Armitage
1962 Thomas Richards Parfitt
1981 John Statham
1990 Canon Peter Peterken
1996 Canon John Coombs Tomlinson
2003 Mark Crowther-Alwyn

Sources: Matlock Parish Church Guide ps. 19-20
                Bryan ps 41-43
                In Lit Hughes 20.01.03

All Saints Church, Matlock Bank – Curates

1876 Edward de Villers Bryams   Curate in charge
1877 Adam Lowe   Curate 1877-86
                                          Vicar 1886-1911
1911 James Bartlett Hyde
1926 William Henry Nixon
1941 William Wallace Hayward Nash
1945 John Mabey Carr
1955 Thomas Neville Vreichvras Churchill Rose Price
1963 Ronald Latimer Davidson
1977 Brian James Coleman
1987 John Oliver Goldsmith
1997 Stuart Ian Mitchell

Assistant Curates:

1909 Oliver William Edward Grant
1912 Arthur Neville Hare
1916 John Brunel le Gassick
1918 George Girdler Marchant   Until 1921
1979 Keith John Orford
Until 1999 – non-stipendiary associate priest

Source: A History of All Saints Church, Matlock Bank   p 70

Holy Trinity – Matlock Bath

1842 William Gibb Barker
1853 Edward Synge
1859 John Martin Maynard MA
1865 Charles Evans MA
1867 Walter Webb Woodhouse
1869 Raymond P Pelly MA
1875 Edward Latham
1883 Charles Baker

1914 William Asquith MA
1921 Edward J M Davies
1929 Clement T Walker MA
1934 Alfred Phidds
1944 William G Lee
1950 Norman B Johnston
1955 L E Waghorn MA
1958 H E Brown MA
1966 James Song (originally Hong Kong Chinese)
1977 Canon Harold Collard
1992 John Wheatley Price (Retired)
1997 John Currin
In Lit: B Smith 20.01.03

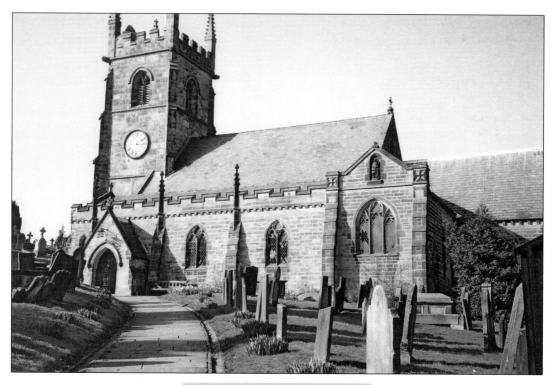

St Giles church from the lych gate

(1) Acolyte - a subordinate office in the Catholic Church
(2) Charborough is probaly Clarborough near Retford, Notts.

Appendix II

War Memorials

There are four war memorials in the Matlocks: Matlock Town on Pic (Pig) Tor, Matlock Bath in the Derwent Gardens, Starkholmes and Riber on the road side and Scarthin on the Promenade. The memorial at Matlock Bath is a particularly fine one in contrast with Matlock Town which is a simple obelisk.

The Great War as it was originally called did not become World War I until World War II had been in progress for a year or so. The first war was meant to be the war to end wars, it was not to be.

The names below are in strictly alphabetical order, the originals on the monuments are not always so.

Matlock Town World War I (The Great War)

The names are on three plaques as indicated

Plaque One

Allen	E
Allen	J T
Allen	T
Allen	W
Allen	W
Andrews	G E
Andrews	H H
Arkwright	F G A

Also on the memorials at Cromford, Starkholmes and in St Mary's Church, Cromford

Ashton	G W
Bagshaw	F
Bagshaw	H
Bagshaw	J
Bagshaw	W
Ballington	G
Barnes	C
Barnes	H
Bates	W
Beard	W
Boden	G W
Boden	S
Booth	J W
Bower	G F
Bradwell	J W
Briddon	W J
Brocklehurst	J E

Bunting	C
Bunting	O
Buxton	F
Buxton	T
Campbell	A B
Checkley	H S
Clarke	C
Clay	H
Clay	J

Also on the Matlock Bath memorial

Clay	G L
Cook	H
Cooper	E
Cowlishaw	H
Croft	F
Crowder	G
Crowther	G
Dakin	F W
Derbyshire	L
Dickinson	L G

Also on the Matlock Bath memorial

Dumas	C D
Eakin	W
Else	G
Else	J
Farnsworth	A
Farnsworth	P
Fearen	T
Fletcher	J
Flint	F

The impressive war memorial in the Memorial Gardens, Matlock Bath, 1922
(Derbyshire County Council, Libraries and Heritage)

Flint	Q
Fox	C
Fox	F
Fox	G
Fox	I S
Fox	J S
Fox	S

Plaque Two

Goodwin	G J W
Gibb	E
Gregory	A
Gregory	E
Gregory	F
Gregory	J J
Grey	H L
Grocott	S
Hall	G S
Hallam	W
Handley	J
Hawley	F
Haynes	E
Hayes	J H
Henstock	E
Henstock	S
Hetherington	F A
Holmes	A
Holmes-Bower A	
Holmes	H
Holmes	J
Holmes	R
Holmes	W
Holland	W
Hopkinson	J
Housley	E L
Hyde	J C
Keeling	A
Keeling	W
Kenworthy	G E
Kersey	J A C
Knowles	C J
Knowles	W R
Land	J
Lewis	F J
Lill	S
Lily	C H
Lovell	A
Lowe	H
Margerrison	J

Milne	B
Milne	R
Mills	J
Mitchell	J P H
Moore	G A
Moxon	J
Muir	J J
Mycock	I
Nixon	F
Oates	W H
Partridge	C
Partridge	G
Poultney	A
Pursglove	H
Radford	J
Rawson	W
Read	A
Read	C E
Riley	W H
Rouse	B
Rylands	W H

Plaque Three
Seedhouse	J
Sellers	G
Sellers	H
Shaw	Al
Shaw	Ar
Simpson	E
Slater	E
Slater	G
Slater	J J
Smith	F
Smith	H
Smith	I
Smith	J
Smith	R
Smith	S A
Smith	W
Spencer	A
Stacey	G
Statham	J

Also on the Matlock Bath memorial

Stone	J
Storey	G W
Swinscoe	H
Taylor	W E
Thomson	G
Thorpe	A

Toft	H
Tomlinson	T F
Toplis	A
Towe	H
Twigg	J W
Vincent	E
Wall	A
Wall	J
Wall	L
Wall	R W
Walters	T
Ward	B
Ward	R
Wheatcroft	A
Wheatcroft	F
Wherrett	T

Also on Starkholmes memorial

White	F
Wildgoose	C
Wildgoose	E H
Wildgoose	J H
Wildgoose	N
Willcock	C C
Wilson	T
Woodhouse	J
Woodhouse	R
Woodiwiss	R
Woodiwiss	W H
Woolley	C W
Woolley	J
Wragg	G P
Wragg	H
Wyatt	J W

Matlock Town World War II

The names are on three plaques as indicated

Plaque One

Alsop	C T P E
Allsop	T
Allwood	J T
Ballington	H
Barnes	C
Bonsall	F K
Bowler	W S
Briddon	S H
Brown	S
Crouch	W

Gaunt	S
Gould	H
Gregory	C C
Grimshaw	H
Ham	M G
Harrison	K G
Hood	A E

Plaque Two

Jones	F A
Kennedy	F J
King	F S
Kirwan	T
Loverock	E J
Lowe	W H
Moore	C B
Mowatt	T R
Owens	F J
Pennington	W
Scotthorne	T A
Sheldon	H
Slater	A L
Slater	C
Slater	G T
Stafford	W S

Plaque Three

Vallance	F B
Vallance	R
Wall	C
Walthall	C
Wherrett	R N R
Wibberley	G T
Wicks	R J S
Wildgoose	F B H
Wilson	K W
Wood	E K
Wood	J
Woolley	A E

A small plaque commemorates the following:

Prime	M F	NI (Northern Ireland)

The memorial has a flower vase inscribed "Matlock Civic Association 1998", the year when they restored this memorial.

There are war graves in this churchyard extension as follows:

Kennedy   F J
Kirwan   T

Ordinary Seaman   P/JX 157970
Serjeant   7109656
Royal Navy
The King's Regiment
29th May, 1940 Aged 18

9th April, 1945   Aged 44

Bowler   W J
Able Seaman   P/JX 161662
Royal Navy   HMS Thane
15th January, 1945 Aged 22

King   F S
Sergeant
Royal Air Force
8th July, 1940

Loverock   E J
Sergeant   950159
Air Gunner
Royal Air Force
18th February, 1943 Aged 21

Simpson   E
Private
Northumberland Fusiliers
16th April, 1917 Aged 18

Gould   H
Private   14714367
The Yorkshire & Lancashire Reg
29th June, 1944   Aged 19

Slater   G T
Midshipman (A)
HMS Heron
15th October, 1942 Aged 18

Mellows   E J
Gunner   920279
Royal Artillery
30th October, 1940 Aged 23

Crowther   G E
Private
Notts. and Derbys. Regiment
8th Decfember, 1918 Aged 37

A single stone records that these two men are buried elsewhere in the graveyard:

Wildgoose   N
Private   147910
5th Battalion Canadian Infantry
27th September, 1916

Allen   J T
Kings Own Scottish Borderers
4th October 1916 Aged 40

Matlock Bath World War I (The Great War)

Boden   Frank Wigley
                    Also on Matlock Town memorial

Boden	George William
Boden	Matthew
Britland	William Henry
Burdett	Thomas Cecil
Buxton	Edgar
Clay	John

Also on the Matlock Town memorial

Coates	Clarence Hugh
Dickinson	Lewis George

Also on the Matlock Town memorial

Elliott	William Henry
Ellis	Ernest
Finney	William John
Gregory	William Henry
Hardstaff	Richard
Hall	Angus Walker
Knight	William Ernest
Morgan	Arthur William (Holmes)
Pickford	Richard
Reynolds	Thomas Bertram
Seedhouse	John

Also on Matlock Town memorial

Sims	Alexander Anthony
Statham	Joseph

Also on Matlock Town memorial

Matlock Bath World War II

Ballington	Herbert
Binks	Ronald Douglas
Edmonds	Cyril Rowland
Grantham	David
Howitt	George
Land	Norman
Moffat	Angus Donald
Morten	Maurice Furniss
Morten	Charles Richard
Walker	Warren

Scarthin World War I (The Great War)

Tomlinson	Joseph
Sherratt	William
Biddulph	Arthur
Keightly	Thomas
Worthy	Thomas
Allen	William H

Kirk	George
Pidcock	John A

Scarthin World War II

Kniveton	Harry
Pidcock	George A
Russell	Arthur H

Starkholmes and Ryber World War I (The Great War)

Arkwright	F G A
Fox	C
Fox	F
Fox	S
Fery	T
Fletcher	J
Growcott	S
Knowley	C J
Knowley	W
Milne	B
Pursglove	H
Read	E
Smith	F
Taylor	W E
Wherrett	T

Starkholmes and Riber World War II

Not shown, anyone from these settlements will be on the Matlock Memorial.

The memorial has a flower vase inscribed "Matlock Civic Association 1998", the year when they restored it.

Appendix III

Population

The population of the Matlocks is presented in graphical form and in separate graphs for Matlock Bank and Bridge, and Matlock Bath.

Before 1911, Matlock Bath was part of the other Matlocks.

It should be noted that the national census was taken from 1801 and every ten years thereafter. No census was taken in 1941 due to hostilities.

The figures for 2001 onwards were not available at the time of writing.

The population of Matlock Bank and Bridge took a dip in 1891 and 1951. The latter can be explained by the introduction of the National Health Act in 1948 which emptied the hydros. The dip in 1891 is a mystery.

The gradual fall in population of Matlock Bath may signify that there are more retired people in this area than young marrieds who would add to the population.

The sudden rise for Matlock Bank and Bridge from 1961 onwards must be due to the Derbyshire County Council occupying Smedley's and the general drift of people moving into the area.

The two Great Wars of the 20th century had a marginal effect as was the case throughout the country. Indeed, the population rose after World War II due to an influx of displaced persons. The emptying of houses to create second homes and holiday lets from the 1970s onwards must have had its effect.

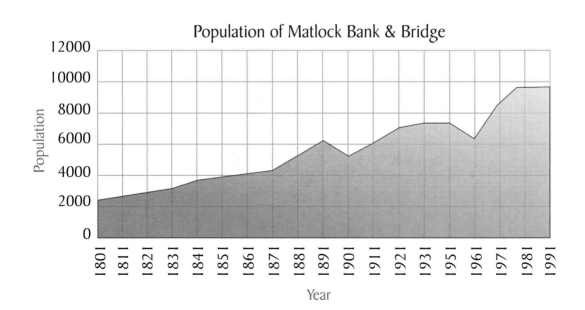

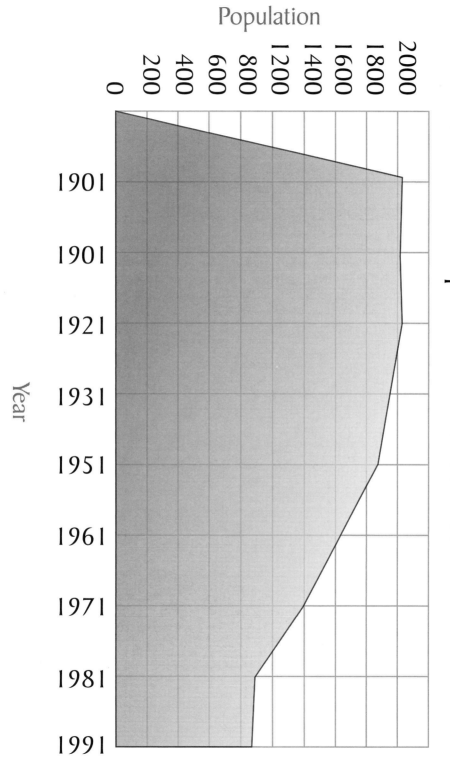

Population of Matlock Bath

Appendix IV
Mayors & Chamberpersons

Matlock Urban District Council – Mayors

Inaugurated 17 May 1983

1983 P F Leighton
1984 P Richardson
1985 B Turner
1986 G E M Stevens
1987 P V Edwards MBE
1988 D T Barker
1989 M S Burfoot
1990 T L Boam
1991 J Henshaw
1992 S Fletcher
1993 D T Barker
1994 J Clegg
1995 A Bond
1996 P A Wildgoose
1997 M Moss
1998 M Moss
1999 S Fletcher
2000 S Burton

Matlock Urban District Council – Chairpersons

1924 J Shaw
1925 Ditto
1926 A Wrigley
1927 Ditto
1928 Ditto
1929 W E Beaumont
1930 Ditto
1931 Ditto
1932 J G Wildgoose
1933 Ditto
1934 Ditto
1935 Ditto
1936 Ditto
1937 Ditto
1938 J W Hibbs
1939 Ditto
1940 F W Beddington
1941 Ditto
1942 G W Burton
1943 Ditto
1944 Ditto
1945 Ditto
1946 C Harrison
1947 Ditto
1948 J S Wain
1949 F R Rhodes
1950 Ditto
1951 A May Greatorex
1952 Ditto
1953 J Turner
1954 Ditto
1955 O R Tinti
1956 Ditto
1957 E C P Stevens
1958 Ditto
1959 L E Twigg
1960 Ditto
1961 T Neville
1962 Ditto
1963 S Elliott
1964 Ditto
1965 W Horobin
1966 Ditto
1967 G H Walters
1968 Ditto
1969 Doris A Johnson
1970 Ditto
1971 H A Briddon
1972 Ditto
1973 J Yates
1974 Ditto

Derbyshire Dales District Council – Chairpersons
(Courtesy Derbyshire Dales District Council In Litt. 27.09.02)
Became West Derbyshire District Council on 19 March 1974
Became Derbyshire Dales District Council on 1 January 1987

1973-75	D A Fisher JP
1975-76	G J Peach MBE
1976-77	E J Smith

1977-78	G T Ward MBE JP
1978-79	Mrs C M N Crowther
1979-80	M Rose OBE
1980-81	W H Doxey MBE JP
1981-82	J Stevenson JP
1982-83	F E Holland
1983-84	G E M Stevens
1984-85	Mrs M E Gillian
1985-86	F W Glossop
1986-87	Mrs J T Naylor
1987-88	C B Hoole
1988-89	K C Bull
1989-90	B Oldfield
1990-91	Mrs E M Plumbly
1991-92	Mrs O M Allen
1992-93	Mrs J A Twigg
1993-94	Mrs P V Edwards MBE
1994-95	C H Birch
1995-96	D R Burton
1996-97	C P Brindley
1997-98	A Hodkinson
1998-99	A S Thomas
1999-2000	J Bevan JP
2000-01	Mrs C M N Crowther
2001-02	T B L Boam
2002-03	I Bates

Matlock Town Council Mayors

1983-84	P F Leighton
1984-85	P Richardson
1985-86	B Turner
1986-87	G E M Stevens
1987-88	V Edwards
1988-89	D T Parker
1989-90	M S Burfoot
1990-91	T L Boam
1991-92	J Henshaw
1992-93	S Flitter
1993-94	D T Parker
1994-95	J Clegg
1995-96	A Bond
1996-97	P A Wildgoose
1997-98	M Moss
1998-99	M Moss
1999-2000	S Flitter
2000-01	S Burton
2002-02	A Elliott
2002-03	B Tipping
2003-04	A Prosser

(Courtesy: Matlock Town Council)

References

Secondary Sources

Adam W	*Gem of the Peak, 5th Edition 1851* - Reprint	Ashbourne	1973
Arkle M J	*Tuppence Up, Penny Down*	Matlock	1983
Austin M	*George Fox and John Wesley in Derbyshire*	Derby	n.d
Barton D A	*Around Matlock*	Stroud	1993
Bogarde D	*Snakes and Ladders*	London	1988
Bradbury E	*All About Derbyshire*	Derby	1884
Brewer E C	*The Dictionary of Phrase and Fable*	Leicester	1990
Bryan B	*Matlock Manor & Parish*	London	1903
Bryan B	DASJ Volume IX On a Cromlech formerly standing on Riber Hill, Matlock	Derby	1887
Burr P E	Notes on the History of Phosgenite and Matlockite from Matlock, England The Mineralogical Record, Volume 23 September-October 1992		
Cameron K	*The Place-Names of Derbyshire*	Cambridge	1959
Cooper N & Cooper N	*Transformation of a Valley*	Cromford	1991
Craven M and Stanley M	*The Derbyshire Country House*	Ashbourne	2001
Crystal D, Ed.	*Cambridge Biographical Encyclopedia*	Cambridge	2000
Drabble E P	*Tansley and Lumsdale Mills* Matlock Field Club – Second Report	Matlock	1972
Dodd A E and Dodd E M	*Peakland Roads and Trackways*	Ashbourne	1974
East Midlands Electricity	In Lit Castle Donington, Derbyshire		23.09.02
Farmer F L	*Matlock over the years 1897-1964*	Matlock	1964
Fay S V	The Matlock Steep-Gradient Tramway, (1893) Forward in the reprint by the Arkwright Society	Matlock	1974
Fineran J	*The Index of Derbyshire Artists connected by* *Birth, Education, Employment or Domicile*	Derby	2000
Firth J B	*Highways and Byeways of Derbyshire*	London	1903
Flindall R & Hayes A	*The Caverns and Mines of Matlock Bath: No 1* *The Nestus Mines: Rutland and Masson Caverns*	Hartington	1976
Ford T D Ed.	*Caves of Derbyshire*	Clapham	1974
Ford T & Rieuwerts J Eds.	*Lead Mining in the Peak District*	Ashbourne	2000
Franklin A	*At a Cinema near you*	Derby	1996
Gage J	*J M W Turner. A Wonderful Turn of Mind*	London	1987
Gosling R	Nottingham Quarterly No.3– Trogs at Matlock	Nottingham	1978
Havin P J N	*The Spas of England*	London	1976
Heath J	*The Illustrated History of Derbyshire*	Buckingham	1982
Hey D	*Packmen, Carriers and Packhorse Roads*	Leicester	1980
Jackson L R	*Darleys in the Dale*	Little Longstone	2002
Jillings J	*Rotary Today*	Matlock	April, 2002
Mitchell I	*A History of All Saints' Church, Matlock Bank, 1876-2000*	Matlock	2000
Mee A	*The King's England, Derbyshire*	London	1974
Monet-Lane H C	*The Romans in Derbyshire* Vol.2	Chesterfield	1988

Morgan P	Domesday Book. Derbyshire	Chichester	1978
Morgan V & Morgan P	Rock around the Peak	Wilmslow	2001
Mullins J	The Divining Rod	Bath	1914
Naylor P J (CD)	Celtic Derbyshire	Derby	1983
Naylor P J (CaH)	Cromford a History	Cromford	2001
Naylor P J (DG)	Derbyshire Graves	Ashbourne	1992
Naylor P J & Porter L	Well Dressing	Ashbourne	2002
Paulson E	The Matlock Monster – A Derbyshire Folk Tale?		N.d.
Pevsner N	The Buildings of England – Derbyshire	Harmondsworth	1986
Rieuwerts J H	History and Gazetteer of the Lead Mine Soughs of Derbyshire	Sheffield	1987
Simpson J	DAJ, Volume XXXVII	Derby	1915
	Megalithic Remains on Bilberry Knoll, Matlock	London	1863
Smedley J	Practical Hydrotherapy 6th Edition		
Spark R E	A View of Masonry in the Matlocks	Matlock	1999
Stephens J V	Wells and Springs of Derbyshire	HMSO	1929
Stokes A H	Lead and Lead Mining in Derbyshire	Bakewell	1973
	Peak District Mines Historical Society – Special Publication No. 2		
Tilley J ("JT")	The Old Halls, Manors and Families of Derbyshire	Derby	1892
Tomkins R	Pipe Organs in Churches and Chapels in the Derwent Valley	Cromford	1995
Tomlinson J M	Derbyshire Black Marble	Matlock Bath	1996
Transco	National Gas Archive, In Litt	Manchester	2002
Wailes R	The Newcomen Society Transactions	London	1966/7
	Vol: XXXIX		1970
Wolley W	History of Derbyshire – Derbyshire Record Society Vol: VI Glover C & Riden P Eds.	Derby	1981

Publications without authors:

Book of Saints 4th Edition (BS)	London	1947
Brown and Gold, Convent High School Magazine	Matlock	1965/6
Cavendish Fields Sports Association – Newsletter Issue 4	Matlock	2002
Gas Works Directory and Statistics. In Lit courtesy Transco		1908/9
Ground Station Zero	Matlock	n.d.
Hall and Sons Ltd – Calendar	Derby	1985
An Inventory of Nonconformist Chapels & Meeting Houses in Central England – Derbyshire	HMSO	1986
The Matlocks and their Past	Matlock	1977
Matlock Parish Church Guide (MPCG)	Matlock	1977
Reflections and reminiscences of old Matlock	Unknown	n.d.
Used for references to the Hydros.(County Library)		
A Short History of Derbyshire Constabulary	Ripley	1983
Tawney House, R.H.Tawney – An Appreciation	Matlock	1962
Ward Lock Guide to Matlock 10th Edition.	London	n.d.

Primary Sources

DAJ	*Derbyshire Archaeological Society Journal*	Derby
DM	*Dales Matters* (Derbyshire Dales District Council)	Matlock
HPN	*High Peak News*	Bakewell
MM	*Matlock Mercury*	Matlock
PA	*Peak Advertiser*	Bakewell
PT	*Peak Times*	Matlock
Reflections	*Reflections*	Chesterfield
WMSS	Wolley Additional Manuscripts	

Acknowledgements

The author records his gratitude to the following individuals who gave of their time and knowledge:

Margaret Elson of Matlock for proof reading and modern photographs.
Dr J H Rieuwerts for allowing me to quote freely from his seminal work *History and Gazetteer of the Lead Mine Soughs of Derbyshire* and Dr T D Ford OBE for guiding the way with Chapter 3
Peter F Attwater of Matlock for permission to reproduce his map of the WWII emplacement on Asker Lane, Matlock
Tony Broome of Matlock
Frank Dickens of Darley Dale

In Litt:

Allen I – Hard of Hearing Club – 16.12.02
Attwater P – Chapter 13 – 12.12.02
Belcher K – Age Concern, Matlock – 30.12.02
Brawn A – Matlock Luncheon Club – 15.12.02
Broome A – 50 years of Rotary in Matlock 1927-77
Carter J – Girls Brigade – 13.12.02
Chief Constable – Information regarding Derbyshire Constabulary – 12.12.02
Chisnall K T, ChCem FRSC MchemA – retired County Analyst, Derbyshire County Council
Christine Sister – Archivist, Presentation Convent – 03.12.02
Dakin A E "Tod" – Matlock Round Table, 1935-1970 – 02.02.03
Davenport E – Omya Ltd – 12.02.03
Derbyshire County Council – Leaflet regarding stained glass windows in County Hall – 28.01.03
Dinnigan N – Re: Simon Dinnigan – 02.02.03
Docherty S – Sub Officer Matlock Fire Station, Derbyshire Fire Service – 14.10.02
Elson M - Age Concern Matlock - 30.12.02
East Midlands Electricity – 12.12.02

Farmer Jason and Peter / Farmer Jonathan – C Farmer Ltd/Farmers Garage Ltd – December, 2002
Flindall R – Chapter 3 – 14.10.12
Ford T D, OBE Dr – Chapter 3 – 31.10.02
Goodall D – M Wright Ltd. – 12.02.02
Hall L – Elmer, Washington, USA – 14.10.02
Hope Dr AML – Archivist for the Religious Society of Friends – 17.02.03
Hughs T – Church Warden – St Giles Church – 20.01.03
Jackson B – daughter of FSJ Broome – 1987
Kay B – Matlock Golf Club – 12.12.02
Lund F – United Reform Church – 21.11.02
Marshall D – Highfields School – 17.12.02
Murray M G – Derbyshire Constabulary – 08.10.02
Mutter A – H J Enthoven and Sons – 12.12.02
Nickolds G – Severn-Trent Water Limited – 09.10.02
Parker K – Matlock Civic Association – 02.12.02
Pilkington T – Boys Brigade – 02.12.02
Pugh A - The Heights of Abraham – 06.11.02
Rieuwerts J H – Chapter 3 – numerous contacts – 12.02 to 02.03
Rowley K – British Red Cross – 30.01.03
Smickersgill L – BBC Television, Leeds – 31.12.02
Smith B – Church Warden – Holy Trinity church – 20.01.03
Smith H – YHA (England and Wales) Ltd. – 21.11.02
Turnbull C – Lions Club – 21.12.02
Walker K – Lilybank Hydro Care Home – 04.12.02
White Young Green for Sainsburys – 12.02.02
Yeomans M – Rockside Hydro – 01.01.03

Loan of Books

Matlock Branch Library,
Janet Ede of Cromford

Archive material

Derbyshire County Council Local Studies Library
Derbyshire County Council Records Office
Census for 1881 - The Church of Jesus Christ of Latter-Day Saints
Census for 1901 - www.pro.gov.uk
Commonwealth War Graves Commission - www.cwgc.org

With apologies to those who have helped and who are not recorded here. Any mistakes are mine and mine alone.

About the Author

Peter Naylor is married and lives in Cromford from which address he operates an engineering consultancy and writes books. He is an incorporated engineer, double graduate, a radio "ham", and a Juryman on the Great Barmote Courts for the Low Peak, High Peak and the Private Liberties of the Duke of Devonshire. This is his sixteenth book and he has another one at draft stage *Discovering Water Supply*.

The Author's Connections with the Matlocks

Being born in and bred close to Nottingham, the author always considered the Matlocks to be his retreat into the countryside, where the mines, crags, trees and rivers fascinated him. During World War II, a trip to High Tor was a regular feature where he would picnic with his parents on cheese and tomato sandwiches. Even today, when he has the same, his mind evokes the scene by the Roman and Fern Caves.

In his teens he stayed at Willersley Castle many times and learned how to rock climb on the nurseries of the Black Rocks and to explore the mines and caves in the area. He arrived permanently to live in Matlock Bath in 1977 via Littleover and Sudbury, eventually to settle in Cromford via Wirksworth Moor.

He feels that he and his family have contributed significantly to the area in many ways:

His great, great uncle founded the Matlock Prize Band, a distant cousin was the first manager of the Matlock Gasworks and yet another distant cousin was head teacher at Cromford School.

Peter had some input with the Town Hall Extension whilst with Hadfield, Cawkwell, Davidson and Partners of Sheffield, with the building of Highfield School and the erection of the cable cars' pylon when with Shand Building division of Lehane, Mackenzie and Shand Ltd. Darley Dale. He also designed the improvements to the pool heating and ventilation at the Matlock Lido and New Bath Hotel whilst with Andrew Engineering Ltd at Chesterfield.

For 12 years he was the Secretary of the Peak District Mines Historical Society later Chairman and is now an honorary member and a progenitor of the Peak District Mining Museum. He was also a partner in the Goodluck Mining Museum.

He was the founder editor of the Derbyshire Heritage Series of books contributing to some of the titles. He also taught as a Nottingham University tutor at Tawney House.

He has come to stay and does not intend to leave.

The index does not include the following:

Appendix I - Incumbents of the Church of England, Appendix II - War Memorials, Appendix III - Population, Appendix IV - Mayors & Chairpersons, References - About the author & The Author's connections with the Matlocks

Index

Symbols

41 Club 101

A

Adam, William 107, 126, 141
Adam's and Vallance's Museum 134
Adelaide, Dowager 107
Adulph, King of the East Angles 28
Agard, Thomas 14
Age Concern 104, 184
Air Raid Protection 159
Alabaster 12, 17, 141
Alderwasley 10, 63, 108
Alexander 13
Alfreton 23, 49, 54, 62
All Saints 16, 19, 54, 59, 92, 93, 94, 97, 119, 135, 153, 170, 182
Allcock 121
Allen, George 128, 129
Allen Hill 30, 41, 57, 89, 97, 98
Allen Hill Spring 97
Allen, John 107
Allotments 38, 48, 85
Amber Valley 81
Amelie, Marie 112
Anderson Shelters 159
Angelina's Cavern 42
Angelus 17
Angling 73, 84, 145, 155
Anglo-Saxon 11
Anne, Queen 12
Apetito's Food Selection 81
Apperknowle 136
Aquarium 31, 41, 45, 72, 128
Arkwright, F C 19, 29, 71, 89, 122
Arkwright, Frederic 14
Arkwright, James 19, 153
Arkwright, Sir Richard 6, 16, 21, 39, 63, 100, 114, 130, 131, 138
Arkwrights 12, 14, 46, 77, 122
Armstrong, Dr 125
Arrock Mines 141
Arthur, James 24
Artists Corner 63, 70, 100, 132
Ascending Douche 50
Ashbourne 4, 11, 12, 28, 50, 91, 104, 135, 182, 183
Ashbourne Turnpike 63
Ashbury Croft 27
Ashford-in-the-Water 80, 141
Ashover 11, 14, 45, 49, 63, 143, 144, 146, 148, 149, 160
Ashover House of Industry 78
Askew, Misses 70
Assembly Hall 117, 155
Athletics 82
Atkins, William 55
Attila 39

B

Bage Mine 7
Bailey family 16, 108, 142, 148
Bailey, Henry Enwin 108
Bailey, Mary Ann 108
Baileys Mill 60
Bailey's Tump 157
Bakepaire, Ralph 11
Bakewell Road 48, 62, 64, 65, 73, 89, 102, 126, 144, 149, 150, 156, 160, 163
Bakewell Union 78
Ball Eye Mine 27
Ball, Sir Albert 52
Bandstand 70, 120
Bank House 51, 54, 55, 58, 133
Bank Road 21, 22, 24, 25, 50, 52, 54, 55, 59, 65, 68, 74, 75, 76, 80, 86, 90, 91, 105, 108, 110, 127, 142
Banks and Barton 29, 44
Barker 13
Barker, Alexander 38
Barmote Court 28, 32, 33, 186
Barnet, Lady Isobel 56
Barrel Edge 8
Barton, George 52
Barton, Mr Geo B 53
Barton, Mrs 53
Barytes 6, 27, 29, 146
Bateman, John 122
Bateman's Park 30, 96, 122, 126
Bath 7, 71, 116
Bath Houses 127
Battalion 77
Beck, Arthur 32
Beech House 145
Beech, Roy 87
Beeching, Dr Richard 67
Belper 10, 21, 22, 54, 62, 63, 64, 66, 76, 78, 115, 125, 153
Belsize Taxi 64
Bennett, Peter J 24
Bentley Brook 6, 18, 30, 47, 60, 68, 70, 88, 120, 140, 142, 144, 145, 147, 148, 163
Beresford, John 13
Bess of Hardwick's 12
Bevington & Sons 20
Biggin, Alex 129
Bilberry Knoll 8, 183
Birchinwood 49
Bishop of Derby 25, 120
Bisley 77
Blackstone Level 31
Blackwell, Thomas 69
Bleach Works 138
Blue John 31, 107, 141
Blue Peter Appeals 92
Boathouse Inn 70
Boating 88, 100
Bobbin Mill 146

Boden 33, 86, 135, 172, 176, 177
Boden, Mr George 33
Boden, Mr Joseph 135
Bogarde, Dirk 108
Bold Slasher 97, 98, 99
Bole Hill 27
Bone Mill 138, 145
Bone Milling 138
Bonfire Night 97
Bonsall 11, 14, 25, 27, 29, 31, 38, 41, 49, 75, 106, 111, 114, 129, 146, 162, 175
Bonsall Hollow 27
Bonsall School Trustees 146
Bonsall, Thomas of 11
Boothby, Brooke 13
Bosch 143
Bourne, Anthony 14
Bourne, Hugh 22
Bow Wood 14, 46
Bowling Green 53, 88, 117
Bown, Phoebe 108
Boy Scouts 92
Boys' Brigade 91, 92
Bradbury, Mr W R 68
Bradley, Horace G 22
Bradley, Joshua 78
Bramald, William 53
Bramwell, Leonard 53
Brass Band 82, 88, 93, 96, 103, 120
Brawn, Anne 90
Breadalbane, Viscount John 20
Breakholes 28
Bridge Hall 53, 117, 130, 162
Brindley & Foster 17, 22
British Legion 96, 102
British Red Cross 56, 95, 105, 185
British School 23
British Spa Federation 7, 164
Broad Stone 99
Bronchocele 15
Broome, John 140
Brown, Richard 141
Browne, Robert 25
Brunswood Terrace 31
Bryan, Benjamin 7, 43
Bull Baiting 96
Bump Mill 148
Bunting, Julie 80, 144, 156
Burdett 60
Burgons 133
Burial Grounds 26
Burne-Jones, Edward Coley 19
Butler and Bayne 16
Buxton 7, 10, 45, 49, 59, 63, 64, 65, 66, 67, 122, 136, 157, 160, 164, 172, 177
Byng, John 130
Byron, George Gordon Byron 109
Byron, Lord 38, 40

C

Cable Tramway 55, 113
Calamine 27, 29, 38
Calcium Fluoride 27
Canadian Officers 157
Canal 65, 84, 140
Candlewick Yarn 148
Canoeing 84
Cardiff Corporation 73
Cardin, J H 44
Carrier Holmes 65
Carsington 8, 59, 63, 111
Carsington Pastures 8
Cash, Dr 52
Castle Top 46, 77, 115
Castle View Primary School 153
Castleton 10, 31, 141
Cattle Market 48, 79
Causeway Lane 62, 64, 78, 82, 83, 89, 106, 120, 134, 144, 156, 160
Cavendish, Edward 89, 122
Cavendish Field Sports Association 86
Cavendish Fields 77, 83, 86, 183
Cavendish School 154
Cavendish, Victor MP 84, 89
Cawdor 8, 30, 31, 32, 65, 133, 163
Cawdor Cottage 133
Cawdor Quarry 8, 32, 65, 163
Celts 8, 10, 80
Central Trains 66
Chadwick, Mrs 43, 44
Challand, H 86
Chandler, Charles 106
Chapel Hill 22
Chapel of St John the Baptist 20
Chapman, Dr E H 100
Chappell, John 12, 13, 38, 169
Chappell, Rev. John 38
Charities 77
Charles Greaves 13
Charles, King I 12, 13, 46
Charles, King II 79
Charles, Prince 111
Charles White School 151, 153
Chatsworth 14, 40, 46, 52, 53, 91, 100, 135, 155, 163, 164
Chaworth, Mary 40, 109
Chellaston 17, 141
Cheltenham 7, 23, 49, 107, 126
Cheshire 21, 105
Cheshire Wichs 59
Chesterfield 10, 23, 24, 25, 45, 49, 52, 53, 58, 59, 62, 63, 71, 76, 77, 82, 86, 88, 93, 95, 103, 113, 141, 145, 154, 156, 169, 182, 184, 186

Chesterfield Road 23, 24, 52, 77, 86, 95, 113
Childs, Rev. L N 17
Christmas 19, 50, 78, 97, 140
Church Of England 169
Church of the Holy Trinity 20
Church Road 24
Church Street 59, 63, 64, 65, 76, 104
Church View 53
Church Wilne 10, 135
Cinema 68, 82, 87, 88, 100, 101, 182
Citizens Advice Bureau 80, 81
City of London 46
Claremont House 132
Clark, Daniel 78
Clark, Mrs Charles 14
Clarke, Mr Charles 20
Clay Cross 75, 93
Clerk, John 112
Cliff House 20
Clifton Road 44, 151
Clowes, William 22
Clubs for Farmers, Workmen, Wives, etc 90
Co-operative Society Shop 19
Coal Pit Rake 31
Coal Supplies 75
Cock Fighting 96
Cock Horse 63
Colin Shewring 16
Colour Works 28, 29, 44, 70
Congregational Church 24
Connor, Mrs S 54
Constable Hart of London 32
Constantines 8
Corby 32
Coritani 10
Corn Mill 47, 60, 108, 138, 142, 146, 147, 148
Cottage Hospital 57, 77, 91, 127
Cotton Spinning 138, 147, 148
Coumbs 14
County and Borough Act 76
County Archives 51
County Hall 51, 94, 184
Court of Chancery 13
Cox, Dr 8
Crich 8, 25, 68, 92
Cricket 50, 83
Cromford Bridge 10, 63, 69, 70, 130
Cromford Bridge House 70, 130
Cromford Court 31, 37, 130, 140
Cromford Hill 8, 10, 59
Cromford Moor 72
Cromfordite 7
Cromlech 8, 129, 182
Crosby, Bing 50
Crossing, Sheep 70, 80
Crowder, Joseph 53, 58
Crown Square 67, 68, 69, 89, 90, 102, 120, 126
Crowther, Mr 44
Crystal Sets 27

Cubley, Henry Hadfield 109
Cuckoostone House 72
Cumberland Cavern 42, 43, 45
Cumming, Dr James 136
Curry, P H 16
Customs 28, 29, 38, 96

D

Dakeyne, Arthur 13
Dale Cottage 109
Dale Road 33, 48, 65, 70, 80, 81, 82, 87, 89, 96, 105, 113, 125, 126, 142, 143, 151, 163
Dalefield Hydro 53
Dalesman Male Voice Choir 94
Darley 11, 75, 79
Darley Bridge 33
Darwin, Erasmus 41, 109, 113
Davie, John 24
Davis, Edwin 23
Davis, George 53, 58
Davis, Mr 19
Davis, Ralph 49, 52, 55, 57, 58
Davis, Thomas 55, 58
Dawber, Sir E Guy 20
Dawes, Sir D'Arcy 12
de Ferrers 12
Dean, Lynne 94
Defoe 40
Dene Hill House 161
Dennis Traditional Pumps 77
Derby Arboretum 136
Derby, Earl of 12
Derbyshire Dales 7, 52, 81, 87, 91, 162, 163, 164, 180, 184
Derbyshire Miners 27
Derbyshire Neck 72
Derbyshire Stone 80
Derbyshire Stone Ltd 29, 32, 33, 143
Derbyshire Wild Life Trust 91
Derwent Avenue 70, 82
Derwent Cottage 132
Derwent Dams 157
Derwent Gardens 36, 122, 163, 172
Derwent Mills 140
Derwent Park 7
Derwent Valley Scheme 71, 73
Des Moines 7
Devonshire Arms Hotel 71
Devonshire Cavern 42, 43, 107
Devonshire, Duke of 53, 86, 107, 115, 123, 140, 141, 186
Dickens, Charles 78
Dimmock, Mrs 55
Dimple 6, 11, 57, 60, 62, 63, 89, 123, 143
Dimple House 143
Dimple Level 30
Dinnigan, Simon R 110
Ditchfield, Edward 13
Dobson and Nell Ltd 42

Dog Fighting 96
Dogs Farm 68
Dolphin, Mr 130
Domesday 11, 16, 28, 46
Domesday Book 28, 183
Domesday Survey 11
Drabble & Sons Ltd 111
Drabble Family 110, 148
Drabble, Frederick Henry 110
Dragons 99
Droitwich Spa 7
Dronfield 136
Duchy of Lancaster 12, 13
Duffield 11
Duffield Frith 11
Duggins, Ron 103
Duke of Lancaster 28
Duke of Wellington Inn 71
Dungeon Tors 137

E

Eadburger, Abbess 28
East Coast Flood Disaster 101
East Midlands Electricity 75, 182, 184
East Moor 63
Ecton Copper Mines 140
Edward, King I 11, 12, 62
Edward the Confessor 11, 12
Electricity 75
Elizabeth, Queen II 110, 111, 120
Ember Farm 84
English Heritage 128, 163
English Sewing Cotton Company 138
Ernest Bailey Grammar School 51, 82, 108, 153, 155
Esculapius 51
Essential Energy School of Theatre 95
Evans & Son 142
Evans the Jewellers 82, 86
Evans, William 142
Evelyn Skenfield 80
Eyam 10, 146

F

Fairy Elves 99
Farm Dam 146
Farmer, Charlie 144
Farmer, Francis Leo 144
Farmer, Hewson 24
Farmer, Robin 144
Farnsworth, Richard 141
Fearn, Fay 104
Fern Cave 42, 43, 44
Ferne, Joseph 124
Fields, Gracie 87
Fillpurse Vein 32
Fin Cop Hill 99
Fire Fighting 76
Firetown 7
Firs Parade 76, 105, 134, 156, 163
Fish Pond Hotel 39, 41, 90, 126, 134
Flair Singers 95
Flavius Wamba 19
Flax Waste 148

Flea Market 79
Fleming, Dr Hans 156
Fletcher, Harold 80
Flight and Robson 17
Flour Milling 142
Fluorspar 33, 42, 44
Fluorspar Cavern 42, 44
Foljambe, Godfrey 14
Foljambe, Roger 14
Football 80, 82, 83, 86, 96, 153, 163
Footbridges 70
Footpaths 121, 136
Forum Club 89, 101
Foster & Andrew of Kingston-upon-Hill 19
Fountain Baths 31, 122
Fox, Harry 90
Fox Memorial Chapel 23
Fox, W G 76
Framework Knitters 51, 138
Frank, Mr Lund 26
Frankpledge 14
Free Methodism 23
Freemasons 100
Fryer, E 25
Fuller, Henry 22
Fun Fair 79
Furida 141

G

Galena 6, 27, 33
Gallic Wars 10
Garnet & Farnsworth 147
Garratt, Thomas 78
Gas 29, 42, 54, 68, 71, 73, 74, 75, 78, 106, 118, 121, 128, 142, 183, 186
Gaskin Mine 42
Gassy-Gessy Parade 74
Gate Inn 50, 58, 63, 65, 127
George Hotel 126
George, St. 98, 99
German Invasion 157
Gessy the Stationer 74
Gilderoy House 108, 151
Girl Guides 92
Girls' Guildry 92
Girl's Life Brigade 92
Gladiators 82, 83
Glenorchy Chapel 20, 21, 23, 62, 63, 85, 113
Glenorchy School 154
Glossop Division 76
Glove Factory 134
Goitre 15
Golf 54, 84, 185
Goodall, Derek 142
Goodwin, Lillian 56
Goose Fair 79
Gothic Warehouse 104
Goward, David 142
Granby Level 30
Grangemill 59
Great and Coalpit Rakes 32
Great Court Baron 14
Great Longstone 63
Great Masson Cavern 42, 43
Great Rutland Cavern 42
Greatorex, Anthony 93

Greatorex, Thomas 93
Greaves, Mrs John 14
Greenhough, Edward 78
Greenwood, Timothy 64
Greyhound Hotel 64
Grinding Mill 147
Grinling Gibbons 17
Groovers 38
Ground Station Zero 160, 161, 183
Groveholt Ltd 163
Grunwell, J M 23
Guide Dogs for the Blind 92
Gulliver's Kingdom 31, 40, 44, 121

H

Hackney 59, 60, 63, 71
Haddon Hall 113, 116
Hadfield, John 33, 143
Hag Mine 31, 140
Haliwellker 36
Hall Dale Quarry 33
Hall Leys Park 7, 46, 67, 69, 70, 82, 88, 89, 100, 102, 120, 135, 136, 160, 163, 165
Harley House 63
Harriet 52
Harrison Almshouses 77, 120
Harrison, Mrs Margaret 120
Harrogate 7, 49
Hartington, Marquis of 116
Harveydale Quarry 33, 163
Harveydale Quarry (Limestone) 33
Hat Making 138
Hayward, Benjamin 41, 124
Haywood, Mr 52
Health 77
Hearthstone 6, 33, 72, 73
Heathcote, George 13
Heights of Abraham 11, 28, 31, 39, 43, 44, 49, 73, 100, 107, 121, 131, 137, 185
Heights of Jacob 40, 44, 121, 137
Helipoma 121
Henry, King VII 11
Henry, King VIII 11, 87
Henry Road 59
Hereward Street 10, 59, 62
Heywood, Benjamin 70
Hickling, Mrs 52
Hickman, Eunice 153
Higginbotham, Mrs 53
Higgot, John 23
Higgs, Rev. John 19
High Leas Farm 73
High Peak 28, 71, 72, 80, 184, 186
High Tor 7, 10, 28, 29, 31, 32, 39, 42, 43, 44, 54, 62, 69, 94, 114, 120, 122, 123, 127, 132, 136, 137, 163, 166, 167, 168, 186
High Tor Hotel 127
High Tor Mine 114
High Tor Players 94
High Tor Pleasure Ground 122

High Tor Recreation Grounds Company Ltd 122
Higham 49, 111
Highfields School 103, 123, 131, 153, 155, 163, 185
Hill, Charles 68
Hillock Croft 78
Hilton, Sir Peter 111
Hockey 86
Hodge, Thomas Hallett 12
Hodgkinson, Edmund 12
Hodgkinson's Hotel 2, 126
Hodgkinson's Hotel 41, 76
Holden, Dr Totty 97
Holland, John 14
Holloway 25, 49, 58, 63
Holmes, Horace 79
Holt Lane 25, 54, 62, 63, 89
Holworthy, James 114
Holy Trinity 16, 20, 78, 92, 102, 151, 170, 185
Holy Trinity Church of England Primary School 151
Holy Well 36
Home Guard 157, 158, 161
Hopton Stone 16
Horseshoe Hotel 96, 126
Howard, Caroline Ann 49
Howden Dam 69
Humber 10, 11, 69
Humber Estuary 10
Humbert, Aelderman 28
Hunt, W 24
Huntsbridge House 23, 95
Huntsbridge Mill 47
Hurst Farm 59, 92, 106, 141
Hurst Rise 161
Hurt, Charles 8, 63, 108
Hurt, Francis 13, 14
Hydro House 51, 52, 53, 54, 55, 57, 58, 67, 154, 155
Hydrogen Gas 73
Hygeia 51

I

Ilkley Hydro 52
Illuminations 88
Imperial Road 23, 52, 65, 80, 84, 117, 123
Imperial Road Church 23
Independent Methodist Connection 23
Industrial Revolution 110, 114, 138, 144
Infantry Rifle Volunteers 77
Information Centre 41, 72, 134
Inner Wheel Club 100, 101
Institute of Advanced Motoring 93, 103
Iron Age 8
Iron Teeth and Bloody Bones 99
Ivy Cottage 145

J

Jackson House 53, 58
Jackson Road 26

Jankin Flat 78
Jeffrey, Dianne 103
John, King 12
John of Allen's Hill 11
John, Wesley 116
Johns, Thomas 78
Joseph Rank Benevolent Trust 24
Joseph, Sir Paxton 93, 132, 133
Joseph's Roman Catholic Voluntary Aided School 154
Jubilee Bridge 70
Jugholes 45
Julius Caesar 10

K

Kelstedge 63
Kennedy, Inspector 76
Kennewara 28
Kiddy, Mr K 82
King's (or Queen's) Field 28, 38
Kingston, Earl of 12
Kinnear, Jane 143
Kit's Koty House 8
Kneedham, Thomas 117
Knights of St Columba 25
Knights, Peter 54
Kniveton 63, 177
Knowles, George 93
Knowles, Henry 120
Knowlestone House 132
Knowlestone Place 48, 56, 132
Kursaal 41, 134

L

Ladies Circle 102
Lady Glenorchy Chapel 20, 63
Lady Whitworth Memorial 77
Ladygate Vein 30
Lancashire 23, 68, 72, 93, 99, 156, 176
Lascelles, Edwin 12
Latham, John 112
Lathkill Dale 141
Lauder, Sir Harry 50
Laugh and Scratch 87
Laughton, Mr 130
Law and Order 76
le Masseden 6, 15
Le Roy, Father George 25
Lea Bridge 46
Lea Brook 136
Lea Mills 14, 48, 49, 50, 51, 84, 110
Lead 6, 10, 11, 14, 16, 27, 28, 29, 30, 33, 36, 37, 39, 40, 42, 43, 44, 59, 60, 62, 63, 65, 69, 75, 89, 94, 124, 126, 140, 144, 145, 146, 147
Lead Smelter 14, 60, 63, 145, 146
Leather Gloves 134
Leawood Pumping Engine 140
Leche 46
Leche, Radulphus 14

Leche, Roger 14
Lee, Lawrence 16
Lee, Mr 54
Leedham, John 77
Leroy, Father 155
Letchworth 133
Lilybank 53, 54, 56, 58, 59, 154, 185
Lime kiln 138
Lime Tree Road 63, 89
Lincoln, Dean of 16
Linnell, Mr Bill 104
Lions Clubs International 90
Little Bolehill 7
Little Chester 10, 59
Local Board 54, 55, 71, 79
Local Defence Volunteers 157
Local Tax Office 54
Logan Stone 8, 9
Lomas's 13
Long Tor Cavern 42
Long Tor Quarry 33
Lords of the Manor 36, 47, 70, 79, 146, 162
Lots Quarry 33
Lovers' Walk 7, 107, 113, 136
Low Peak 28, 38, 186
Lower Towers 39, 43
Lucius 8
Lumb Smelting Mill 140
Lumbs Dale 6, 60, 142
Lumb's Mill 47, 146
Lumsdale 29, 33, 47, 62, 75, 76, 99, 110, 111, 138, 139, 141, 142, 144, 145, 147, 149, 153, 155, 163, 182
Lumsdale and Cuckoostone Quarries 33
Lutudaren 10
Lynchets 46
Lysons 41

M

Macleod, Dr 49
Maessa's Valley 6, 15
Maggert Machine 7
Maidens Garlands 17
Mail 75
Malvern 7, 67
Malvern House 54, 67
Mam Tor 10
Manchester House 54
Manifold Valley Railway 149
Manor of Matlock 12, 36, 38
Manoral Corn Mill 142
Market Tolls 79
Markets and Fairs 70
Marks, G Croydon 68
Marsden-Smedley, Mr S E 14
Martial Arts 86
Mary Knight School 7
Mason County 7
Masson 6, 7, 8, 15, 20, 28, 30, 32, 33, 36, 37, 38, 39, 42, 43, 59, 62, 63, 65, 69, 75, 78, 84, 85, 88, 93, 106, 110, 123, 131, 138, 140, 160, 163, 164, 167, 182
Masson Cavern 28, 42, 43,

Masson Dale 6, 36, 37, 138
Masson Fluorspar Opencast 33
Masson Lodge 131
Masson weir 136
Matlock and Cromford Angling
    Association 84
Matlock and District Talking
    Newspaper 104
Matlock Auction 143
Matlock Bank 5, 6, 16, 19,
    23, 30, 36, 46, 47, 48, 49,
    51, 52, 53, 54, 58, 63, 65,
    68, 90, 93, 94, 97, 104, 114, 121,
    127, 128, 141, 142, 144, 153, 154,
    155, 159, 178, 182
Matlock Bath 2, 5, 6, 7, 8,
    9, 11, 14, 15, 16, 20, 21,
    22, 28, 30, 31, 33, 35, 36, 37,
    39, 42, 44, 46, 47, 49, 62, 63,
    65, 66, 67, 69, 70, 72, 73, 74, 75,
    76, 77, 78, 83, 84, 85, 87,
    88, 90, 91, 92, 94, 96, 97,
    99, 100, 102, 107, 108, 109,
    111, 112, 113, 115, 116, 119,
    121, 122, 123, 124, 125, 126,
    127, 128, 130, 131, 134, 135,
    136, 138, 140, 141, 142, 144, 151,
    154, 158, 162, 164, 166, 167, 170,
    172, 173, 174, 176, 177,
    178, 182, 183, 186, 187
Matlock Bath Bridge 69, 70
Matlock Bath Cinema 87
Matlock Brass Band 93, 120
Matlock Bridge 6, 7, 11, 14,
    28, 39, 41, 46, 48, 52, 60,
    62, 63, 65, 66, 67, 68, 69, 72,
    73, 74, 75, 76, 79, 81, 88,
    89, 93, 96, 97, 100, 106, 110, 117,
    120, 122, 123, 126, 127, 130, 132,
    133, 135, 137, 140, 142, 143, 144,
    151, 163, 165
Matlock Bridge Rifle Band 93
Matlock Camera Club 104
Matlock Carnival 96
Matlock Cavendish Rovers 83
Matlock Chamber of Trade
    100
Matlock Choir 94
Matlock Circuit 22, 23
Matlock Civic Association 89,
    175, 177, 185
Matlock Cliff 96
Matlock College 52, 53, 54,
    55, 57, 152, 158, 164
Matlock Cottage Hospital 77
Matlock Cricket Club 83
Matlock Cycling Club 87, 103
Matlock District Sunday School
    Union 25
Matlock Electric 7
Matlock Field Club 91, 149,
    182
Matlock Garden School 154
Matlock Gas Light and Coke
    Company 73
Matlock Gilbert and Sullivan
    Society 94
Matlock Gorge 33
Matlock Green 6, 23,
    24, 30, 47, 48, 56, 68, 70,

76, 79, 80, 86, 92, 95, 96,
    101, 117, 120, 126, 127, 132, 145,
    148, 153, 156, 161
Matlock Hard of Hearing Club
    104
Matlock Luncheon Club 90,
    184
Matlock Manor and Parish 7
Matlock Mercury 80, 103,
    104, 156, 184
Matlock Modern School
    54, 154
Matlock Moor 6, 8, 22, 72,
    123, 145
Matlock Motor Club 103
Matlock Philatelic Society 104
Matlock Picture Palace 87
Matlock Poultry Society 103
Matlock Pre-school Play Group
    104
Matlock Railway Club 104
Matlock Rectory 132
Matlock Round Table 101,
    184
Matlock Rugby Club 82, 153
Matlock Sketchbook 114
Matlock Social Institute
    Company 90
Matlock Station 33, 67, 133
Matlock Teacher Training
    College 155
Matlock Town Church of
    England Primary School
    151
Matlock Town Football Club
    80, 82, 163
Matlock Town Hall 23, 101,
    117
Matlock Tramway 21, 54
Matlock Urban District Council
    71, 72, 76, 102, 117,
    128, 162, 180
Matlock Victorian Weekend 91
Matlock Volunteers 77
Matlock Wakes 96
Matlock Water Company 71
Matlockite 7, 27, 182
Matriculation 153
Mawe, Mr 141
Maycock, W 53
Mayors & Chamberpersons
    180
Meals on Wheels 81
Meeting House 26, 127
Megdale Farm 8
Melville, Revd W R 14
Mercia 11
Mestesford 6, 11, 70
Methodism, Primitive 22
Methodist 21, 22, 23, 24,
    26, 49, 80, 92, 112, 116, 130
Michael, Imperial Grand Duke
    of Russia 112
Mid Derbyshire Riding Club
    103
Middleton, John 13
Midland Organ Builders of
    Derby 19
Midland Railway 65, 66, 67
Mild Water Cure 53
Militia 77

Mill Pond 70, 146, 147, 148
Mills, Elsie F 24
Milnes, William 13, 14
Miniature Railway 120
Mission Room 16, 19, 20
Model T Ford 75
Moletrap Vein 31, 32
Monyash 25, 141
Moore, Arthur 13
Moorland Fires 77
Moot Hall 28, 29
Morphy, Edmund 14
Morris, Michael 54, 112
Morrison Shelters 159
Moss, Martyn 86
Mosse, ffrancis 13
Motoring and Cycling 103
Mow Cop 22
Mullins, John 71
Museum Mine 42
Mussolini 90

N

Nagle Preparatory School
    54, 154
Nairn, Scotland 32
Nantwich 21
Napoleonic Wars 77
National Health Act 51, 96,
    178
National School 151, 153,
    154
Need, Samuel 21
Needham, Bernard 25
Nelson, Lord 64
Nestalls 28
Nesterside 11
Nestus 11, 28, 29, 31, 35,
    44, 182
Nestus Mine 28, 29
New Bath Hotel 31, 36, 41,
    43, 62, 72, 84, 85, 90, 100,
    101, 113, 122, 124, 167, 186
New Opportunities Fund 81
New Street 134, 153, 155
Newhaven 62, 63
Newholme Hospital 79
Newnes, Sir George 113
Nightingale, Florence 14, 16
Nightingale, Peter 14, 16,
    47, 130
Nightingale, W E 14, 130
Nightingale, W H 14
Nightingales 14
Norman 11, 16, 177
Norman Conquest 11
Norman, George 146
North Midland Railway 65
North Parade 41, 70, 76
Nottingham, Lloyd of 22, 23
Novello, Ivor 50
Nuttall, John 14, 48, 122
Nutthall, George 77

O

Oak Tree House 55
O'Brien, Drill Sergeant 19
Oddfellows Society 99
Old Baileans RFC 82

Old Bank House 54, 55
Old Bath Hotel 36, 38, 40,
    41, 44, 62, 65, 107, 109,
    112, 114, 115, 119, 124,
    125, 134, 135, 136, 166
Old Bath Terrace 39
Old English Hotel 88
Old English Road 125, 135
Old Matlock 6, 16, 47, 67,
    110, 183
Old Meeting House 26
Old Museum 134
Old Nestus Pipe Vein 44
Old Picture Palace 143
Olympic Peninsular 7
Omya UK Ltd 143
One Ash Grange 25
Operation Millennium 158
Orchard Holme 122
Orme, Dr Marie 65
Ornaments 107, 126, 134,
    141
Osowhite Step Powder 33
Owlett Hole Mine 43, 44
Oxfam 105

P

Packhorse Routes 59
Paint Mill 146
Palethorpe Farm 8, 72
Paper Mill 31, 36, 138, 140
Park Head 67, 100, 102,
    133, 165
Parker and Unwin 133
Parker, Barry 55
Parochial Hall 117
Pavilion 36, 39, 40, 44, 70,
    72, 87, 111, 119, 134, 135, 162
Paxton House 132
Paxton, Joseph 66, 93, 132,
    133
Paxton, Sir Joseph 66
Paxton Tor 132
Peak Advertiser 149, 156, 184
Peak District Mines Historical
    Society Ltd 44
Peak District Mining Museum
    30, 32, 35, 41, 44,
    134, 140, 186
Peak Rail PLC 67
Peak Ranger 64
Peak Times 143, 156, 184
Pedro, Dom II of Brazil 113
Pennell 36, 38, 39, 41, 62,
    124
Pentrich 8
Petrifying Wells 39, 40, 42,
    44, 135
Petty Sessions 76, 117
Peveril of the Peak 64
Pic Tor 70, 89, 100, 102,
    137, 163
Pickard, Ms Jan Sutch 24
Pierpoint, Robert 12
Pierpoints 12
Pikehall 63
Pinfold 80
Plain of Abraham 39
Plough Bullocks 97
Plough Sunday 97